RESEARCH IN GLOBAL STRATEGIC MANAGEMENT

Volume 7 • 1999

INTERNATIONAL ENTREPRENEURSHIP:
GLOBALIZATION OF EMERGING BUSINESSES

RESEARCH IN GLOBAL STRATEGIC MANAGEMENT

INTERNATIONAL ENTREPRENEURSHIP: GLOBALIZATION OF EMERGING BUSINESSES

Series Editor: ALAN M. RUGMAN
Templeton College
Oxford University

Volume Editor: RICHARD W. WRIGHT
Faculty of Management
McGill University

VOLUME 7 • 1999

 JAI PRESS INC.
Stamford, Connecticut

CONTENTS

LIST OF CONTRIBUTORS

Nancy J. Adler

Faculty of Management
McGill University
Montreal, QC, Canada

Paul W. Beamish

Richard Ivey School of Business
University of Western Ontario
London, ON, Canada

James D. Bell

Division of Commerce
University of Otago
Dunedin, New Zealand

Odd Jarl Borch

Nordland Research Institute
Bodo, Norway

Leo Paul Dana

School of Accountancy & Business
Nanyang Technological University
Singapore

Hamid Etemad

Faculty of Management
McGill University
Montreal, QC, Canada

Eileen Fischer

Schulich School of Business
York University
Toronto, ON, Canada

Len Korot

Graziadio School of
    Business & Management
Pepperdine University
Culver City, CA

Patricia P. McDougall

Kelly School of Business
Indiana University
Bloomington, IN

Rod B. McNaughton   Division of Commerce
                                 University of Otago
                                 Dunedin, New Zealand

Bill Merrilees   School of Management
                                 University of Newcastle
                                 Callaghan, Australia

Benjamin M. Oviatt   J. Mack Robinson College of
                                    Business
                                 Georgia State University
                                 Atlanta, GA

A. Rebecca Reuber   Joseph L. Rotman School of
                                    Management
                                 University of Toronto
                                 Toronto, ON, Canada

James H. Tiessen   Michael G. DeGroote School of
                                    Business
                                 McMaster University
                                 Hamilton, ON, Canada

George Tovstiga   TSM Business School
                                 University of Twente
                                 Enschede, Netherlands

Richard Wright   Faculty of Management
                                 McGill University
                                 Montreal, QC, Canada

INTRODUCTION

The world is changing dramatically. Government-imposed barriers and structural impediments, which segmented and protected domestic markets, are falling rapidly, while technological advances in production, transportation, and telecommunications—especially the Internet—allow even the smallest firms access to customers, suppliers, and collaborators around the world. Economic growth and innovation, both domestically and internationally, are fuelled increasingly by small companies and/or entrepreneurial enterprises. These trends will impact profoundly on management strategies, on public policies, and on the daily lives of all of us.

The focus of this volume in the *Research in Global Strategic Management* series is the phenomenon of globalization, and specifically its relevance to and impact on small business and entrepreneurship.

On the surface, the activities of small or entrepreneurial businesses and those of multinational enterprises seem highly divergent. Until recently, they have in fact operated in largely separate realms, each in its own competitive space, and each with characteristics markedly different from those of the other. However, globalization has begun to dismantle the barriers that traditionally segmented local business opportunities and local firms from their international counterparts. Local markets are becoming integral parts of broader, global markets. Consequently, internationally oriented entrepreneurs can now view a much broader range of opportunities, unrestricted by national boundaries. In this integrating global environment, entrepreneurs and emerging businesses need to learn about global business in order to thrive alongside larger firms already in the international marketplace. Conversely, multinational businesses need to acquire greater insight into the strategies and processes of small and entrepreneurial enterprises, with whom they increasingly share the same economic and competitive space. New strategic synergies are being created in the global arena through collaborative arrangements between small, entrepreneurial firms and large, international firms, with small firms frequently entering the global value-added chains of the larger multinationals.

One result of the breakdown of the lines of demarcation, that formerly segregated these disparate fields of management, is the emergence of a new subfield of research—*international entrepreneurship.* To explore and develop this rising area of research, a pioneering, three-day conference was held at McGill University, in Montreal, Canada, under the joint auspices of McGill's Centre for International Business Studies, and the Dobson Centre for Entrepreneurial Studies. The objective of the conference was to bring together leading scholars both from international business, and from small business/entrepreneurship, to begin integrating research in what had previously been widely divergent fields. Selected papers from that conference were subjected to a vigorous process of peer review and comments. Each paper was revised extensively to incorporate and reflect the perspectives of other disciplines. The final product is the series of leading-edge research papers presented in this volume.

The book is organized into four sections. Part I consists of two related papers presenting theoretical overviews of the emerging field of international entrepreneurship. Leo-Paul Dana, Hamid Etemad, and Richard W. Wright review the theoretical foundations of its two main component fields—entrepreneurship and international business—emphasizing the dichotomy which has traditionally existed between these two areas, in management practice as well as research. They show how current trends toward globalization are fusing the two formerly disparate fields into the emerging discipline of international entrepreneurship. Their analysis underscores the need for new, forward-looking models that will help us to better understand the phenomenon of accelerated internationalization of new and small firms.

Benjamin M. Oviatt and Patricia P. McDougall, who had originally observed the phenomenon of international new ventures, address this need in the following chapter by identifying a framework for such a theory. They begin by defining the objectives of the theory, along with the research questions it should answer when it is fully delineated. They identify rapidly changing technology as the foundation of international economic dynamism, and then explore four building blocks that they believe provide the framework for an improved theory of accelerated small-firm internationalization: political economy, industry conditions, firm effects, and the management team.

Taken together, these two opening chapters provide both a comprehensive overview of the component elements of mainstream international business and entrepreneurship theories, and a framework for a new theoretical approach to better understanding the increasingly important role of SMEs in the global economy. It is hoped that the ideas and concepts in these two chapters will stimulate discussion, as well as theoretical and empirical efforts, that will lead eventually to a contemporary dynamic theory of small-firm internationalization and its acceleration.

Part II focuses on the use of alliances and networks to facilitate the entry of small businesses into the global arena. Paul W. Beamish opens this section with a vision of the role of alliances in the emerging field of international entrepreneurship, drawing from the practices and experiences of larger firms, as well as from his own extensive experience as an alliance facilitator. Beamish first presents a brief history of the use of alliances. He than discusses what he sees as the four main liabilities which potential international alliance users must overcome—newness, size, foreignness, and relational orientation—as well as the need for congruent measures of performance. He provides both practical guidelines for SME managers, and suggestions for a future research agenda.

Rod B. McNaughton and James D. Bell further illustrate this relationship between networks and SME internationalization, focusing on brokered networks as a means by which small firms can avoid the liabilities outlined by Beamish. They first synthesize the literature on networks, SME growth, and internationalization to establish a theoretical underpinning for brokered networks of SMEs. They argue that networking offers managers of SMEs an alternative to internally oriented strategies for growth and internationalization. But successful networking requires participants to exercise managerial skills that may be unfamiliar to entrepreneurs used to managing within the environment of their own firm. McNaughton and Bell argue that networks of firms are a form of social capital providing a supportive environment to offset the inherent instability and constraints of small firm size. The material of this chapter has important implications both for SME managers, and for governments.

The third part of the book provides the results of three empirically based research studies designed to better understand the market forces and managerial characteristics which appear to underlie the success of SMEs in the global arena. In each of the chapters the authors relate the objectives and methodologies of their research, and they also discuss the implications of their findings for competitive strategy, for public policy, and for future research.

A. Rebecca Reuber and Eileen Fischer examine the influences of industry characteristics—particularly the consequences of domestic market size—on the internationalization of SMEs. Their underlying assumption is that firms in a small domestic market are more likely to develop the international business competences than are firms in larger domestic markets, because they have a greater need to enter foreign markets. Their study compares firms in an industry with a relatively large domestic market (the food and beverage industry) with those in an industry with a relatively small domestic market (software products). They show that SMEs in the smaller market demonstrate greater international business competence, greater innovative competence, and less product-specific competence. The strong differences between industries in their findings highlight the importance of industry characteristics in the international behavior of SMEs. One interesting conclusion emerging from their research is that internationalization may not be a phenomenon that should be equally encouraged or comparably supported in all industries.

In the following chapter Odd-Jarl Borch reports on his research on strategic change in an industry facing a radical transition of structure, from regional fragmentation to global integration: the agro-food industry. He focuses on how firms in a rapidly globalizing industry manage the challenges of the removal of trade barriers and increased cross-border competition. Borch first conceptualizes several business substrategies at the level of the business unit. He then uses cluster analysis to define prototypes of five business strategy patterns for coping with change in the firms which he studied. He discusses each of these clusters or strategic prototypes at length, relating strategy to performance. His findings give us useful insights about the responses of firms in industries in transition toward global integration.

Finally, James H. Tiessen and Bill Merrilees extend our examination of the process of SME internationalization, by reporting on and analyzing case studies of six entrepreneurial firms, from different industries. The firms studied vary widely in terms of age, size, industry, and the percentage of revenues developed outside the home country. All, however, exhibited a strong entrepreneurial stance, leveraging their domestic capability internationally. Tiessen and Merrilees proceed, from their individual case analyses, to develop an entrepreneurial model of SME internationalization, to help us identify how the key entrepreneurial functions of leveraging and generating variety can be used to create an international competitive advantage. Their discussion of sequential internationalization versus born-globals, and their observations on the use of networking by SMEs to gain global access, link directly to the material of previous chapters of this book.

The last section looks to the future, with two visionary contributions on forces which will shape the successful international firm of the future. While the material of these chapters is relevant to large and small alike, they are especially germane to the rapidly growing, flexible, creative SMEs emerging in the global arena. First, Len Korot and George Tovstiga examine the role of knowledge as the key source of competitive advantage in the twenty-first-century firm. They lay out a framework for better understanding the role of knowledge in the firm, examining the way in which the Network Age enterprise manages its knowledge base and infrastructure, its culture and its practices. They look also at the new demands being made on its primary source of competitive advantage: its knowledge workers. After defining their profile of the twenty-first-century firm, Korot and Tovstiga introduce a diagnostic profiling instrument designed to assess an organization's knowledge culture and processes, and to gauge its progress toward achieving that profile.

Nancy J. Adler focuses on global leadership, and the type of leader needed for the twenty-first century. In particular, she includes the increasingly important role and contribution of women leaders into a field that has been understood primarily from the perspective of history's male leaders. Adler raises and demolishes a number of commonly held myths about the role of women leaders, whether in business, politics, or entrepreneurial enterprises. Her chapter underscores the importance of the growing number of female chief executives of global entrepreneurial and family firms. Adler discusses the importance of this phenomenon, not just for global business and entrepreneurial activity, but for the very future of twenty-first-century society.

Globalization poses dramatic new competitive challenges as well as new opportunities for SMEs. Success in the emerging global arena will require strategies and mindsets which blend the skills and experiences of both small, entrepreneurial businesses, and large, established international companies. It is not surprising, then, that the emerging research discipline of international entrpreneurship draws as well from different backgrounds. That diversity is reflected in this volume, which juxtaposes the views and approaches of researchers from a variety of disciplines. The common thread which unites the nine papers is the extent to which globalization calls for new strategic approaches by small firms, large firms, and governments alike. It is hoped, particularly, that the research findings and insights reported in this volume will assist managers of SMEs to better understand and anticipate these dramatic changes, and to design appropriate corporate strategic responses.

Richard W. Wright
Volume Editor

PART I

THEORETICAL FRAMEWORK

THEORETICAL FOUNDATIONS OF INTERNATIONAL ENTREPRENEURSHIP

Leo-Paul Dana, Hamid Etemad, and Richard W. Wright

I. INTRODUCTION

Until recently, the fixed costs of learning about and penetrating foreign markets were very high, leading Caves (1971, 1996) and others to conclude that foreign direct investment would be mainly an activity of large players. Traditional logic held that a firm had to be big in order to compete globally (Chandler 1990). Consequently, international business and small business/entrepreneurship were largely separate fields, both academically and practically. With the exception of exporting, the international business literature focused on the behavior of large, multinational companies, while the small business/entrepreneurship literature dealt mainly with the evolution of new companies and the management of small businesses in a domestic context.

This demarcation, however, is no longer sustainable. Government-imposed barriers and structural impediments, which segmented and protected domestic markets, are falling rapidly, while technological advances in production, transportation, and telecommunications—especially the Internet—allow even the smallest firms better access to customers, suppliers, and collaborators around the

Research in Global Strategic Management, Volume 7, pages 3-22.
Copyright © 1999 by JAI Press Inc.
All rights of reproduction in any form reserved.
ISBN: 0-7623-0458-8

world. Acs (1996) showed that the long-term trend toward increasing firm size has decelerated and may even have been reversed. Thus, a research subdiscipline is emerging, fusing elements of what formerly had been considered international business with what used to be small business/entrepreneurship. Researchers (Coviello and Munro 1993, 1994; Oviatt and McDougall 1994) have begun to focus on why and how small enterprises internationalize.

This chapter examines and elaborates on the two constituent foundations of this emerging field. It then considers the relevance of their fusion, both for the practice of international entrepreneurship, and for the pursuit of academic research.

II. ENTREPRENEURSHIP IN A GLOBAL CONTEXT

The origin of the word "entrepreneurship" can be traced to the German *unternehmung* and the French *entreprendre* (Cantillon 1755), literally meaning taking from below or undertaking, and understood as taking charge or responsibility or challenge from the root/source/beginning/origin. For our purposes, entrepreneurship refers to the practice of undertaking an enterprise, while assuming a majority of the control and underlying risks; as such, few if any strategy specialists are employed, and the owner/manager or entrepreneur is the sole or principal decision maker. Thus, the word entrepreneurship is used here in its classical sense and excludes the concept of organizational entrepreneurship (or "intrapreneurship") which applies to large, mature corporations as investigated, for example, by Morris, Davis, and Allen (1994).

Capital limitations, time constraints, and the entrepreneur's desire to control are among the factors which limit the size of the business venture, which is often referred to as a small- or medium-sized enterprise or SME (Buckley 1989; Erramilli and D'Souza 1993). Buckley (1997) uses the term small- and medium-sized enterprises (SMEs) in reference to firms with fewer than 500 employees, although the size threshold varies. In the United States a small-scale enterprise has fewer than 500 employees; in Europe 300 employees is the dividing mark. Recent research (Admiraal 1996; Fujita 1995) shows that small firms are expanding internationally despite these constraints. Shuman and Seeger (1986) emphasize that small enterprises are not little versions of big businesses, because small firms have unique, size-related issues and therefore behave differently in their analyses of, and interaction with, external variables.

Until recently, an entrepreneur who wished to avoid the uncertainties inherent in foreign markets, could simply keep a business local, refrain from expanding internationally, and thereby avoid the challenges of competing overseas. Today, the successful entrepreneur can move beyond these self-imposed constraints by identifying new opportunities, beyond national confines. Opportunities for entrepreneurship are becoming less restricted to domestic markets. As the domestic/foreign distinction begins to disappear, entrepreneurs need a new orientation with new attitudes, new skills, new knowledge, and new sensitivity to different cultures.

III. THE CONSTITUENT DISCIPLINES OF ENTREPRENEURSHIP

As noted by Stearns and Hills (1996), entrepreneurship, as an academic field, was legitimized in the 1990s. However, academia does not yet have a universally accepted definition of entrepreneurship. Although Cole (1942) endorsed an interdisciplinary approach as far back as 1942, disciplines have regarded the phenomenon differently, resulting in a wide range of contributions. How have anthropologists, economists, psychologists, and others viewed this emerging field?

A. Anthropology

Anthropologists study the entrepreneur in the context of culture. Barth (1963), a founder of decision-making theory, viewed the entrepreneur as an agent for social change. His (1967) model is based on the individual entrepreneur: his alternatives, his choice, and variation. Although he did not attempt to develop a model to analyze how entrepreneurial activity affects the community in which it occurs, his anthropological model explains that entrepreneurs create innovations that affect the community in which they are active. More recently, anthropologists have focused on small enterprises owned by entrepreneurs who belong to ethnic minorities. Rothstein's (1992) Latin American study suggests that migratory minorities are low-cost producers. However, this cost advantage did not necessarily result in international competitiveness. Along the same lines, Blim (1992) discovered that although kinship networks contributed to new-venture startups, they were too limited to facilitate international competitiveness.

B. Economics

Cantillon (1755) was the first to use the term entrepreneur. Subsequently, economists defined the term in the context of economic growth. Say (1803, 1815) linked the growth of England's economy to the skills of her entrepreneurs. Ely and Hess (1893) explained that to simplify economic analysis, economists should group factors of production into four categories: "labour, land, capital and the enterprise or entrepreneur" (1893, p. 95). The last, a particularly elusive term, is applied to the ultimate owners of business enterprises, who make the final decisions and assume the risks involved.

Tuttle (1927) examined entrepreneurship in the context of early economic literature. He focused on ownership considerations. While Keynes (1936) was concerned with equilibrium, Schumpeter (1911) concentrated on disequilibrium created by entrepreneurs. According to Schumpeter, the activity of the entrepreneur is to function as *an agent of change in an otherwise repetitive social economy*. In his view entrepreneurial activity was doing things that were often already being done, but in new and innovative combinations, resulting in nonreversible disturbances of equilibrium. Schumpeter's entrepreneurs were movers of society, who had a joy of creating private dynasties. He emphasized dramatic innovation which fostered long-term growth. Innovators destroyed the positions of stagnant enterprises—a process termed creative destruction. Entrepreneurship was thus a means of transforming and improving society (Schumpeter 1911, 1928, 1942, 1947, 1949).

Economic theory assumes that markets move toward equilibrium, and entrepreneurs cause disequilibrium when they innovate and create profit opportunities. According to this school of thought, profit opportunities created by entrepreneurs generate disequilibria, which improve the incomes of all affected. Knight confirmed, "It is unquestionable that the entrepreneur's activities affect an enormous saving to society, vastly increasing the efficiency of economic production" (1921, p. 278). Baumol described the entrepreneur as "one of the most intriguing and one of the most elusive characters in the cast that constitutes the subject of economic analysis" (1968, p. 64).

In contrast to Schumpeter, who saw entrepreneurs as creating disequilibrium, Kirzner (1973) believed that an entrepreneur could simply *identify* disequilibrium, without necessarily creating it. He discusses the entrepreneur in the context of opportunities, alertness, and economic processes, using the approach of the Austrian school of economics (Kirzner 1982). Accordingly, entrepreneurship has to do with the identification of where the next imperfection will be found. Entrepreneurship therefore corrects socioeconomic waste or inefficiencies. Kirzner further explained that entrepreneurship is unlikely to come from the government or public sector, because even when innovation exists, entrepreneurship will always depend on the profit motive. Extensive state intervention in an economy results in artificial barriers to business entry. It has been argued that this prompts innovators to concentrate on finding ways to beat the system in order to get the necessary resources (Baumol 1990; Murphy, Shleifer, and Vishny 1993). Unlike the Schumpeterian entrepreneur who innovates and thus disturbs equilibrium by introducing something new into the marketplace, Kirznerian entrepreneurs profit from their alertness in existing disequilibrium. Market imperfections give them something to do. Rather than seeing innovation as central to entrepreneurship, in Kirzner's view an imitator, as well as an innovator, can be an entrepreneur and profit from disequilibrium.

Binks and Coyne (1983) remained loyal to Schumpeter, stating that the entrepreneur is an innovator, a force for change linked to the growth of an economy. Casson explained that the "entrepreneur is someone who specializes in making judgmental decisions about the co-ordination of scarce resources" (1982, p. 23).

C. Marketing

Peter Drucker (1974) explained that the most important aspect of entrepreneurship is a focus on the market. To him, this focus is more important than financial foresight. In the area of international marketing, the export behavior of small firms has been studied extensively (Anderson 1995; Bilkey 1978; Brush 1995; Cavusgil, Bilkey, and Tesar 1979; Dichtl, Leibold, Koeglmayr, and Mueller 1984; Gemunden 1991; Tesar and Tarleton 1982). Aaby and Slater (1989) reviewed 55 export studies. Dichtl, Leibold, Koeglmayr, and Mueller (1990) conducted an extensive study comparing German, Finnish, Japanese, South African, and South Korean firms. They concluded that an important determinant of export performance was the foreign market orientation of decision makers. Simon (1992) found that successful entrepreneurs in Germany had a customer orientation. Adams and Hall (1993) studied 1,132 SMEs across Europe. They determined that personal factors were important causal variables of export performance, while Cavusgil and Kirpalani (1993) linked export success to a favorable management attitude and a commitment to export.

Other studies have examined licensing and foreign direct investment by entrepreneurs. Carstairs and Welch (1982) suggested that the key success factor for licensing among entrepreneurs was the development of a long-term, effective interaction with the licensee, which contributes market information, and leads to commercial viability. Sherman (1996) addressed international franchising, and suggested strategies for international cooperation.

D. Psychology

McClelland (1961) based his research on the concept of need for achievement, which he referred to as the "*n*-ach." He found a positive correlation between entrepreneurial behavior and the need for achievement. Researching in the United States, Italy, and Poland, he attributed the individual entrepreneur's need for achievement as the variable that influenced behavior. His results suggest that individuals with high needs for achievement would be influenced by that need and would consequently pursue entrepreneurial behavior. Hornaday and Aboud confirmed, that "Compared to men in general, entrepreneurs are significantly higher on scales reflecting need for achievement" (1971, p. 147). Kets de Vries (1985) also suggested a link between entrepreneurs and an achievement orientation.

McClelland also compared cultural influences across cultures, concluding that some cultures have a greater need for achievement than others do. His research influenced numerous other studies, which subsequently established a link between a high need for achievement and a belief in internal locus of control. Brockhaus (1982) and Begley and Boyd (1987) contended that entrepreneurs generally have a more internally oriented locus of control than do managers. Sexton and Bowman (1985), however, did not find a significant difference.

Shapero (1975) examined entrepreneurship as a psychological response to displacement. To Shapero (1984) the entrepreneurial event is innovative, the result of one's decision to change one's path in life and to start a new business. Often, negative forces, such as frustration or the loss of a job prompt this action.

Other significant contributions dealing with the theme of psychological traits include Gasse (1977); Hornaday and Bunker (1970); Kets de Vries (1977); and Zaleznik and Kets de Vries (1976). Such research has resulted in lists of characteristics pertaining to typical entrepreneurs. These traits may predispose an individual to become an entrepreneur.

Stevenson and Jarrillo-Mossi (1986) found that the classic bureaucrat and the entrepreneur were poles apart. The former prefers the status quo and the entrepreneur seeks change. They also suggested that entrepreneurship included the ability and desire to recognize and to pursue opportunity. More recently, as noted by Bygrave and Hofer (1991), there has been a gradual shift away from this traditional focus.

E. Sociology

Sociologists have long studied entrepreneurship, and the literature emerging from this field is a rich one. The basic premise is that entrepreneurs do not make rational and isolated decisions in a vacuum. Instead, they are influenced by their surroundings. Weber pioneered the field with his work ethic theory (1904-1905). More recently, Shapero and Sokol (1982) studied the social dimensions of entrepreneurship. Other significant contributions have come from, among others, Aldrich and Waldinger (1990); Auster and Aldrich (1984); Bonacich (1973); Bonacich and Modell (1980); Brenner and Toulouse (1990); Cherry (1990); Dana (1995); Jensen and Portes (1992); Kasdan (1965); Min (1984, 1986-1987, 1987); Min and Jaret (1985); Portes (1981); Portes and Bach (1985); Portes and Jensen (1987, 1989, 1992); Portes and Walton (1981); Reynolds (1991); Sanders and Nee (1987); Waldinger (1984, 1986a, 1986b); Waldinger and Aldrich (1990); Waldinger, Aldrich, and Ward (1990); Waldinger, McEvoy, and Aldrich (1990); Wilson and Portes (1980); Young (1971); and Zhou and Logan (1989).

Sociology has also given rise to a very fertile literature about entrepreneurship networks. Networking involves calling upon a web of contacts for information, support, and assistance. Aldrich and Zimmer (1986) integrated social network theory into the study of entrepreneurship. They linked entrepreneurship to social networks. Carsrud, Gaglio, and Olm (1986) also found networks important to the understanding of new venture development. Boissevain and Grotenbreg (1987), in their study of the Surinamese in Amsterdam, suggested that access to a network of contacts is an important resource for entrepreneurs. Their study noted that networks may provide introductions to wholesalers, and warnings of government inspections. Aldrich, Rosen, and Woodward (1987), as well, determined that network accessibility is significant in predicting new venture creation. Dubini and Aldrich (1991) found networks central to entrepreneurship.

In their study of Koreans in Atlanta, Min and Jaret (1985) found family networks to be a source of manpower for entrepreneurs. Analyzing Asian entrepreneurs in Britain, Aldrich, Jones, and McEvoy found that they "benefit from...certain advantages denied non-ethnic competitors" (1984, p. 193). They also discovered a strong internal solidarity in the ethnic enclave.

Given that the possibility of exploiting opportunities appears to be linked to the internal organizing capacity of a group (such as creating an ethnic network), Auster and Aldrich (1984) concluded that an ethnic enclave reduces the vulnerability of small firms by providing both an ethnic market, as well as general social and economic support, including credit. Others who focused on ethnic enterprise include Cummings (1980); Light (1972, 1984); Light and Bonacich (1988); Ward (1987); Ward and Jenkins (1984); Wong (1987) and Wu (1983). Anderson (1995) and Johanson and Associates (1994) examined the effect of business networks on the internationalization of firms, concluding that networks may affect positively a firm's degree of internationalization.

IV. THEORETICAL FOUNDATIONS OF INTERNATIONAL BUSINESS

While entrepreneurial studies continue to draw on the supporting disciplines of anthropology, economics, psychology, and sociology to better understand and to predict entrepreneurship patterns, international business has progressed beyond its constituent fields. As an older discipline, international business has developed a cumulative methodological and theoretical "tradition of its own" (Culnan and Swanson 1986). The following is a summary of some of the main theoretical streams of international business, and their contributions as viewed through an international entrpreneurship lens.

A. Product Life-Cycle Theory

Product life-cycle theory, as discussed by Vernon (1966, 1979), Stopford and Wells (1972), Wells (1972), Knickerbocker (1973), and Davidson (1980), attempts to explain world trade and foreign direct investment (FDI) in manufactured products based on stages in a product's life. Briefly, the theory of international product life cycle (PLC) states that certain kinds of products go through a continuum, or cycle, that consists roughly of four stages—introduction, growth, maturity, and decline—and that the location of production will shift internationally, depending on the stage of the cycle.

Vernon observed that most new products are produced in the innovating country—in the 1960s it as the United States; in the 1980s it was Japan—and sold mainly in the domestic market, with some exports to other major markets. Over time, however, demand for the new product starts to grow in other advanced countries, and competition begins to develop from other producers both at home and abroad. At that point the firm may choose to set up production facilities in wholly owned subsidiaries in those advanced countries where demand is growing, to service those markets more effectively. At later stages, as price competition begins to loom ever larger, it shifts production to low-cost developing countries, exporting the product back to the original home market and to other developed markets. Thus the cycle is complete.

The PLC theory, despite its relevance to large multinationals, is not applicabile to entrepreneurship. In reality, entrepreneurs, with new ventures, often sell their products—prior to maturity—in niche markets where there is little or no competition.

B. Oligopolistic Reaction Theory

Knickerbocker (1973) postulated that in oligopolistic industries, enterprises react to the moves of their competitors, and imitate them to reduce the risk of being different. Two findings formed the basis of his theory. The first one referred to evidence indicating the tendency of firms in a number of American industries to cluster their direct investments in foreign countries. The second originated from data which suggest that American enterprises in the forefront of international expansion are typically in oligopolistic industries. Knickerbocker's exposition suggests that there exists a relationship between the clustering of foreign investments and the desire of oligopolists to react to the moves of rivals. His research pointed to a comfort zone characterized by firms replicating the actions of others to re-create a perceived level playing field. Once one company in an oligopolistic industry decides to enter or produce in a particular overseas market, competitors are prone to follow quickly, rather than let the first mover gain an advantage. Thus, the decision is based not so much on the benefits to be gained, but rather on the greater losses sustained by not entering the field. The question for many multinational enterprises facing investment decisions is, "Do I lose less by moving abroad or by staying at home?" This theory helps to explain the herding nature of FDI patterns, as well as the large number of producers relative to the size of the market in some countries. A problem with this theory, however, is that it does not apply to international entrepreneurs, as they are not in oligopolistic industries (by definitition). As explained by Schumpeter (1911), entrepreneurs create and innovate. They often have first-mover instincts for taking advantage of present opportunities—even launching born-global new ventures. Such behavior is not explained adequately by the oligopolistic reaction theory.

C. Monopolistic Advantage/Market Imperfections Theories

Modern monopolistic advantage theory arises from the work of Hymer (1976) in the 1960s. He demonstrated that FDI occurred largely in oligopolistic industries rather than in industries operating in near-perfect competition. This means that the firms in these industries must possess advantages not available to local firms. Hymer argued that the advantages can include economies of scale, superior technology, or superior knowledge in marketing, management, or finance. FDI takes place because these product- and factor-market imperfections allow the multinational corporation to gain and maintain monopolistic advantages not accessible to local firms.

Caves (1971) expanded on Hymer's work to show that superior knowledge permitted the investing firm to produce differentiated products that consumers prefer to similar, locally made goods, thus producing an advantage over indigenous firms. In supporting these contentions, he noted that companies investing overseas were in industries that typically engaged in heavy product research and marketing.

Monopolistic advantage theories are helpful in explaining why large firms invest heavily in a special class of assets—long-lasting, protectable, and proprietary—which can give them long-term competitive advantages abroad. They are, however, much less useful in explaining entrepreneurial advantages, which are likely to be of a much different type: entrepreneur-based, more ephemeral, and more narrowly defined than those of larger firms.

D. Internalization Theory

Internalization theory, expounded by Buckley and Casson (1976), Rugman (1979, 1981), Teece (1985), and others, is an extension of market imperfections theory. The multinational corporation is observed to derive firm-specific advantages in technological, marketing, or management know-how. It is reluctant to transfer its assets to a nonrelated firm through a contractual agreement such as licensing, as there is a risk of dissipation of its firm-specific advantages. By investing in its own foreign subsidiaries, rather than licensing, the company is able to exploit its knowledge across borders, while maintaining control and realizing a longer, better, and safer return on its investment. Internalization theory was tested and confirmed by Morck and Yeung (1991, 1992) among others.

Internalization does not necessarily explain decisions of entrepreneurs to locate enterprises as a function of personal preference for a particular environment—certain locations may be preferred by an entrepreneur for religious, linguistic, or cultural reasons. To the entrepreneur, these are all constituent—albeit nonmonetary—influences that are not captured by economic-based theories such as internalization. However, Casson (1982) argued that all the internalization principles did apply to entrepreneurship.

E. The Eclectic Paradigm

Dunning's (1973, 1977, 1980, 1988) contributions provide a framework designed to synthesize internalization theories with the international business literature to explain the nature and direction of FDI. His model includes:

- *Ownership-specific advantages,* including patents, trademarks, and management know-how;
- *Location-specific advantages* that arise from using resource endowments or assets tied to a particular foreign location, which a firm finds valuable to combine with its own unique assets; and
- *Internalization,* or the multinational enterprise's use of its own internal market—its network of headquarters and sister subsidiaries—which allows it to further enhance its other advantages.

Dunning advanced his model as a "three-legged stool," with each part interdependent on the others; it would be a mistake to use any one part of his eclectic theory independently. Dunning's location-specific advantage refers to all the advantages that accrue to MNEs because of transferring investment and production to a specific location (in contrast with those of local firms). Explicit in the theory is that ownership advantages will further augment location-specific advantages. Thus, MNEs, in spite of their high transaction costs (Williamson 1975), may be more competitive in foreign markets than local firms.

Internalization theories and the related eclectic paradigm provide useful insights into how large firms create internal markets for their own advantage. However, they identify a very limited set of source-specific advantages for the international firm. International entrepreneurship often appears to be based on a much greater diversity of resources and processes. Entrepreneurs focus on the advantage, regardless of its source, and the distinction of source specificity may be largely irrelevant to them. While internalization implies limiting the scope of exploiting an advantage to within an organization or family of enterprises (such as sister subsidiary networks), international entrepreneurs, in contrast, may draw on a wide range of outside resources and external organizations to facilitate their internationalization.

F. Incremental Internationalization

The Uppsala Model (Johanson and Wiedersheim-Paul 1975) identified four stages of entry into international markets. This was further elaborated in Johanson and Vahlne (1977). Bilkey and Tesar (1977) opted for a six-stage model. Newbould, Buckley, and Thurwell (1978) also examined such a stage approach to international business. Cavusgil (1980, 1984) considered five stages. Bilkey (1978); Bartlett and Ghoshal (1989); Buckley, Newbould, and Thurwell (1988);

Cavusgil (1984); Cavusgil and Nevin (1981); Johanson and Vahlne (1990, 1992); Leonidou and Katsikeas (1996) were among others to adhere to this approach. Essentially, this approach views internationalization as a series of involvements through incremental modes of activity. Each involvement is a more progressive stage in the process of understanding the global environment and the competition. Typical stages include (i) indirect exporting/importing/sourcing; (ii) direct exporting/importing/sourcing; (iii) licensing; (iv) joint ventures; and finally (v) wholly owned subsidiaries.

A major limitation of this approach is the assumption of a span of time through which the various stages evolve in a controlled fashion. But born-global ventures, for example, represent entrepreneurial behavior that cannot possibly follow incremental stages. Often, a firm must internationalize immediately, perhaps because its domestic market is too small to sustain it. In such cases there are no time-delayed increments. The same is true of many small businesses with high-tech products or demand conditions which defy conventional patterns. Coviello and Munro (1993) determined that small, high-tech firms rarely follow the step approach to internationalization. Other research, which further challenges stage theories, include Bell (1995); Bloodgood, Sapienza, and Almeida (1996); McDougall, Shane and Oviatt (1994); Sullivan and Bauerschmidt (1990); and Turnbull (1987).

G. National Competitive Advantage

Porter has made several significant contributions (1980, 1985, 1986, 1990) to the theoretical understanding of international business. Based on an extensive study of 100 industries in 10 nations, Porter and his associates attempted to explain why some nations are internationally competitive. His thesis is that four broad attributes of a nation shape the environment in which local firms compete, and they can promote or impede the creation of a competitive advantage. These attributes are:

- *Factor endowments:* a nation's position in factors of production, such as skilled labor, or the infrastructure necessary to compete in a given industry.
- *Demand conditions:* the nature of domestic demand for the industry's product or service.
- *Related and supporting industries:* the presence or absence in a nation of supplier industries and related industries that are internationally competitive.
- *Firm strategy, structure, and rivalry:* the conditions in the nation governing how companies are created, organized, and managed and the nature of domestic rivalry.

Porter speaks of these four attributes as constituting a diamond. He argues that firms are most likely to succeed in industries or industry segments where the diamond is most favorable. Porter maintains that two additional variables—chance and government—can influence the national diamond in important ways. One apparent shortcoming is the theory's lack of explicit recognition for the role of entrepreneurship, particularly its inability to explain the possibility of entrepreneurial success in small-niche markets which lack rivalry.

H. International New Ventures

As explained by Oviatt (1995), the increasingly global nature of demand is encouraging the formation of global startups—emerging firms, which do not begin domestically with a subsequent internationalization process. Knight and Cavusgil (1996) identified "born globals," while Oviatt and McDougall (1997) wrote of "international new ventures." Consequently, an emerging field of research involves studies of new ventures that are engaged in international business from the time of inception. McDougall, Shane, and Oviatt (1994) showed that international new ventures are not explained by existing theories of international business. Oviatt and McDougall (1994) pioneered a new theory relevant to such enterprises as international new ventures. Examples of related research include Cavusgil (1994); McDougall (1989); McMullan (1994); Ray (1989); and Shane, Kolvereid, and Westhead (1993). In a two-year study of U.S. technology-based firms, McDougall (1996) found that early international sales are associated positively with relative market share, but not necessarily with return on investment. Giamartino, McDougall, and Bird (1993) addressed the growth of the international entrepreneurship field. Reuber and Fischer (1997) found similarities between firms that internationalize early and those that internationalize at inception. The emergence of this new field of global startups illustrates the degree to which international business and entrepreneurship have begun to converge.

V. GLOBAL ENTRPRENEURSHIP: THE EMERGING FIELD

A dominant characteristic of the international business theories reviewed above is their orientation toward *large firms* (multinational enterprises) and *established processes* (foreign direct investment). Entrepreneurs have motives and processes which are more subjective and individualistic. On the surface, then, the activities of large firms, and those of entrepreneurs, seem highly divergent. However, globalization has begun to dismantle the barriers that traditionally segmented local business opportunities and local firms (SMEs) from their international counterparts, the multinational enterprises (MNEs). Local markets are becoming integral parts of broader, global markets. Consequently, internationally oriented entrepreneurs can now view a much broader range of opportunities, unrestricted by national boundaries.

A. Implications for Businesses

As explained by Oviatt and McDougall, "facile use of low-cost communication technology and transportation means that the ability to discover and take advantage of business opportunities in multiple countries is not the preserve of large, mature corporations" (1994, p. 46). These trends, coupled with decreasing government protection in many countries, are enabling new entrants to join the competitive field and are causing multinationals to seek ever-greater efficiency. Large, established firms increasingly find this efficiency by subcontracting to smaller businesses, owned and managed by entrepreneurs. Buckley (1997) discovered that small and medium firms can fill crucial niche roles, especially within business network systems. There is a new symbiosis between large and small business, with large firms providing new niche opportunities for smaller firms. Such relationships have long characterized economies such as Japan (Wright 1989) and Korea (Dana 1994), and they are increasingly apparent in North America and Europe as well.

Given these sweeping changes in the global business environment, entrepreneurs and small-business owners need to more than ever to examine the received tradition of international business, as they function increasingly in the same competitive environments as MNEs. Another choice for SMEs is to become partners with MNEs in business networks, for example, as key suppliers or key contractors (Rugman and D'Cruz 1997). At the same time, multinational companies and the agents of international business—and research in international business—need to examine and understand what gives rise to and sustains the competitive advantages of entrepreneurial firms, against which they may increasingly be competing. Bridging these two formerly disparate fields, and facilitating their fusion, is the fertile new research field of international entrepreneurship.

ACKNOWLEDGMENTS

The authors acknowledge with gratitude the financial support of the Dobson Centre for Entrepreneurial Studies, the Business and Management Research Centre, and the Centre for International Business Studies, all of the Faculty of Management, McGill University. They wish also to express their deepest gratitude to Peter Johnson, Director of the Dobson Centre, for his encouragement and support, and to Paul W. Beamish, Benjamin M. Ovitatt, David A. Ricks, and Alan M. Rugman for their constructive comments and suggestions.

REFERENCES

Aaby, N., and S.F. Slater. 1989. "Management Influence on Export Performance: A Review of Empirical Literature 1978-1988." *International Marketing Review* 6 (4): 7-26.

Acs, Z.J. 1996. *Small Firms and Economic Growth.* Cheltenham: Edward Elgar.

Adams, G., and G. Hall. 1993. Influences on the Growth of SMEs: An International Comparison. *Entrepreneurship and Regional Development* 5: 73-84.

Admiraal, P.H. 1996. *Small Business in the Modern Economy.* Oxford: Blackwell.

Aldrich, H.E., T.P. Jones, and D. McEvoy. 1984. "Ethnic Advantage and Minority Business Development." In *Ethnic Communities in Business: Strategies for Economic Survival,* edited by R. Ward and R. Jenkins. Cambridge: Cambridge University Press.

Aldrich, H., B. Rosen, and W. Woodward. 1987. "The Impact of Social Networks on Business Foundings and Profit in a Longitudinal Study." In *Frontiers of Entrepreneurship Research,* edited by Babson College. Wellesley, MA: Babson College.

Aldrich, H.E., and R.D. Waldinger. 1990. "Ethnicity and Entrepreneurship." In *Annual Review of Sociology* 16: 111-135.

Aldrich, H.E., and C. Zimmer. 1986. "Entrepreneurship Through Social Networks." In *The Art and Science of Entrepreneurship,* edited by D. L. Sexton and R. W. Smilor. Cambridge, MA: Ballinger.

Anderson, P.H. 1995. *Collaborative Internationalization of Small and Medium-Sized Enterprises.* Copenhagen: DJOF.

Auster, E., and H.E. Aldrich. 1984. "Small Business Vulnerability, Ethnic Enclaves and Ethnic Enterprise." In *Ethnic Communities in Business: Strategies for Economic Survival,* edited by R. Ward and R. Jenkins. Cambridge: Cambridge University Press.

Barth, F. 1963. *The Role of the Entrepreneur in Social Change in Northern Norway.* Bergen: Norwegian Universities' Press.

_____. 1967. "On the Study of Social Change." *American Anthropologist* 69 (6): 661-669.

Bartlett, C.A., and S. Ghoshal. 1989. *Managing Across Borders: The Transnational Solution.* Boston: Harvard Business School Press.

Baumol, W.J. 1968. "Entrepreneurship in Economic Theory." *The American Economic Review* 58 (2): 64-71.

_____. 1990. "Entrepreneurship: Productive, Unproductive and Destructive." *Journal of Political Economy* 98 (5); 893-921.

Begley, T.M., and D.P. Boyd. 1987. "Psychological Characteristics Associated With Performance in Entrepreneurial Firms and Smaller Businesses." *Journal of Business Venturing* 2: 79-93.

Bell, J.D. 1995. "The Internationalisation of Small Computer Software Firms." *European Journal of Marketing* 29 (8): 60-75.

Bilkey, W.J. 1978. "An Attempted Integration of the Literature on the Export Behavior of Firms." *Journal of International Business Studies* 9 (1): 33-46.

Bilkey, W.J., and G. Tesar. 1977. "The Export Behavior of Smaller Sized Wisconsin Manufacturing Firms." *Journal of International Business Studies* 8 (1): 93-98.

Binks, M., and J. Coyne. 1983. *An Analytical and Empirical Study of the Growth of Small Firms.* London: The Institute of Economic Affairs.

Blim, M.L. 1992. "Small-Scale Industrialization in a Rapidly Changing World Market." In *Anthropology and the Global Factory: Studies of the New Industrialization in the Late Twentieth Century,* edited by F. A. Rothstein and M. L. Blim. New York: Bergin and Garvey.

Bloodgood, J.M., H.J. Sapienza, and J.G. Almeida. 1996. "The Internationalization of New High-Potential US New Ventures." *Entrepreneurship Theory and Practice* 20 (4): 61-76.

Boissevain, J., and H. Grotenbreg. 1987. "Ethnic Enterprise in the Netherlands: The Surinamese of Amesterdam." Pp. 105-130 in *Entrepreneurship in Europe: The Social Process,* edited by R. Goffee and R. Scase. London: Croom Helm.

Bonacich, E. 1973. "A Theory of Middleman Minorities." *American Sociological Review* 38(5): 583-594.

Bonacich, E., and J. Modell. 1980. *The Economic Basis of Ethnic Solidarity: Small Business in the Japanese American Community.* Berkeley, CA: University of California Press.

Brenner, G., and J. Toulouse. 1989. "Business Creation Among the Chinese Immigrants in Montreal." *Journal of Small Business and Entrepreneurship* 7(4): 38-44.

Brockhaus, R.H., Sr. 1982. "The Psychology of the Entrepreneur." In *Encyclopedia of Entrepreneurship,* edited by C. A. Kent, D. L. Sexton, and K. H. Vesper. Englewood Cliffs, NJ: Prentice Hall.

Brush, C.G. 1995. *International Entrepreneurship: The Effect of Firm Age on Motives for Internationalization.* New York: Garland.

Buckley, P.J. 1989. "Foreign Direct Investment by Small and Medium-Sized Enterprises." *Small Business Economics* 1: 89-100.

_____. 1997. "International Technology Transfer by Small and Medium-Sized Enterprises." *Small Business Economics* 9: 67-78.

Buckley, P.J., and M. Casson. 1976. *The Future of the Multinational Enterprise.* London: Macmillan.

Buckley, P.J., G.D. Newbould, and J. Thurwell. 1988. *Foreign Direct Investment by Smaller UK Firms.* London: Macmillan.

Bygrave, W.D., and C.W. Hofer. 1991. "Theorizing About Entrepreneurship." *Entrepreneurship, Theory and Practice* 26 (2): 13-22.

Cantillon, R. 1755. *Essai sur la Nature du Commerce en Général.* London and Paris: R. Gyles; translated (1931) by Henry Higgs. London: MacMillan.

Carsrud, A.L., C.M. Gaglio, and K.W. Olm. 1986. "Entrepreneurs –Mentors, Networks and Successful New Venture Development: An Exploratory Study." In *Frontiers of Entrepreneurship Research,* edited by Babson College. Wellesley, MA: Babson College.

Carstairs, R.T., and L.S. Welch. 1982. "Licensing and Internationalization of Smaller Companies: Some Australian Evidence." *Management International Review* 22(3): 33-44.

Casson, M. 1982. *The Entrepreneur: An Economic Theory.* Oxford: Martin Robinson.

Caves, R.E. 1971. "International Corporations: the Industrial Economics of Foreign Investment." *Economica* 38(1).

_____. 1996. *Multinational Enterprise and Economic Analysis, 2nd ed.* Cambridge: Cambridge University Press.

Cavusgil, S.T. 1980. "On the Internationalisation of Firms." *European Research,* 8.

_____. 1984. "Differences Among Exporting Firms Based on Their Degree of Internationalization." *Journal of Business Research* 12 (2): 195-208.

_____. 1994. "Born Globals: A Quiet Revolution Among Australian Exporters." *Journal of International Marketing Research* 2(3): editorial.

Cavusgil, S.T., W.J. Bilkey, and G. Tesar. 1979. "A Note on the Export Behavior of Firms." *Journal of International Business Studies* 10(1): 91-97.

Cavusgil, S.T., and V. Kirpalani. 1993. "Introducing Products into Export Markets: Success Factors." *Journal of Business Research* 27(1): 1-15.

Cavusgil, S.T., and R.J. Nevin. 1981. "International Determinants of Export Marketing Behavior." *Journal of Marketing Research* 28: 114-119.

Chandler, A.D. 1990. "The Enduring Logic of Industrial Success." *Harvard Business Review* 68(2): 130-140.

Cherry, R. 1990. "Middleman Minority Theories: Their Implications For Black-Jewish Relations." *The Journal of Ethnic Studies* 17(4): 117-138.

Cole, A. 1942. "Entrepreneurship as an Area of Research." *The Tasks of Economic History* (Supplement to the *Journal of Economic History:* 118-126.

Coviello, N.E., and H. J. Munro. 1993. "Linkage Development and the Role of Marketing in the Internationalization of the Entrepreneurial High Technology Firm." In *Research at Marketing/*

Entrepreneurship Interface, edited by G. Hills, R. W. LaForge, and D.F. Muzyka. Chicago: University of Chicago Press.

_____. 1994. "International Market Development and Growth of Entrepreneurial Firms." In *Research at the Marketing/Entrepreneurship Interface*, edited by G. Hills and S. T. Mohan-Neil. Chicago: University of Chicago Press.

Culnan, M.J., and E.B. Swanson. 1986. "Research in Management Information Systems, 1980-1984: Points of Work and Reference." *MIS Quarterly* (September): 289-301.

Cummings, S. 1980. *Self-Help in Urban America: Patterns of Minority Business Enterprise*. Port Washington, New York: Kennikat.

Dana, L.P. 1994. *Enterprising in the Global Environment*. Delhi: World Association for Small and Medium Enterprises.

_____. 1995. "Entrepreneurship in a Remote Sub-Arctic Community." *Entrepreneurship: Theory and Practice* 20(1): 57-72.

Davidson, W.H. 1980. "The Location of Foreign Direct Investment Activity." *Journal of International Business Studies* 11: 9-22.

Dichtl, E., M. Leibold, H. Koeglmayr, and S. Mueller. 1984. "The Export-Decision of Small and Medium-Sized Firms." *Management International Review* 24(2): 49-60.

_____. 1990. "International Orientation as a Precondition for Export Success." *Journal of International Business Studies* 21(1): 23-41.

Drucker, P.F. 1974. *Management, Tasks, Responsibilities, Practices*. New York: Harper and Row.

Dubini, P., and H.E. Aldrich. 1991. "Personal and Extended Networks are Central to the Entrepreneurship Process." *Journal of Business Venturing* 6(5): 305-313.

Dunning, J.H. 1973. "The Determinants of International Production." *Oxford Economic Papers* (November): 289-336.

_____. 1977. "Trade, Location of Economic Activity and MNE: A Search for an Eclectic Approach." Pp. 395-418 in *The International Allocation of Economic Activity: Proceedings of A Nobel Symposium Held at Stockholm*. London: Macmillan.

_____. 1980. "Toward an Eclectic Theory of International Production: Empirical Tests." *Journal of International Business Studies* 11(1): 9-31.

_____. 1988. "The Eclectic Paradigm of International Production: A Restatement and Some Possible Extensions." *Journal of International Business Studies* 19(1): 1-31.

Ely, R.T., and R.H. Hess. 1893. *Outline of Economics*. New York: Macmillan.

Erramilli, M.K., and D.E. D'Souza. 1993. "Venturing into Foreign Markets." *Entrepreneurship: Theory and Practice* 18: 29-41.

Fujita, M. 1995. "Small and Medium-Sized Transnational Corporations." *Small Business Economics* 7(3): 183-204.

Gasse, Y. 1977. *Entrepreneurial Characteristics and Practices: A Study of the Dynamics of Small Business Organizations and Their Effectiveness in Different Environments*. Sherbrooke, Quebec: René Prince.

Gemunden, H. 1991. "Success Factors of Export Marketing: A Meta-analytic Critique of the Empirical Studies." In *New Perspectives on International Marketing*, edited by S. J. Paliwoda. London: Routledge.

Giamartino, G.A., P.P. McDougall, and B.J. Bird. 1993. "International Entrepreneurship: The State of the Field." *Entrepreneurship: Theory and Practice* 18(1): 37-41.

Hornaday, J.A., and J. Aboud. 1971. "Characteristics of Successful Entrepreneurs." *Personnel Psychology* 24 (2): 141-153.

Hornaday, J.A., and C.S. Bunker. 1970. "The Nature of the Entrepreneur." *Personnel Psychology* 23 (1): 47-54.

Hymer, S. 1976. *International Operations of National Firms: A Study of Direct Foreign Investment*. Cambridge, MA: MIT Press.

Jensen, L., and A. Portes. 1992. "Correction." *American Sociological Review* 57(3): 411-418.

Johanson, J., and Associates. 1994. *Internationalization, Relationships and Networks.* Stockholm: Almquist and Wiksell International.

Johanson, J., and J. Vahlne. 1977. "The Internationalization Process of the Firm – A Model of Knowledge Development and Increasing Foreign Market Commitments?" *Journal of International Business Studies* 8: 23-32.

_____. 1990. "The Mechanism of Internationalization." *International Marketing Review* 7(4): 11-24.

_____. 1992. "Management of Foreign Market Entry." *Scandinavian International Business Review* 1(3): 9-27.

Johanson, J., and F. Wiedersheim-Paul. 1975. "The Internationalization of the Firm: Four Swedish Cases." *Journal of International Management Studies* 12 (3): 36-64.

Kasdan, L. 1965. "Family Structure, Migration and the Entrepreneur." *Comparative Studies in Society and History* 7: 345-357.

Kets de Vries, M. 1977. "The Entrepreneurial Personality: A Person at the Crossroads." *The Journal of Management Studies* 14(1): 34-57.

_____. 1985. "The Dark Side of Entrepreneurship." *Harvard Business Review* 63(6): 160-167.

Keynes, J.M. 1936. *The General Theory of Employment, Interest and Money.* New York: Harcourt, Brace and Co.

Kirzner, I.M. 1973. *Competition and Entrepreneurship. Chicago:* University of Chicago.

_____. 1982. *Method, Process and Austrian Economics.* Lexington, MA: Lexington Books.

Knickerbocker, F.T. 1973. *Oligopolistic Reaction and Multinational Enterprise.* Boston: Graduate School of Business Administration, Harvard University.

Knight, F.H. 1921. *Risk Uncertainty and Profit.* Boston and New York: Houghton Mifflin.

Knight, G.A., and S.T. Cavusgil. 1996. "The Born Globalization: A Challenge to Traditional Internationalization Theory." In *Advances in International Marketing*, edited by S.T.Cavusgil and T. K. Masden. Greenwich, CT: JAI Press.

Leonidou, L.C., and C.S. Katsikeas. 1996. "The Export Development Process." *Journal of International Business Studies* 27(3): 517-551.

Light, I. 1972. *Ethnic Enterprise in America: Business and Welfare among Chinese, Japanese and Blacks.* Berkeley, CA: University of California.

_____. 1984. "Immigrant and Ethnic Enterprise in North America." *Ethnic and Racial Studies, 7(2),* pp. 195-216.

Light, I., and E. Bonacich. 1988. *Immigrant Entrepreneurs: Koreans in Los Angeles 1965-1985.* Berkeley, CA: University of California Press.

McClelland, D.C. 1961. The *Achieving Society.* Princeton, NJ: D. Van Nostrand.

McDougall, P.P. 1989. "International Versus Domestic Entrepreneurship: New Venture Strategic Behavior and Industry Structure." *Journal of Business Venturing* 5(4): 387-400.

_____. 1996. "New Venture Internationalization, Strategic Change, and Performance: A Follow-Up Study." *Journal of Business Venturing* 11(1): 23-40.

McDougall, P.P., S. Shane, and B.M. Oviatt. 1994. "Explaining the Formation of International Joint Ventures: The Limits of Theories from International Business Research." *Journal of Business Venturing* 9: 469-487.

McMullan, W., ed. 1994. "Going Global on Start-Up: A Case Study." *Technovation* 14 (3):141-143.

Min, P.G. 1984. "From White-Collar Occupation to Small Business: Korean Immigrants' Occupational Adjustment." *Sociological Quarterly* 25(3): 333-352.

_____. 1986-7. "Filipino and Korean Immigrants in Small Business: A Comparative Analysis." *Amerasia* 13(1): 53-71.

_____. 1987. "Factors Contributing To Ethnic Business: A Comprehensive Synthesis." *International Journal of Comparative Sociology* 28(3-4).

Min, P.G., and C. Jaret. 1985. "Ethnic Business Success: The Case of Korean Small Business in Atlanta." *Sociology and Social Research* 69(3): 412-435.

Morck, R., and B. Yeung. 1991. "Why Investors Value Multinationality." *Journal of Business* 64(2): 165-187.

———. 1992. "Internalization: An Event Study Test." *Journal of International Economics 33:* 41-56.

Morris, M.H., D.L. Davis, and J.W. Allen. 1994. "Fostering Corporate Entrepreneurship: Cross-Cultural Comparisons of the Importance of Individualism Versus Collectivism." *Journal of International Business Studies* 25(1): 65-90.

Murphy, K.M., A. Shleifer, and R.W. Vishny. 1993. "Why is Rent-Seeking Costly to Growth?" *American Economic Review* 82(2): 409-414.

Newbould, G.D., P.J. Buckley, and J.C. Thurwell. 1978. *Going International - The Enterprise of Smaller Companies Overseas.* New York: John Wiley and Sons.

Oviatt, B.M. 1995. "Entrepreneurs on a Worldwide Stage." *Academy of Management Executive* 9(2): 30-43.

Oviatt, B.M., and P.P. McDougall. 1994. "Toward A Theory of International New Ventures." *Journal of International Business Studies* 25(1): 45-64.

———. 1997. "Challenges for Internationalization Process Theory." *Management International Review* 37(2): 85-99.

Porter, M.E. 1980. *Competitive Strategy: Techniques for Analyzing Industries and Competitors.* New York: Free Press.

———. 1985. *Competitive Advantage.* New York: Free Press.

———. 1986. "Changing Patterns of International Competition." *California Management Review* 28: 9-40.

———. 1990. *The Competitive Advantage of Nations.* New York: Free Press.

Portes, A. 1981. "Modes of Structural Incorporation and Present Theories of Immigration." In *Global Trends In Migration: Theory and Research On International Population Movements*, edited by M. Kritz, C. Keely, and S. Tomasi. New York: Center For Migration Studies Press: 279-297.

Portes, A., and R.C. Bach. 1985. *Latin Journey.* Berkeley, CA: University of California Press.

Portes, A., and L. Jensen. 1987. "What's an Ethnic Enclave? The Case For Conceptual Clarity." *American Sociological Review* 52(6): 768-771.

———. 1989. "The Enclave and the Entrants: Patterns of Ethnic Enterprise in Miami Before and After Mariel." *American Sociological Review* 54(6): 929-949.

———. 1992. "Disproving the Enclave Hypothesis." *American Sociological Review* 57(3): 418-420.

Portes, A., and J. Walton. 1981. *Labor, Class and the International System.* New York: Academic Press.

Ray, D.M. 1989. "Strategic Implications of Entrepreneurial Ventures 'Born' International: Four Case Studies." Paper presented at the 1989 Babson Conference; abstracted in *Frontiers of Entrepreneurship Research*, edited by R. H. Brockhaus, N. C. Churchill, J. Katz, B. A. Kirchoff, K. H. Vesper, and W. E. Welzel. Wellesley, MA: Babson College.

Reuber, A.R., and E. Fischer. 1997. "The Influence of the Management Team's International Experience on the Internationalization Behavior of SMEs." *Journal of International Business Studies* 28(4): 807-825.

Reynolds, P.D. 1991. "Sociology and Entrepreneurship: Concepts and Contributions." *Entrepreneurship, Theory and Practice* 16(2): 47-70.

Rothstein, F. 1992. "What Happens to the Past? Return Industrial Migrants in Latin America." In *Anthropology and the Global Factory: Studies of the New Industrialization in the Late Twentieth Century*, edited by F. Rothstein and M. Blim. New York: Bergin and Garvey.

Rugman, A.M. 1979. *International Diversification and the Multinational Enterprise.* Farborough: Lexington.

———. 1981. *Inside the Multinationals: The Economics of Internal Market.* New York: Columbia University Press.

Rugman, A.M., and J.R. D'Cruz. 1997. "The Theory of the Flagship Firm." *European Management Review* 15 (4): 403-412.

Sanders, J.M., and V. Nee. 1987. "Limits of Ethnic Solidarity in the Enclave Economy." *American Sociological Review* 52(6): 745-767.

Say, J.B. 1803. *Traite d'économie politique ou simple exposition de la manière dont se forment, se distribuent, et se consomment les richesses*; revised (1819); translated (1830) by C. R. Prinsep, as *A Treatise on Political Economy: On Familiar Conversations On the Manner in Which Wealth is Produced, Distributed and Consumed by Society.* Philadelphia: John Grigg and Elliot.

_____. 1815. *Catechisme d'économie politique*; translated (1821) by John Richter, as *Catechism of Political Economy.* London: Sherwood.

Schumpeter, J.A. 1911. *Theorie der wirtschaftlichen Entwicklung*, Munich and Leipzig: Dunker und Humblat; translated (1934) by R. Opie, as *The Theory of Economic Development.* Cambridge, MA: Harvard University Press.

_____. 1928. "The Instability of Capitalism." *Economic Journal* 38: 361-386.

_____. 1942. *Capitalism, Socialism and Democracy.* New York: Harper and Row.

_____. 1947. "The Creative Response in Economic History." *Journal of Economic History* 7: 149-159.

_____. 1949. "Economic Theory and Entrepreneurial History." In *Change and the Entrepreneur*, Cambridge, MA: Harvard University Press.

Sexton, D., and N. Bowman. 1985. "The Entrepreneur: A Capable Executive and More." *Journal of Business Venturing* 1: 129-140.

_____. 1990. "Female and Male Entrepreneurs: Psychological Characteristics." *Journal of Business Venturing* 5: 29-36.

Shane, S., L. Kolvereid, and P. Westhead. 1993. "Do International and Domestic Entrepreneurs Differ at Start-Up?" In *Entrepreneurship Research: Global Perspectives*, edited by S. Birley and I. MacMillan. North Holland, The Netherlands: Elsevier Science.

Shapero, A. 1975. "The Displaced, Uncomfortable Entrepreneur." *Psychology Today* 9(11): 83-133.

_____. 1984. "The Entrepreneurial Event." In *The Environment for Entrepreneurship*, edited by C. Kent. Lexington, MA: DC Health.

Shapero, A., and L. Sokol. 1982. "The Social Dimensions of Entrepreneurship." In *Encyclopedia of Entrepreneurship*, edited by C. Kent, D. Sexton, and K. Vesper. Englewood Cliffs, NJ: Prentice Hall.

Sherman, A.J. 1996. "International Franchising: Strategies for Building Bridges Between Asia and North America." *Journal of International Business and Entrepreneurship* 4(1): 1-28.

Shuman, J.C., and J.A. Seeger. 1986. "The Theory and Practice of Strategic Management in Smaller Rapid Growth Companies." *American Journal of Small Business* 11(1): 7-18.

Simon, H. 1992. "Lessons From Germany's Midsize Giants." *Harvard Business Review* 70 (2): 115-123.

Stearns, T.M., and G.E. Hills. 1996. "Entrepreneurship and New Firm Development: A Definitional Introduction." *Journal of Business Research* 36(1): 1-4.

Stevenson, H.H., and J.C. Jarrillo-Mossi. 1986. "Preserving Entrepreneurship as Companies Grow." *Journal of Business Strategy* 7: 10-23.

Stopford, J., and L.T. Wells, Jr. 1972. *Managing the Multinational Enterprise.* New York: Basic.

Sullivan, D., and A. Bauerschmidt. 1990. "Incremental Internationalization." *Management International Review* 30(1): 19-30.

Teece, D. 1985. "Multinational Enterprise, Internal Governance and Economic Organization." *American Economic Review* 75: 233-238.

Tesar, G., and J.S. Tarleton. 1982. "Comparison of Wisconsin and Virginia Small and Medium Sized Exporters: Aggressive and Passive Exporters." In *Export Management: An International Context*, edited by M. R. Czinkota and G. Tesar. New York.

Turnbull, P. W. 1987. "A Challenge to the Stages Theory of the Internationalization Process." In *Managing Export Entry and Expansion*, edited by P. J. Rosson and S. D. Reids. New York: Praeger.

Tuttle, C. 1927. "The Entrepreneur in Economic Literature." *Journal of Political Economy* 35: 501-521.

Vernon, R. 1966. "International Investment and International Trade and the Product Cycle." *Quarterly Journal of Economics* (May): 190-207.

_____. 1979. "The Product Cycle Hypothesis in a New International Environment." *Oxford Bulletin of Economics and Statistics* 41: 255-267.

Waldinger, R.D. 1984. "Immigrant Enterprise in the New York Garment Industry." *Social Problems* 32(1): 60-71.

_____. 1986a. "Immigrant Enterprise: A Critique and Reformulation." *Theory and Society* 15(1-2): 249-285.

_____. 1986b. *Through the Eye of the Needle: Immigrants and Enterprise in New York's Garment Trades.* New York: New York University Press.

Waldinger, R.D., and H.E. Aldrich. 1990. "Trends in Ethnic Business in the United States." In*Ethnic Entrepreneurs: Immigrant Business in Industrial Societies,* edited by R. Waldinger, H. Aldrich, R. Ward, and Associates. Newbury Park, CA: Sage.

Waldinger, R.D., H.E. Aldrich, and R. Ward. 1990. "Opportunities, Group Characteristics and Strategies." In *Ethnic Entrepreneurs: Immigrant Business in Industrial Societies,* edited by R. Waldinger, H. Aldrich, R. Ward, and Associates. Newbury Park, CA: Sage.

Waldinger, R.D., D. McEvoy, and H.E. Aldrich. 1990. "Spatial Dimensions of Opportunity Structures." In *Ethnic Entrepreneurs: Immigrant Business in Industrial Societies,* edited by R.Waldinger, H. Aldrich, R. Ward, and Associates. Newbury Park, CA: Sage.

Ward, R. 1987. "Ethnic Entrepreneurs in Britain and in Europe." In *Entrepreneurship in Europe,* edited by R. Scase and R. Goffee. London: Croom Helm.

Ward, R., and R. Jenkins. 1984. *Ethnic Communities in Business: Strategies For Economic Survival.* Cambridge: Cambridge University Press.

Weber, M. 1904-1905. Die protestantische Ethik und der Geist des Kapitalismus. *Archiv fur Sozialwissenschaft und Sozialpolitik* 20-21; translated (1930) by Talcott Parsons, as *The Protestant Ethic and the Spirit of Capitalism.* New York: George Allen and Unwin.

Wells, L.T., Jr. 1972. *The Product Life Cycle and International Trade.* Boston: Harvard.

Williamson, O.E. 1975. *The Economic Institutions of Capitalism.* New York: Free Press.

Wilson, K.L., and A. Portes. 1980. "Immigrant Enclaves: An Analysis of the Labor Market Experiences of Cubans in Miami." *American Journal of Sociology* 86(2).

Wong, B. 1987. "The Role of Ethnicity in Enclave Enterprises: A Study of the Chinese Garment Factories in New York City." *Human Organization* 66(2): 120-130.

Wright, R.W. 1989. "Networking, Japanese Style." *Business Quarterly* 54(2): 20-24.

Wu, Y.L. 1983. "The Role of Alien Entrepreneurs in Economic Development: An Entrepreneurial Problem." *American Economic Review* 73(2): 112-117.

Young, F.W. 1971. "A Macrosociological Interpretation of Entrepreneurship." In *Entrepreneurship and Economic Development,* edited by P. Kilby. New York: Free Press.

Zaleznik, A., and M.F.R. Kets de Vries. 1976. "What Makes Entrepreneurs Entrepreneurial." *Business and Society Review* 17: 18-23.

Zhou, M., and J. Logan. 1989. "Returns on Human Capital in Ethnic Enclaves: New York City's Chinatown." *American Sociological Review* 54(5): 809-820.

A FRAMEWORK FOR UNDERSTANDING ACCELERATED INTERNATIONAL ENTREPRENEURSHIP

Benjamin M. Oviatt and Patricia P. McDougall

I. INTRODUCTION

From many sources we are learning that increasing numbers of new and small firms in many countries conduct business across national borders. Perhaps one to two percent of emerging businesses are now international at inception, and a quarter of all small- and medium-sized businesses (SMEs) around the world derive a major portion of their revenues (i.e., more than 10%) from foreign countries (OECD 1997). Furthermore, there is increasing evidence that the speed with which emerging businesses internationalize is accelerating. Many businesses have international revenue within four or five years of start-up now; whereas, in the 1980s it might have taken a decade (OECD 1997). The Organisation for Economic Co-operation and Development predicts that within seven years a third of all SMEs will derive a major portion of their revenues from international sources. Indeed, recognition of such facts is a major impetus for the conference on "Globalization and Emerging Businesses."

Research in Global Strategic Management, Volume 7, pages 23-40.
Copyright © 1999 by JAI Press Inc.
All rights of reproduction in any form reserved.
ISBN: 0-7623-0458-8

A dynamic theory of the process of firm internationalization relevant to the economic conditions of the 1990s is lacking (Dunning 1993a). Thus, our ability to explain accelerated internationalization is limited, especially for emerging businesses. The purpose of this paper, therefore, is to identify a framework for such a theory and, through the identification of research questions and propositions, stimulate discussion plus theoretical and empirical efforts that may eventually lead to a contemporary dynamic theory of firm internationalization and its acceleration. We begin by defining the problem in greater detail. We follow by describing the objective of the theory along with the research questions it should answer when it is fully delineated. The foundation of international economic dynamism—rapidly changing technology—is identified. Subsequent sections of the paper explore four building blocks that we believe provide the framework for an improved theory of firm internationalization: political economy, industry conditions, firm effects, and the management team.

II. THE THEORETICAL PROBLEM

First, we must be clear about what we mean by internationalization. We are referring to a process, over time, in which a firm develops increasing involvement in operations outside the firm's home country (Welch and Loustarinen 1988). Such involvement may include inputs and/or outputs of the firm and may also touch some or many parts of its value chain. For example, a new venture may depend on research and development work done in another country for the design of its initial product. It may use skilled human resources located overseas. And it may sell its product in an increasing number of foreign countries over time. Thus, it is obvious that a firm may internationalize along a variety of dimensions.

The accelerated process of internationalization appears to be a historically significant change in the way business is conducted. Toward the end of the 1980s and beginning of the 1990s the popular business press noted with interest that some businesses were internationalizing at a younger age and with a smaller size than was usually expected (Brokaw 1990; *The Economist* 1992, 1993; Mamis 1989; Gupta 1989). Additional evidence was provided by a study of new ventures in Australia that uncovered surprisingly aggressive international activities (McKinsey and Co. 1993). The United Nations surveyed small transnational corporations around the world and found falling barriers to small firm internationalization and an increasing number of small firms that bypassed the traditional, incremental, step-wise pattern of internationalizing (UNCTAD 1993a). In some industries most firms, regardless of their young age or small size, were forced by competitive forces to go international (Burrill and Almassey 1993). Universally respected scholars of international business have noted the increasing importance of small- and medium-sized businesses in the international economy (Dunning 1995). The OECD (1997) report on the internationalization of small enterprises, mentioned earlier, is probably the most comprehensive account of how pervasive the phenomenon is throughout the world.

Unfortunately, received international business theory focuses on other, albeit related, phenomenon. To explain the dynamic process of accelerated internationalization, a theory must be dynamic. However, most international economic theories, such as the eclectic theory, are static (Dunning 1993a). A recent explanation of why international new ventures[1] exist also presents a static model (Oviatt and McDougall 1994). The dynamic product cycle theory is acknowledged by its author to be increasingly less applicable as time passes (Vernon 1979). Stopford and Wells's (1972) dynamic theory is primarily applicable to the development of structure and process in established multinational enterprises. Stage models of exporting have been criticized for their inadequate theory and for their reliance on largely cross-sectional empirical evidence, which cannot support a dynamic model (Andersen 1993). The most widely recognized theory concerning the dynamics of internationalization and one that has been relevant for young and small firms in the past—the Uppsala model (Johanson and Vahlne 1990, 1977)—relies on assumptions that applied nearly a generation ago.

In the 1970s international telephone connections were expensive and not very reliable. International air transport was available only from a limited number of cities. Mainframe computers with less calculating power than today's desktops were available only to the largest corporations. Foreign direct investment inflows and outflows were less than $50 billion per year in the 1970s; whereas, they are now approaching $400 billion annually (UNCTAD 1997). Electronic commerce and global start-ups were the stuff of science fiction. Thus, for a small emerging business in the 1970s to make investments or even to trade internationally was unusual, expensive, and fraught with uncertainty.

It is no wonder that the primary goal of the Uppsala model was to explain the typically incremental internationalization process of firms at that time. For the environment of the 1970s, Johanson and Vahlne (1977) valuably highlighted managers' experiential (i.e., tacit) knowledge of foreign markets as the primary determinant of how much a firm was committed to international business and where such business was conducted. They believed at the time that the influence of tacit foreign market knowledge had been overlooked. At the beginning of the 1990s, while acknowledging that such knowledge had become more widespread, they continued to believe that its influence was insufficiently recognized (Johanson and Vahlne 1990). They and others also believed that the Uppsala model applied best to the early stages of the internationalization process (Hadjikhani 1997; Johanson and Vahlne 1990). Such beliefs are supported by the universal observation that the majority of emerging businesses that internationalize do so incrementally, albeit perhaps with greater speed in recent years (OECD 1997; UNCTAD 1993a).

Nevertheless, empirical research since the 1980s has found significant numbers of firms that did not follow the internationalization path predicted by the Uppsala model (Bloodgood, Sapienza, and Almeida 1996; Coviello and Munro 1997; McDougall, Shane, and Oviatt 1994; OECD 1997; Preece, Miles, and Baetz 1999; Sullivan and Bauerschmidt 1990; Turnbull 1987; UNCTAD 1993b). Thus, international new ventures and accelerated firm internationalization are not anomalies, but represent current trends and perhaps windows on the future of international business. We believe academic effort should be devoted, not to further theoretical elaboration about the past, but to explaining the lesser understood and still accelerating internationalization of today's and tomorrow's businesses.

III. THE THEORETICAL OBJECTIVE: AN EXPLANATION OF ACCELERATED INTERNATIONALIZATION

Why do businesses, especially newly emerging ones, internationalize more rapidly than they have done in the past? That is the general research question which governs our search for a new dynamic theory of internationalization. Significant corollary issues involve the breadth and modes of accelerated internationalization and how the role of an emerging firm within its business system influences the speed of internationalization. We will briefly consider each of these issues below.

A. Breadth of Internationalization

Internationalization may not accelerate at a unified pace throughout the entire breadth of a firm's value chain (Welch and Loustarinen 1988). For example, some inputs may be sourced from foreign countries before foreign revenues are generated, especially commodity inputs for emerging firms headquartered in highly developed economies. On the output side of the value chain, packaging, sales, and distribution may be international sooner than core production activities (OECD 1997). A rich theory of accelerated internationalization will explain why some parts of the value chain tend to internationalize more rapidly. In addition, the theory would identify important relationships among the parts. For example, perhaps if vital inputs are sourced from a foreign country by a small emerging firm before it begins sales efforts, it is sensitized to the opportunity for sales in that country regardless of its cultural distance. Attention to such foreign opportunities seems likely to lead to early internationalization.

B. Modes of Internationalization

It is clear that modern internationalization is a complex process. Firms, even small ones, may simultaneously purchase foreign inputs, establish alliances with foreign firms, make direct investments in foreign sales offices, and export (OECD 1997; UNCTAD 1996). Thus, the traditional expectation that firms will internationalize through a graduated series of increasingly risky modes of entry and investment may be wrong for a significant number of firms. Indeed, firms that are committed to multinational markets from their inception may internationalize rapidly through a simultaneous combination of modes. Yet we have little understanding about why the combinations are chosen and which ones are typical and successful.

C. Role of Emerging Businesses

As noted earlier, the recent significant internationalization of small and emerging businesses is one of the most important challenges to the Uppsala model (Oviatt and McDougall 1997). Some scholars believe the situation is due to the increasing focus of established multinational firms on their core competencies and their concomitant downsizing (Dunning 1993a, 1995; Johanson and Vahlne 1990). It is seen as the continuation of a subcontracting trend among large firms, which symbiotically create new niche opportunities for the small firms. In Japan such relationships have been common for many years (Wright 1989). Typically, the small emerging firms are depicted as weak dependents of multinational corporations, and undoubtedly, that is true for many firms.

Informed observers, however, seem to have identified at least three distinct roles for small internationalizing firms (Dunning 1995; OECD 1997). First, the most dependent small firms tend to emerge in mature, global industries, such as automobiles, pharmaceuticals, and aerospace, where investments in research and development are enormous and scale economies essential. In mature but less concentrated industries, such as textiles and furniture, small firms may depend on large multinational corporations for distribution or other types of alliances. Second, in new industries and niche markets, such as precision instruments and specialist software, small firms and new ventures internationalize quite independently perhaps because specialized and unique knowledge is the key to being a successful competitor. New ventures with such knowledge either do not need partners or are concerned that partners will appropriate their competitive advantage. Finally, some small emerging firms in particular locations may internationalize as part of an interdependent industrial network of small firms (Dunning 1995), like Italian ceramic tile makers do. We call these three roles of emerging international businesses: dependence, independence, and interdependence. Even our brief description suggests that industry competitive conditions influence which role a firm assumes, perhaps more than the Uppsala theory's tacit knowledge about foreign markets. Furthermore, there is some evidence that the rather independent firms in new industries and niche markets may internationalize most rapidly (OECD 1997), but systematic study is needed to understand how these differing roles influence the speed of firm internationalization.

In summary, an improved theory of internationalization must explain its acceleration, its breadth, its modes of entry and investment, and the roles of emerging international businesses. We suspect that, while some explanatory influences on firm internationalization processes will be more important than others, any attempt to highlight a single determinant of the process, as was done in the Uppsala model, will result in a misleadingly simple theory. At the same time, one of the virtues of the Uppsala model that has contributed to its popularity is its parsimony, and if an improved theory of the process of firm internationalization is to be useful, it must also be reasonably succinct.

IV. THE FOUNDATION OF CHANGING TECHNOLOGY

In the last two decades changes in the international business environment have stimulated and facilitated the accelerated internationalization of new, small, and medium-sized ventures. One can identify a variety of environmental influences: increasingly liberal regulations for the international marketplace, changing demand patterns among consumers, and rapidly evolving advances in technology (Knight and Cavusgil 1997; UNCTAD 1997). We believe technological change is the foundation for accelerated internationalization and may be increasing in importance relative to the Uppsala model's tacit foreign market knowledge.

Firm technology, or the production and organizational capacity that determines how resources are converted to outputs, has been changing with increasing speed throughout the twentieth century (Dunning 1993b). Following World War II, trade and foreign direct investment were focused on the natural resource sector (i.e., agriculture, mining, petroleum) and in resource-based manufacturing, but their importance has faded (UNCTAD 1993b). By the 1990s foreign direct investment was greatest in services and technology-intensive manufacturing, and those investments often supported the expansion of trade (UNCTAD 1993b, 1996). Because technological change is now so rapid and valuable in many industries, it is generally believed that the ability to create, acquire, and use technological innovations is one of the most important keys to success and growth for firms in all societies (Dunning 1993b; Porter 1990; UNCTAD 1995). New and small firms play an essential part in the continuing process of global innovation, and many of the innovations that they initiate enable their own accelerated internationalization.

Concerning the part they play in the global innovation process, small firms produce more innovations per employee than large firms (Acs and Audretsch 1990). Even in industries where large firms dominate, most innovations occur in the industry's small firms (Acs and Audretsch 1988). A primary role for large established firms seems to be the development and transmission of those innovations around the world by purchasing the exports of small firms and by building networks of small firm alliances (Acs, Morck, Shaver, and Yeung 1997; Dunning 1995). This process may be observed in the technological innovations emerging from recombinant DNA, which began in the 1970s (Barley, Freeman, and Hybels 1992). Entrepreneurs who observed the commercial potential of those discoveries encouraged and assisted molecular biologists to form biotechnology firms for the purpose of pursuing applied and basic research. Such firms were generally small and numbered perhaps 500 by the mid-1980s. Most joined international networks of new and established firms for the purpose of development and/or commercialization, and such networks continued to expand in the 1990s. Thus, the relatively rapid internationalization of small firms and new ventures, either as part of a multi-firm network or on their own, is essential to innovation in the global biotechnology industry. Some of the most significant changes ever seen in medicine may emerge in the twenty-first century through biotechnologies that are still emerging (Carey 1999).

At this point, however, the development of the microprocessor is an innovation which may have had a more significant impact (Hill 1998), and it directly facilitates the accelerated internationalization of small firms and new ventures. The microprocessor has made computers an indispensable business tool around the world. It has also brought about advances in communications that make international business no longer the preserve of large, mature corporations (Oviatt and McDougall 1994). More efficient, easier to use, and lower cost global communication technologies have eroded the advantages that large multinational corporations once held over small and new ventures. By 1990 the fax machine was a major technological tool for the global entrepreneur, multiplying market access and information (McDougall and Oviatt 1991; McKinsey and Company 1993).

Yet the impact of the Internet may dwarf that of the fax machine (Ostry 1998). The most obvious implication is that firms as small as one employee can become international through a Web site. While a small firm may not have an explicit international expansion strategy, the Web site automatically positions the firm in the international marketplace. Unsolicited international orders have often served as a trigger for internationalization in the past. The receipt of foreign orders over the Internet may even more rapidly propel firms to explore the international marketplace, even firms that, contrary to the Uppsala model's predictions, have little tacit knowledge of foreign markets. With the predicted explosion in electronic commerce, the Internet may greatly decrease the time to internationalize and may increase the level of internationalization of among the smallest businesses of the twenty-first century.

Knight and Cavusgil (1997) identified advances in communications technology as a "facilitating factor" in the rise of born-global firms and noted that communication tools such as the fax, e-mail, and the Internet have greatly reduced the need for expensive face-to-face meetings. Thus, it is possible for resource-poor ventures to conduct international business from home. Increasingly competitive international airfares and telephone rates further level the playing field for small businesses. If the predictions regarding the falling cost of international telephone calls (*Economist* 1995) become reality, then entrepreneurs may soon be able to dial up a company 10,000 miles away almost as cheaply as placing a call 100 miles away. In summary, the dramatic increases in the speed, quality, and efficiency of international communication and transportation have reduced the transaction costs of international exchange, thereby making internationalization feasible even for emerging firms (Porter 1990). Reduced international transaction costs mean that business risk is reduced and tacit foreign market knowledge may be less important for internationalization.

New production technologies have also had an impact on the ability of emerging firms to compete with large firms. Computer-aided design and special software programs enable the rapid development of prototypes and put the cost of their development within the reach of small emerging firms (*Business Week* 1994). The outsourcing of manufacturing provides opportunities for smaller firms and reduces the size, and therefore the competitive threat, of established multinational corporations. The advantage of economies of scale is further reduced by advances in microprocessor controls which allow small-scale, batch-type production to be economically feasible (Wheelwright and Hayes 1985). These innovations in production technologies allow emerging firms to successfully compete in the international arena by reducing one more advantage once held by the large established firm. Indeed, such innovations have probably contributed to the cessation and possible reversal of the long-term trend of increasing firm size sometime during the 1970s (Acs and Preston 1997).

In summary, three factors make changing technology the most likely foundation of accelerated internationalization. First, it is clear that advancing technology is essential to social progress in all countries. Second, it is apparent that small emerging firms play a vital part in the discovery of technological innovations that are used worldwide. Finally, it has been observed that these firms use some of their own communication and production innovations plus those of other emerging firms to facilitate their own rapid internationalization. Thus, we believe changing technology, not the Uppsala theory's tacit knowledge of foreign markets, is the foundation of accelerated internationalization among new and small ventures.

Proposition 1.   Technological innovation is increasing in importance relative to tacit managerial knowledge of foreign markets as a determinant of the speed, breadth, and mode of internationalization, and the role of emerging firms.

Changing technology, while serving as the foundation, cannot by itself explain accelerated internationalization among small and new firms. Therefore, changing technology is best depicted as the foundation that influences all the other theoretical building blocks of accelerated internationalization. Those building blocks are considered in the following sections.

V. BUILDING BLOCKS OF ACCELERATED INTERNATIONALIZATION THEORY

We believe four building blocks—political economy, industry conditions, firm effects, and the management team—will explain much about the speed, breadth, and modes of internationalization and the role of emerging businesses in the internationalization process. The first three of these influences closely match the three primary uncertainties of international business identified by Miller (1992): general environmental uncertainties, industry uncertainties, and firm uncertainties. We have added the management team to the list because the personal decision-making power of a few top managers and owners in emerging firms typically substitutes for some bureaucratic decision structures and processes in large established firms.

A. Political Economy

Although national and international regulatory regimes greatly affect the geographic direction and speed of technology diffusion around the world, the causal effect can also run the other way (Dunning 1998). That is, changes in technology can cause regulatory regimes to be revised, and there is evidence that this influence may be gaining strength. For example, it is believed by some that information available on Cable News Network, which relies on advanced cable and satellite television technologies for worldwide distribution, may have played a part in the fall of Communism in Eastern Europe (Davis 1999). Perhaps less dramatic although still quite important, the Uruguay Round of negotiations about the General Agreement on Tariffs and Trade, initiated in 1986 and completed in 1993, was the first round to consider regulations regarding services, intellectual property, and investment (Ostry 1998). All three issues are vital to the development and diffusion of advanced technology. At the 1997 G-7 Summit talks, it was proposed that the OECD explore the many policy dimensions of electronic commerce (Ostry 1998), a largely unregulated technologically based activity that is spreading rapidly around the world. Dunning's (1993b) encyclopedic *Multinational Enterprises and the Global Economy* devoted two chapters to technological developments, much of it on how governments can and should react to the accelerating changes. In general, governments have refocused their attention from the development of regulatory and rent distribution policies concerning multinational corporations to how they can attract knowledge-based foreign direct investment into their countries (Rugman and Verbeke 1998). This historical reversal of attitude among governments is one reason why we believe that, while the political economy is certainly one of the vital building blocks of a theory of accelerated internationalization, changing technology is a better candidate for its foundation. Over time, the increasing value governments have placed on open and less regulated markets has guaranteed the increasing influence of technology simply because its diffusion is less constrained by regulation.

Proposition 2. Technological innovation is increasing in importance relative to international regulation as a determinant of the speed, breadth, and mode of internationalization, and the role of emerging firms.

One of the reasons firms internationalize is to seek new markets for growth (Dunning 1993b). When small and new businesses first internationalize, they usually enter countries whose culture and business customs most resemble their home (OECD 1997). Indeed, that observation supports the Uppsala model of internationalization because managers are more likely to have tacit knowledge about the operation of foreign markets most similar to their own. We believe, however, that the pull of foreign growth opportunities is vying with the pull of cultural proximity to explain international initiatives by emerging firms. With increasing numbers of entrepreneurs familiar with foreign cultures and international operations, concerns about strange foreign locations and risks may be attenuated (Hedlund and Kverneland 1985), while attention to locations with profitable growth opportunities may be accentuated. Consistent with that belief was Shrader's (1996) finding that among successful, growth-oriented, newly public, international new ventures started in the United States during the 1980s, Japan was the most frequently entered country, not Canada, which is culturally and geographically closer.

Proposition 3. Opportunities for foreign growth are increasing in importance relative to tacit managerial knowledge of foreign markets as a determinant of the speed, breadth, and mode of internationalization, and the role of emerging firms.

When the worldwide economy is growing, business opportunities in foreign countries are numerous. No matter what conditions are like in the home country, businesses feel a greater pull to internationalize than when the worldwide economy grows more slowly or when it is not growing. At the nadir of a worldwide business cycle, of course, the pull may not be felt. Indeed, such conditions may cause withdrawals from foreign markets, and the effect is felt by both large established multinational corporations and newly emergent international ventures. However, where the primary role of the latter is as dependent suppliers of the former, as some have speculated (e.g., Dunning 1995), then the prevalence, profitability, and failure rate of emergent international new ventures will vary more significantly over time than they will for established multinational corporations. That is because large, established multinational corporations are likely to pass along at least some of their economic distress to their suppliers, which are likely to be more fragile. Of course, when regional economies sour, such as occurred in

Asia in 1997 and 1998, or when the economies of specific countries grow significantly, such as in some South American countries in the first half of 1998, the location of viable business opportunities shifts.

Proposition 4. Over time, the prevalence of emerging businesses experiencing accelerated internationalization will vary significantly more that the prevalence of established multinational enterprises.

There may also be an economic push effect. The OECD (1997) reports that in small open economies, firms may internationalize sooner after start-up than in some large economies. The explanation seems to be that growth-oriented businesses begun in small economies may have insufficient local opportunities. The OECD cautions, however, that the association does not always appear. When national governments offer significant competitive protection to their indigenous businesses, the size of the country's economy has little effect on the speed of firm internationalization. Apparently when protection is provided and domestic profit, therefore, increases, there is little incentive to grow internationally. For example, in Portugal, where the economy is relatively small but protection has been significant, firms tend to be relatively slow to internationalize.

Proposition 5. The size of a country's economy has a negative association with the speed of internationalization among the country's firms.

Proposition 6. A high degree of regulatory protection provided by a national government for its indigenous firms slows their internationalization and overcomes the effect of the economy's size.

In summary, we believe the variety and dynamism of the international political economy will serve as a powerful cornerstone of any theory that is to successfully explain accelerated firm internationalization. As increasing numbers of entrepreneurs become familiar with foreign markets, the opening, closing, and shifting of foreign business opportunities is an increasingly salient influence on the process of firm internationalization.

B. Industry Conditions

The theoretical building block of industry conditions focuses on technological and competitive characteristics of the arena in which emerging businesses operate. The traditional theory of comparative advantage indicates that the goods produced for foreign markets will be those that derive unique advantage from the location in which they are produced. Such theory has historically focused on understanding the natural advantage of geographic location (e.g., mineral deposits). However, in modern technologically advanced, knowledge-based industries, where accelerated internationalization is most obvious, the resources that provide decisive advantage are human (Dunning 1998; Porter 1990). We recently observed a four-person venture less than a year old traveling to India to seek inexpensive software code writers as well as sales contracts. Thus, the venture was simultaneously "market seeking" and "strategic asset seeking," and both motivations for internationalization had their foundation in advanced, knowledge-based technology (Dunning 1998).

In some technology-based industries, sizeable research and development investments typically precede revenue generation (Dunning 1993a). New ventures in such situations may be seen, for example, in microelectronics and in the biotechnology industry (Barley, Freeman, and Hybels 1992). For companies inhabiting those arenas, such investments are a requirement of participation. Venture capitalists, venture angels, or large established companies may serve as sources of investment in return for significant ownership of the venture and the hope of very significant financial returns when the venture goes public or is acquired. For some of those companies, such returns could not even be hoped for without a worldwide market for their outputs. If sales were restricted to a single region, even one as vast and rich as North America, revenue would be insufficient to justify the research and development investment. For example, we interviewed a top manager of a Silicon Valley firm that produced electron microscopes for semiconductor fabrication plants. Research and development was expensive and time consuming, and he was quite certain that his company could not recoup that investment without sales in foreign countries.

Closely related to this issue is the fact that some industries are simply so globally integrated that even the newest and smallest competitors must be international. That has been true for some time in many segments of the electronics industry (Burrill and Almassey 1993). Cost control and access to world-class inputs in hotly contested industries often require early internationalization. For example, Japanese small- and medium-sized enterprises are said to enter other Asian countries in order to control costs and to enter Europe to learn new technologies (OECD 1997). We observed one small U.S. maker of digital controls for heating, air conditioning, and security systems in large buildings frightened into internationalizing by the sudden entry of foreign competitors into its domestic market.

Over the last two decades services have become the largest sector of the world economy (UNCTAD 1996). Service businesses have internationalized during this period to the point that by the mid-1990s services accounted for about 65 percent of worldwide foreign direct investment flows. Service firms often do not have tradeable outputs. Thus, foreign direct investment is often the first mode of internationalization by service firms, although traditional theory, which focuses on manufacturing, assumes that exporting precedes foreign direct investment (UNCTAD 1996). Emerging international service firms often use partnerships and joint ventures as their initial foreign entry modes (Coviello and Munro 1997).

The Uppsala model of internationalization virtually ignores the kinds of industry forces described above. However, we believe they are powerful determinants of rapid internationalization. Furthermore, modern industry forces for internationalization are clearly built on our foundation of knowledge-based, advanced technology. Any theory that ignores such industry conditions is severely crippled in its ability to explain current processes of firm internationalization. Thus,

Proposition 7. Industry conditions are increasing in importance relative to tacit managerial knowledge of foreign markets as determinants of the speed, breadth, and mode of internationalization, and the role of emerging firms.

C. Firm Effects

The primary firm level influences on the process of internationalization, including that of emerging firms, appear to be firm size and firm strategy. Among scholars interested in the internationalization of small- and medium-sized businesses, the effect of firm size seems to have received the most attention. However, the empirical results of its effect are ambiguous (e.g., Bilkey and Tesar 1977; Bonaccorsi 1992; Cavusgil 1984). The OECD (1997) provides perhaps the most interesting explanation. The larger a firm is, the more likely it is to be international. Once a firm has internationalized, however, its size has conflicting effects on internationalization. On the one hand, some evidence suggests that investment abroad requires a certain minimum number of employees, perhaps 50, to manage the complexity of the effort. On the other hand, small firm size is associated with flexibility and greater responsiveness to customers.

We believe these intriguing speculations based on minimum data are worthy of further empirical investigation. We have studied successful international new ventures that did not have 50 employees, but our own evidence is thin. We have also heard repeatedly that smaller firms are unusually flexible and responsive. However, some of those statements come from the managers of small firms, who, of course, are not objective observers.

It is also likely that as digital technology diffuses, the average firm size required to manage foreign assets will decrease. High-speed data transmission lines, satellite communications, and the decreasing price of microprocessor power permits even the smallest companies to communicate with partners overseas and even to operate equipment from remote locations. Advanced computer and communication technology may permit younger and smaller firms to internationalize and to manage more complex foreign transactions than in the past. Thus, the theoretical building block of firm effects, like the other building blocks, also has a foundation in technological change.

Perhaps firm size interacts with firm strategy to influence the success of accelerated internationalization. It is clear that some international new ventures enter foreign countries following clients that are established multinational corporations (OECD 1997). Perhaps such ventures rely on the financial and social support of those large corporations and are, therefore, able to internationalize at a smaller size than they would without such supports. In addition, perhaps ventures that are part of a large, internationalized, industrial network of firms, such as may be found in Silicon Valley or northern Italy, can also enter foreign markets while they are smaller due to their established network of support (Dunning 1998). With either strategy, much of the required tacit knowledge about foreign markets, which is highlighted by the Uppsala model, would come from the firm's support system, not from within the firm itself.

Proposition 8. Technology, support from interfirm alliances, the need for flexibility, and the complexity of a firm's cross-border transactions interact to determine the firm size required for international operations.

Proposition 9. Firm effects (i.e., technology, alliances, flexibility, transaction complexity) are increasing in importance relative to tacit managerial knowledge of foreign markets as determinants of the speed, breadth, and mode of internationalization, and the role of emerging firms.

Many of the international new ventures that we have studied have higher quality, more innovative products, a higher level of service to customers, and extremely aggressive growth goals (McDougall 1989; Oviatt and McDougall 1995; Shrader 1996). They often compete using a global niche strategy (Knight and Cavusgil 1997). Nevertheless, many small- and medium-sized firms still internationalize in an unplanned and passive way (OECD 1997). The new venture with a more aggressive strategy usually experiences more rapid internationalization than the more passive firm. A key empirical question is, under what conditions is each type of strategy most successful?

D. The Management Team

The influence of human resources on the process of firm internationalization is, of course, the only influence considered by the Uppsala model. It predicts a firm will move into foreign markets when its "decision-making system" acquires tacit knowledge of those markets (Johanson and Vahlne 1977). The relevant decision-making system consists of managers, the culture in which they are embedded, and the decision-making routines of their organizations. In emerging firms, which have minimal formal systems, the system is largely in the mind of the founders/entrepreneurs (McDougall et al. 1994). The fact that many, if not most, emerging firms continue to internationalize incrementally suggests the continued relevance of the Uppsala model. However, as already noted, we believe the dominance of that explanation is waning. The OECD (1997) estimated that in 1995 about 40 percent of all small businesses were insulated from the effects of globalization (commonly the smallest very localized service firms), but by 2005 only 20 percent would be in that position. If that is true, tacit experiences with foreigners will soon be forced upon many currently domestically minded small business owners.

Increasing numbers of new ventures appear to internationalize proactively (OECD 1997). Among such emerging firms, a "global orientation" on the part of entrepreneurs may be an important predictor of early internationalization (Knight and Cavusgil 1997). Indeed, in case studies of international new ventures, the founder often has a strong global vision from inception (McDougall et al. 1994). It is useful to ask how such an orientation is learned. It is apparent that many international entrepreneurs learned it by working for companies with international strategies prior to starting their own businesses (Hedlund and Kverneland 1985). Those companies may have adopted international strategies in order to compete effectively in industries that were strongly internationalized. Thus, it may be concluded that both industry- and firm-level influences forced foreign experiences upon many more entrepreneurs today than was true in past decades, a trend which seems likely to expand (OECD 1997). Moreover, we have already noted that industry-and firm-level influences are likely to be at least partially determined by rapidly changing technology. Thus, the slow, incremental, and risk-averse internationalization process described by the Uppsala model may apply best where competitive industry conditions are only weakly international.

Proposition 10. The Uppsala model is most relevant for the decreasing proportion of firms that compete in industries insulated from the forces of globalization.

VI. CONCLUSIONS

This chapter has attempted to further our understanding of accelerated internationalization by identifying relevant research questions, by specifying a framework around which a theory may be formed, and by deriving certain propositions from the foundation and building blocks of the framework. The difficulty of finally devising a rich yet parsimonious theory that explains accelerated firm internationalization is significant. The theory must attend to a sufficient number of influences that the theory is clearly embedded in complex reality, while limiting the number of influences so that complexity does not overwhelm informed scholars and entrepreneurs.

An issue that deserves further exploration is the relationship among the foundation and the building blocks of theory that we have identified. That is, the primary building blocks of theory—political economy, industry conditions, firm effects, and the management team—are not only influenced by the foundation of changing technology, but also by each other. Economic opportunities influence industry conditions, and those conditions influence firm strategies, which in turn effect entrepreneurs' awareness of foreign markets. We have identified some relationships between technological change and the building blocks, but we have only mentioned some of the possible relationships among the building blocks themselves. We hope our effort has been sufficient to stimulate further empirical and theoretical work on our framework so that the future founders of emerging businesses have a better idea about how to determine the best speed, breadth, and modes of internationalization, and the role of their firms in the international business system.

NOTE

1. "International new ventures" are sometimes known as born-globals, born internationals, global start-ups, innate exporters, and infant internationals. For one formal definition see Oviatt and McDougall (1994).

REFERENCES

Acs, Z., and D. B. Audretsch. 1988. "Innovation in Large and Small Firms: An Empirical Analysis." *American Economic Review* 78(4): 678-690.

———. 1990. *Innovation and Small Firms*. Cambridge, MA: The MIT Press.

Acs, Z., R. Morck, J. M. Shaver, and B. Yeung. 1997. "The Internationalization of Small and Medium-sized Enterprises: A Policy Perspective." *Small Business Economics* 9(1): 7-20.

Acs, Z., and L. Preston. 1997. "Small and Medium-sized Enterprises, Technology, and Globalization: Introduction to a Special Issue on Small and Medium-sized Enterprises in the Global Economy." *Small Business Economics* 9(1): 1-6.

Andersen, O. 1993. "On the Internationalization Process of Firms: A Critical Analysis." *Journal of International Business Studies* 24(2): 209-231.

Barley, S. R., J. Freeman, and R. C. Hybels. 1992. "Strategic Alliances in Commercial Biotechnology." In *Networks and Organizations*, edited by N. Nohria and R. G. Eccles. Boston: Harvard Business School Press.

Bilkey, W. J., and G. Tesar. 1977. "The Export Behavior of Smaller-sized Wisconsin Manufacturing Firms." *Journal of International Business Studies* 8: 93-98.

Bloodgood, J. M, H. J. Sapienza, and J. G. Almeida. 1996. "The Internationalization of New High-potential U.S. New Ventures: Antecedents and Outcomes." *Entrepreneurship Theory and Practice* 20(4): 61-76.

Bonaccorsi, A. 1992. "On the Relationship between Firm Size and Export Intensity." *Journal of International Business Studies* 23: 605-635.

Brokaw, L. 1990. "Foreign Affairs." *Inc.*, November: 92-104.

Burrill, G. S., and S. E. Almassey. 1993. *Electronics '93 The New Global Reality: Ernst and Young's Fourth Annual Report on the Electronics Industry*. San Francisco: Ernst and Young.

BusinessWeek. 1994. "The Information Revolution."

Carey, J. 1999. "This Drug's for You." *BusinessWeek*, January 18, 98-100.

Cavusgil, S. T. 1984. "Organisational Characteristics Associated with Export Activity." *Journal of Management Studies* 21: 3-21.

Coviello, N., and H. Munro. 1997. "Network Relationships and the Internationalisation Process of Small Software Firms." *International Business Review* 6(4): 361-386.

Davis, B. 1999. *The Wall Street Journal*, January 11, R14.

Dunning, J. H. 1993a. "The Changing Dynamics of International Production." Pp. 51-77 in *The Globalization of Business*, edited by J. H. Dunning. Routledge: London and New York.

_____. 1993b. *Multinational Enterprises and the Gobal Economy*. Wokingham, England: Addison-Wesley.

_____. 1995. "Reappraising the Eclectic Paradigm in an Age of Alliance Capitalism." *Journal of International Business Studies* 26(3): 461-491.

_____. 1998. "Location and the Multinational Enterprise: A Neglected Factor?" *Journal of International Business Studies* 29(1): 45-66.

The Economist. 1992. "Go West, Young Firm," May 9: 88-89.

_____. 1993. America's little fellows surge ahead. July 3, 59-60.

_____. 1995. "The Death of Distance: A Survey of Telecommunications," Sept 30: 128.

Gupta, U. 1989. "Small Firms aren't Waiting to Grow Up to Go Global." *The Wall Street Journal*, December 5: B2.

Hadjikhani, A. 1997. "A Note on the Criticisms Against the Internationalization Process Model." *Management International Review*, Special Issue 2: 43-66.

Hedlund, G., and A. Kverneland. 1985. "Are Strategies for Foreign Markets Changing? The Case of Swedish Investment in Japan." *International Studies of Management and Organization* 15(2): 41-59.

Hill, C. W. L. 1998. *International Business*, Boston: Irwin/McGraw-Hill.

Johanson, J. and Vahlne, J-E. 1977. "The Internationalization Process of the Firm—A Model of Knowledge Development and Increasing Foreign Market Commitments." *Journal of International Business Studies* 8(1): 23-32.

_____. 1990. "The Mechanism of Internationalization." *International Marketing Review* 7(4): 11-24.

Knight, G.A., and S. T. Cavusgil. 1997. "Emerging Organizational Paradigm for International Marketing: The Born Global Firm." Paper presented at the Annual Meeting, Academy of International Business, Honolulu, HI.

Mamis, R. A. 1989. "Global Start-up." *Inc.*, August: 38-47.

McDougall, P. P. 1989. "International versus Domestic Entrepreneurship: New Venture Strategic Behavior and Industry Structure." *Journal of Business Venturing* 4: 387-399.

McDougall, P. P., and B. M. Oviatt. 1991. "Global Startups: New Ventures without Ggeographic Limits." *The Entrepreneurship Forum*, Winter: 15.

McDougall, P. P., S. Shane, and B. M. Oviatt. 1994. "Explaining the Formation of International New Ventures: The Limits of Theories from International Business Research." *Journal of Business Venturing* 9: 469-487.

McKinsey and Co. 1993. *Emerging Exporters: Australia's High ValueAdded Manufacturing Exporters*. Melbourne: Australian Manufacturing Council.

Miller, K. D. 1992. "A Framework for Integrated Risk Management in International Business." *Journal of International Business Studies* 23(2): 311-331.

Organization for Economic Co-operation and Development. 1997. *Globalisation and small and medium enterprises*. Paris: OECD.

Ostry, S. 1998. "Technology, Productivity and the Multinational Enterprise." *Journal of International Business Studies* 29(1): 85-99.

Oviatt, B. M., and P. P. McDougall. 1994. "Toward a Theory of International New Ventures." *Journal of International Business Studies* 25(1): 45-64.

_____. 1995. "Global Start-ups: Entrepreneurs on a Worldwide Stage." *Academy of Management Executive* 9(2): 30-44.

_____. 1997. "Challenges for Internationalization Process Theory: The Case of International New Ventures. *Management International Review*, Special Issue 2: 85-99.

Porter, M. E. 1990. *The Competitive Advantage of Nations*. New York: The Free Press.

Preece, S. B., G. Miles, and M. C. Baetz. 1999. "Explaining the International Intensity and Global Diversity of Early-stage Technology-based Firms." *Journal of Business Venturing* 14(3): 259-281.

Rugman, A. M., and A. Verbeke. 1998. Multinational Enterprises and Public Policy." *Journal of International Business Studies* 29(1): 115-136.

Shrader, R. 1996. *Influences on and Performance Implications of Internationalization by Publicly Owned U.S. New Ventures: A Risk Taking Perspective.* Unpublished doctoral dissertation, Georgia State University.

Stopford, J. J., and L. T. Wells, Jr. 1972. *Managing the Multinational Enterprise.* New York: Basic Books.

Sullivan, D., and A. Bauerschmidt. 1990. "Incremental Internationalization: A Test of Johanson and Vahlne's Thesis." *Management International Review* 30(1): 19-30.

Turnbull, P. W. 1987. "A Challenge to the Stages Theory of the Internationalization Process." In *Managing Export Entry and Expansion*, edited by P. J. Rosson and S. D. Reid New York: Praeger.

United Nations Conference on Trade and Development. 1993a. *Small and Medium-sized Transnational Corporations.* United Nations: New York.

_____. 1993b. *World Investment Report 1993.* United Nations: New York.

_____. 1995. *World Investment Report 1995.* United Nations: New York.

_____. 1996. *World Investment Report 1996.* United Nations: New York.

_____. 1997. *World Investment Report 1997.* United Nations: New York.

Vernon, R. 1979. "The Product Cycle Hypothesis in a New International Environment." *Oxford Bulletin of Economics and Statistics*, Special Issue 41 (4): 255-267.

Welch, L. S., and R. Loustarinen. 1988. "Internationalization: Evolution of a Concept." *Journal of General Management* 14(2): 34-64.

Wheelwright, S., and R. Hayes. 1985. "Competing Through Manufacturing." *Harvard Business Review* 63 (1): 99-108.

Wright, R. W. 1989. "Networking, Japanese Style." *Business Quarterly* 54 (2): 20-24.

PART II

NETWORKS AND ALLIANCES

THE ROLE OF ALLIANCES IN INTERNATIONAL ENTREPRENEURSHIP

Paul W. Beamish

I. INTRODUCTION

This chapter presents a vision for the role of alliances in the emerging field of international entrepreneurship, and some suggestions for a future research agenda. The basic thrust of the chapter starts with the fact that, in what has been called the "age of alliance capitalism" (Dunning 1995), alliances will be an increasingly important organization form to the global entrepreneur. Yet alliances constitute a large, but necessary, risk for any entrepreneur. So the task will be to determine when alliances are appropriate and if they are, to find ways to reduce the risks associated with their usage.

Limited resources is perhaps the most fundamental reality confronting entrepreneurs—international or otherwise. The cost of making a big mistake is disproportionately higher in the entrepreneurial organization than in the large multinational enterprise. This leads directly then to my vision: that academic research become more helpful to practitioners. In the context of limited financial resources and alliances, this can be expressed more explicitly as "What are the things entrepreneurs have to get right in their international alliances if they are to prosper?"

Research in Global Strategic Management, Volume 7, pages 43-61.
Copyright © 1999 by JAI Press Inc.
All rights of reproduction in any form reserved.
ISBN: 0-7623-0458-8

The remainder of the chapter proceeds through four sections. Section II provides a brief history of alliance usage, including definitions, and a description of the methodology employed. Section III lays out the four liabilities which the potential international alliance participant must overcome. Section IV discusses one of the single most important issues for the international entrepreneur contemplating an alliance—the need for congruent measures of performance. Section V concludes with a future research agenda in support of the stated vision.

II. A BRIEF HISTORY OF ALLIANCE USAGE

International—like domestic—alliances have traditionally been formed to achieve one of four basic purposes: to strengthen the firm's existing business; to take the firm's existing products into new markets; to obtain products which can be sold in the firm's existing markets; and to diversify into a new business. For the entrepreneur, the first two purposes are most relevant. Entrepreneurs generally form alliances to strengthen their existing (or proposed) business, or in order to achieve successful market entry.

Alliances have been used in different ways over the past 30 years. In the 1960s and 1970s alliances were primarily used in peripheral markets and with a firm's peripheral technologies. There existed an "alliance frontier" which firms seldom crossed. In the 1980s this began to change with major alliances formed between such organizations as Ford-Mazda, Philips-Siemens, and Rolls-Royce and the Japanese. This crossing of the technology and market "alliance frontier" was a function of several converging realities: globalization; escalating costs of new technologies; and increased experience with, and awareness of, the potential benefits of alliance formation. By the 1990s joint venture and alliance usage had exploded particularly among larger MNEs. For these, and other firms, the new alliance issues involved the use of nonequity versus equity ventures, and how to construct effective shorter-term alliances quickly (see Figures 1-3).

International alliance usage has grown because alliances allow firms to:

- establish or expand businesses faster, or with more certainty, than going it alone.
- better compete, and
- achieve superior performance (for example, Japanese investments using joint ventures (or wholly owned start-ups) are far superior to acquisitions in terms of both financial profitability, and stability).

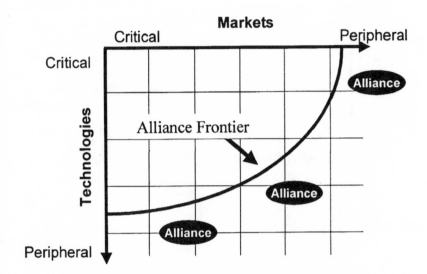

Figure 1. In the 1960s & 1970s Alliances were
Primarily Used in Peripheral Markets and Technologies

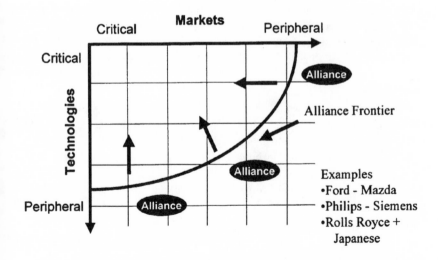

Figure 2. In the 1980s the Alliance Frontier Moved to
Encompass More Important Markets and Technologies

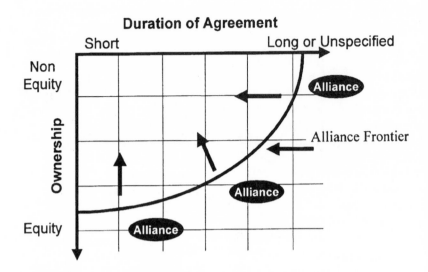

Figure 3.   In the 1990s New Alliance Frontier are Being Crossed

A. Definitions

In any emerging field it is particularly important that it be clear how the key terms under discussion are defined; and that the boundaries of the issues being considered are made clear.

An international alliance is defined as a formal and mutually agreed commercial collaboration between companies from different countries, where the partners pool, exchange, or integrate specific business resources yet remain separate businesses. Numerous types of alliances exist, including joint R&D, joint marketing, co-production, licensing, equity joint venture, and so forth. Each is designed for different purposes (see Beamish and Killing 1999).

Internationalization is defined as the process by which firms both increase their awareness of the direct and indirect influences of international transactions on their future, and establish and conduct transactions with other countries (Beamish 1990). It is a process which may include various modes (Calof and Beamish 1995; Johanson and Vahlne 1977) for which there are positive performance implications, both with respect to the attitude or centric profile of the entrepreneur (Calof and Beamish 1994) and number of markets served (Geringer, Beamish, and daCosta 1989). There is value in internationalization itself, because geographic scope has been found to be related to higher firm profitability, even when controlling for the competing effect of the possession of proprietary assets (Delios and Beamish 1999).

Small firms are defined as stand-alone enterprises with fewer than 100 employees. Medium-sized firms are defined as stand-alone enterprises with 100-499 employees. Most small and medium-sized enterprises (SMEs) have a domestic focus. In Canada, SMEs generate 58 percent of the country's private sector output, but less than 10 percent of its exports.

Entrepreneurship is defined as "the process of creating or seizing an opportunity and pursuing it regardless of the resources currently controlled. Entrepreneurship involves the definition, creation and distribution of value and benefits to individuals, groups, organizations and society" (Timmons 1994, p. 7).

A flexible business network is "a group of already successful SMEs, which cooperate and collaborate, to resolve a business challenge and/or to seek a new business opportunity" (Roy 1998). A network is quite distinct from an alliance according to the ease of entry/exit, focus, the investment required, the relative emphasis, the typical size and the configuration of the relationship, and the structure (see Table 1). Consequently, international alliances in an SME context (including how they are viewed in this paper) will typically involve medium rather than small enterprises, and do not include networks.

B. Methodology

This paper draws upon extensive study of alliances, using a number of data sources: secondary data sets, questionnaires, and interviews. Over 500 interviews were conducted as a researcher, case writer, consultant, and joint venture facilitator. A number of the cases involved global entrepreneurs in alliance situations.[1] Where relevant, the five cases briefly described below are drawn upon to illustrate various points in this paper.

Table 1. Interfirm Cooperation:
Networks versus Alliances

	Networks	Alliances
Ease of Entry/Exit	Very Low	Medium-High
Focus	Narrow, Functional	Broader-Based
Investment Required	Primarily Time (Self Financing/Fees)	Time and Money
Elements of Alliance Process Emphasized	Strategic Logic	Strategic Logic + Partnership & Fit + Shape & Design
Typical Firms	4-5 Small (sometimes Med.)	2-3 Large (sometimes Med.)
Structure	Loose	More Formal, with Legal Agreements

A. Russki Adventures (Ivey case number 9-92-G02). From the perspective of two young entrepreneurs, this case examines the feasibility of establishing a helicopter skiing operation in Russia. One of the options for proceeding was to joint venture with an existing (French) operator.

B. Coral Divers Resort (9A96M01). This case deals with the needs of a small, Caribbean-based scuba-diving operation to change its current focus. Options include an emphasis on operational efficiency, targeting adventure diving or targeting family diving. The latter option might involve a form of strategic buyer-supplier coalition with a travel agency which specialized in family vacations.

C. Neilson International in Mexico (9-95-G003). This case deals with the first major international foray of a small division (nine people) of a medium-sized company which produces chocolate bars. The case examines a proposed nonequity marketing joint venture which would introduce their brands to Mexican consumers. One of the proposed partners would be a division of the much larger MNE, Pepsico.

D. International Decorative Glass (9A97D010). This case is about a small Canadian manufacturer of glass door panels. Most of its manufacturing is done in China via a joint venture arrangement. Due to growing demand the company must decide whether to expand its existing Canadian or Chinese facilities, or to form a new jointly owned manufacturing facility with a supplier in Viet Nam.

E. Nora-Sakari (9-95-G002). This case deals with a proposed equity joint venture between a medium-sized Malaysian company (Nora) and a large Finnish company (Sakari). The case requires resolution of many of the most common issues involved in a joint venture negotiation: equity split, technology to be transferred, royalty payable, expatriate salary levels, and arbitration location.

III. THE FOUR LIABILITIES AND A VISION

Entrepreneurs are not forced to use alliances: they can always not go international, or use alternative modes of internationalization such as exporting or wholly owned investments. Yet a *D*omestic and *D*o-it-yourself (DoDo) approach (see Figure 4) will constrain an organization's ability to maximize its product and market growth. As a consequence, reluctantly or not, entre- preneurs with international aspirations must consider the use of alliances. To borrow from a children's rhyme: Jack may be nimble, and Jack may be quick, (and Jack may be smart, and Jack may be hard working) but, Jack is only Jack; he has limited resources, and the cost of missteps is very high. So Jack, or any entrepreneur, must understand what an alliance can do (or not) for Jack's organization.

A. The Four Liabilities

The reasons for alliance formation are well known, often advocated, and comprehensively described in both the practitioner and academic literatures. Much less understood, are the limitations associated with alliance usage, particularly from the perspective of the international entrepreneur.

There are at least four major liabilities to be overcome by the international entrepreneur contemplating an alliance. These respectively relate to being a new/small entrepreneur anywhere, entering the international arena, and using alliances versus wholly owned approaches.

Liability of Newness

Stinchcombe (1965, pp. 148-149) a sociologist, first articulated the liability of newness argument:

(a) New organizations, especially new types of organizations, generally involve new roles, which have to be learned...(b) The process of inventing new roles, the determination of their mutual relations and of structuring the field of rewards and sanctions so as to get the maximum performance, have high costs in time, worry, conflict and temporary inefficiency...(c) New organizations must rely heavily on social relations among strangers. This means that relations of trust are much more precarious in new than old organizations...(d) One of the main

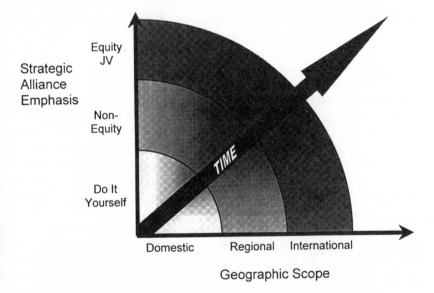

Figure 4.   The Age of International and Alliance Capitalism

resources of old organizations is a set of stable ties to those who use organizational services (i.e., old customers).

These are both internal and external constraints on the legitimacy (or taken-for-granted social status) of the new organization (Aldrich and Fiol 1994). Fledgling organizations must create an internal structure that entails costly learning, as well as break into an existing organizational field and compete for network connections and resources. Overcoming initial lack of trust (both internally and externally) imposes additional start-up costs (Nelson and Winter 1982). Consequently, young organizations initially suffer high failure rates that decline as these problems are solved through experience. Large-scale empirical studies suggest that mortality rates decrease with age and this has been attributed to the increased reliability and accountability that organizations achieve over their growth period (Hannan and Freeman 1989; Carroll and Delacroix 1982).

The liability of newness can be illustrated by several examples. In the Russki Adventures case, one of the reasons that the two entrepreneurs were considering allying with an existing business for their start-up was because they recognized that their network in Russia was quite limited. Also, they recognized that they would be forced to establish new organization structures (which their potential partner already had in place) if they went alone.

Similarly, in the Coral Divers example, to shift emphasis toward a family-based operation was going to require a major reorientation in terms of roles, social relations, and target customer. The potential "partner" for Coral Divers in this nonequity alliance (a specialty travel agency called Rascals in Paradise) was attractive because their emphasis on a family clientele was not new to them—it was what they did best.

Liability of Size

Size of the organization often is a mark of its success as well as an indicator of the resources available to that organization. Large organizational size confers several advantages. The resource pool is larger and thus the organization can withstand environmental fluctuations. They have access to a larger pool of knowledge and capabilities as well as access to premium labor markets (Baum 1996). In contrast, small firms sometimes can not take full advantage of their existing capabilities, often due to the fact that exploitation of these capabilities demand exorbitant investment in complementary capabilities which they cannot afford. The lack of slack resources, both managerial and financial, suggests that they are prone to extreme duress in case of a misstep or sudden changes in the market demand (Baum 1996). Smaller firms also find that they have minimal voice in shaping the industry or any legislation governing the industry, and hence many times are faced with conditions that indirectly favor large firms (Ranger-Moore 1997). Despite the fact that large firms tend to be slow to change and are likely to lose market share to more agile and innovative small firms, several empirical studies suggest that smaller firms have a disproportionately higher likelihood of failure (Hannan and Freeman 1989).

The liability-of-size issue can be illustrated by considering Neilson's entry to Mexico. Effective market penetration for a low-priced consumer product (chocolate bars) in a market of 90 million people requires enormous distribution. For a small company such as Neilson, even though they possess a proprietary product, require complementary capabilities (such as distribution and joint branding) if they are to maximize success. For this reason, Neilson investigated carefully a variety of options but eventually chose to partner with a Pepsico subsidiary because of its ability to provide distribution to 450,000 outlets.

Liability of Foreignness

Entrepreneurs may enter foreign markets using a variety of modes ranging from exporting to investment, and some in fact enter foreign markets from inception (Oviatt and McDougall 1994). Yet most entrepreneurs do not enter foreign markets at all. Why? In part this can be traced to a liability of foreignness. Many small, domestically oriented firms may lack international business competency (Reuber and Fischer 1997) or confidence. Foreign market knowledge is normally not the cornerstone characteristic of most domestic entrepreneurs. The typical firm-specific asset would instead relate to technology.

This additional challenge which entrepreneurs are faced with was highlighted by Hymer (1960) in his work on foreign direct investment (FDI) activities. He noted that in any economy, foreign firms faced a liability of foreignness. While the cost of acquiring better information about the country—its economy, its language, its law, and its politics—is a disadvantage, he noted that it is more a fixed cost, that is, once incurred by establishing a foreign operation, it need not be incurred again. In describing the external constraints Hymer (1960, p. 34) states:

> Of a more permanent nature is the barrier to international operations arising from discrimination by government, by consumers, and by suppliers. It is not the general treatment that is important: this affects the domestic firms as well as the foreign firms, but it does not give one firm an advantage over another. What is important is the fact that in given countries, foreigners and nationals may receive very different treatment....Sometimes it is found to be important, but little is known about this aspect of the stigma of being foreign.

Empirical studies of Canadian medical devices firms entering the U.S. market support this liability of foreignness (Mitchell, Shaver, and Yeung 1994).

Firms (including entrepreneurs) may look to foreign countries as a market to sell in and/or as a market in which to produce for re-export. The liability of foreignness exists under either scenario. Consider the example of International Decorative Glass, a small British Columbia-based company which produces glass door panels. IDG began to source glass door panels from a joint venture with a

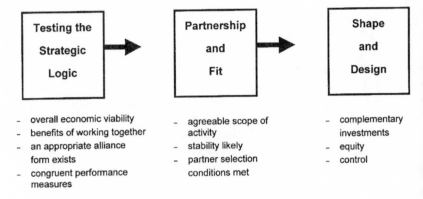

Figure 5.   Designing the Successful Alliance

Chinese partner as a response to the higher labor costs associated with producing labor-intensive goods in North America. They chose to joint venture rather than go it alone because of their need for knowledge of the local economy, politics, and culture. Continuing cost pressures (now even on Chinese-produced goods), and their ongoing need for local market knowledge, were now driving them again toward the use of an alliance, as they now considered adding a manufacturing site in lower-cost Viet Nam.

Liability of Relational Orientation

The challenges facing the international entrepreneur are complex such that he or she has to face the three liabilities discussed above, often simultaneously. It is here that alliances potentially offer substantial advantage to the entrepreneur. By setting up relationships with one or more firms in the foreign market, the entrepreneur has the potential to simultaneously overcome all these constraints. Alliances can provide access to new resources, new ways of managing businesses, market information, as well as access to new customers and suppliers.

Some entrepreneurs may have achieved initial success in part because of relational skills. Oliver (1990) notes how a JV can serve as a means of establishing legitimacy. Baum, Calabrese, and Silverman (1998) predict that new ventures can improve their performance "by establishing alliances and configuring them into an efficient network..., and by allying with potential rivals." While this may well be true for some organizations, other entrepreneurs may have achieved initial success because of their single-minded pursuit of objectives. It is these entrepreneurs—those with a do-it-themselves (wholly owned) rather than a relational (cooperative) orientation—who may have difficulty making alliances work.

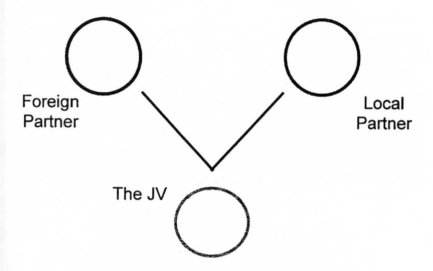

Foreign Partner

Local Partner

The JV

Figure 6. Measuring JV Performance: The Search for Congruity

The liability of relational orientation can be illustrated with the Nora-Sakari case. Both Nora and Sakari had extensive previous experience with various forms of alliances prior to their initial discussions. Neither firm had a do-it-themselves mentality, and as a consequence each readily acknowledged the advantages of allying. (Notwithstanding their willingness to use joint ventures, the partners nonetheless did argue over control—as reflected in their desired equity holdings. Control is but one example of the larger question of relational orientation.)

IV. ACHIEVING SUPERIOR ALLIANCE PERFORMANCE

A reading of the extant academic literature suggests that the answer to the question of what are the things entrepreneurs have to get right in their international alliances if they are to prosper is "Nobody knows," or at least, "Nobody knows with any certainty." There is no end of suppositions put forward in the existing literature about what firms need to do to succeed with their alliances. These include a focus on such things as:

- control (let one partner dominate; share it; split it)
- partner selection (criteria; fit)
- equity (majority; equal; minority)
- conflict (minimize it)

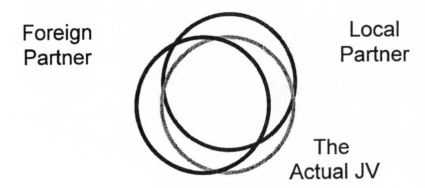

Foreign Partner   **Local Partner**

The Actual JV

IDEAL: Strongly overlapping measures

Figure 7. Measuring JV Performance:
The Search for Congruity

- trust and commitment
- congruity of performance measure
- the ability to insulate the firm against jolts (Woo et al. 1994)

These issues can be organized according to a simple framework (Figure 5).
Other studies sometimes adopt a contingency approach, saying performance depends on:

- industry
- level of competition
- type of country (developed versus emerging)
- number of partners
- cultural distance
- organizational chemistry

Overlaid on the dozen (or more) explanations for alliance failure are a series of theoretical perspectives. These include social exchange, prospect theory, procedural justice, transaction costs, and so on (see also Beamish and Killing 1997).

Conceptually, while all of the explanations and all of the theoretical perspectives may have merit, in their totality what message do they send out to the practitioner? It would be nice to think it is one of vibrancy, steady progress, and consistency of message. This of course is not reality.

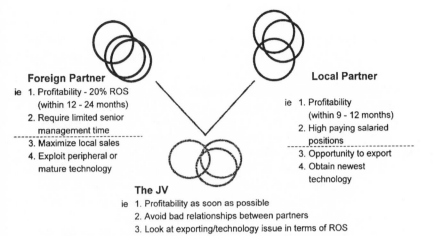

Foreign Partner
ie 1. Profitability - 20% ROS
       (within 12 - 24 months)
    2. Require limited senior
       management time
    3. Maximize local sales
    4. Exploit peripheral or
       mature technology

Local Partner
ie 1. Profitability
       (within 9 - 12 months)
    2. High paying salaried
       positions
    3. Opportunity to export
    4. Obtain newest
       technology

The JV
ie 1. Profitability as soon as possible
    2. Avoid bad relationships between partners
    3. Look at exporting/technology issue in terms of ROS

Figure 8.   Measuring JV Performance:
The Search for Congruity

A. Focus on Performance Measure Incongruity

As noted in Figure 5, we can think about the design of any successful joint alliance in terms of three stages, (1) testing the strategic logic, (2) partnership and fit, and (3) shape and design. The comments here will be focused on a particular element of the strategic logic which must be understood and in place for any alliance to succeed. It was chosen over other elements for reasons of practical relevance, and theoretical support (Beamish and Delios, 1997). The discussion below is relevant to all types of alliances but focuses on the equity joint venture form of alliance because this is the form where the stakes are highest for the international entrepreneur.

The key consideration when one is testing the strategic logic of any proposed alliance is to ask the questions: "How will we each measure performance?" and "Is there congruity between our proposed measures?" Joint venture performance can be measured in numerous ways. These include financial measures such as return on equity, return on sales, return on assets; survival measures; stability measures such as whether there have been any organization changes or changes in equity level; satisfaction measures: my satisfaction, our satisfaction; or other measures such as market share, whether the joint venture is to export, and so forth. Any of these measures may be appropriate for a particular joint venture. The key question here however is whether or not there is congruity between the measures used to assess joint venture performance between the foreign partner, the local partner and the joint venture general manager (i.e., can the organization move from the perspective illustrated in Figure 6 to something closer to that in Figure 7). In a great number of joint ventures, no such congruity exists. This is at the root of why some joint ventures will never succeed. As we think about the search for congruity within any proposed or existing joint venture, it is necessary to understand these three key perspectives.

To illustrate, let us consider the foreign partner and how it often measures performance. As the left side of Figure 8 suggests, the foreign partner may often have several explicit performance measures. For example, profitability levels of a 20 percent of return on sales within a 12- to 24-month period and human resource requirements that perhaps will require only a limited amount of senior management time. These measures of performance are explicit and widely understood. Below the dotted line, however, there are several other performance measures that in fact are in place although not often necessarily made explicit. For example, these may typically include a desire to maximize local sales and perhaps a desire to exploit peripheral or mature technology. Several problems immediately jump out at us as we consider the foreign partners' proposed measure of performance. First of all, we observe a lack of internal consistency. Achieving good profitability while exploiting peripheral or mature technology may not be feasible. A venture that required limited senior management time yet wants to maximize local sales again may not be internally consistent. As well the fact that some of these measures are explicit and some are implicit should be a concern.

Congruity is seldom observed within the senior management team of either partner in terms of how they propose to measure performance. If each member of the senior management teams are privately asked to jot down the four key ways in which they propose to measure performance in the joint venture under consideration, seldom if ever will complete congruity within a senior management team be observed. More significantly here is the fact that this is not referring simply to the order in which the performance measures will be applied, but in fact the lack of congruity in terms of the actual measures to be used.

A similar situation exists with the local partner (see right side of Figure 8). The local partner has a desire of course for profitability, however in this case, often within a shorter nine- to 12-month period. In addition they may hope to establish a joint venture where there are going to be some high-paying salaried positions for themselves or their associates. These are the explicit measures. The implicit measures often include a desire to export, and an understandable desire to obtain the newest technology. Again a similar problem as before jumps out. First of all, the lack of internal consistency. A desire to have quick profitability and high-paying salaried positions may not be compatible. A desire to have quick profitability, yet to obtain the newest technology again may not be internally consistent. As well, some of these measures are implicit and others are explicit. So once again there is a lack of congruity, but this time within the local partner.

The third stage of course is to look at how the joint venture general manager proposes to measure performance (see bottom of Figure 8). Joint venture general managers tend to measure performance first of all in terms of achieving profitability as soon as possible. They do not necessarily set a particular time frame, rather their desire is just to get it done as quickly as they can. The second measure that they typically employ to measure performance is the avoidance of bad relationships between the partners. In essence they look to reduce the noise level within the joint venture. A third measure that they may utilize is to look at issues such as whether the joint venture exports or acquires old versus new technology in terms of its impact on return on sales and impact on the actual needs of the particular market. So, they tend to take a more contingent approach. Again we do not have completely congruent performance measures.

The difficulty of establishing congruity is further exaggerated when the partners are of vastly unequal size (such that the alliance is proportionately more important to one than the other) or when only one of the partners has previous alliance experience (so can better manage the inevitable differences of opinion). In observing the JV negotiations between a division of a Fortune 100 company, and a very small privately held company (names withheld due to confidentiality) the size differences were further exacerbated by the lack of respect of each management team for the other. Here, those in the small, entrepreneurial company thought their counterparts were "overpaid specialized administrators" who knew little about how to really start, or manage a business. Conversely, those in the large MNE thought their counterparts were unsophisticated and ill-trained. (Fortunately, this alliance discussion ended with the agreement not to form a joint venture).

When we consider these three perspectives in total, it becomes eminently clear that many joint ventures can never succeed due to the lack of congruity in performance measure. What are we to do then? First of all, we recognize that we aren't dealing with some Disney-like situation. We acknowledge that there will never be perfectly congruent measures. But what we need to do is to work toward an ideal of strongly overlapping measures between the foreign partner, the local partner, and the joint venture general manager. To do this we suggest a five-stage approach.

Step I—Ask yourself, "How do I propose to measure joint venture performance?" and "Why do I propose to measure it this way?"

Table 2.

	Equity Joint Venture	NonEquity Alliance
Large MNEs		
Global Entrepreneur		

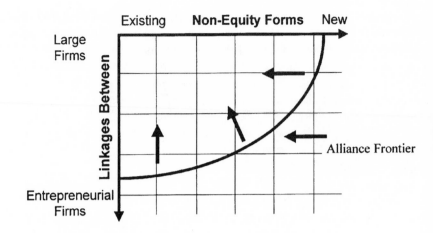

Figure 9. In the 2000s, Alliances will Increasingly Occur
Between Entrepreneurial and Large Firms, and New
Forms of Non-Equity Alliances will Develop

Step II—Ask your colleagues—the other members of your own senior management team—how they propose the performance of the joint venture be measured. Inevitably, differences of opinion will exist. Now is the time to hash these out.

Step III—Ask your partners how they propose to measure joint venture performance. Again ask them to be as explicit as possible and to lay out their rationale for performance.

Step IV—This step applies to joint ventures which already exist or ones that are far enough along where the joint venture general manager has been selected. Again here the same process is in place. Ask the joint venture general manager how he or she is measuring performance and why. Again what we are looking for is congruity.

Step V—The final step is to keep asking. Keep asking yourself, your colleagues, your partners and the joint venture general manager about performance. Conditions will often change in a particular country market or joint venture. Flexibility is required because currency values change, market conditions evolve, and so on. It is sometimes necessary to modify how one assesses joint venture performance but if we can't establish strongly overlapping measures then we should simply not use the joint venture organization form.

Joint ventures can be an extremely effective way of implementing an international strategy but they are no panacea. There are certain conditions under which they make sense and conditions when they don't make sense. One of the key considerations is the need to establish congruent measures of performance before we use the joint venture organization form as an element of our international strategy.

V. A FUTURE RESEARCH AGENDA

Most of what we do know in the alliances area is related to the experience of large multinational enterprises in equity joint ventures (as in upper left hand quadrant of Table 2).

While there is an emerging literature on the nonequity alliance experience of large MNEs (and certainly some literature on domestic, non-international practices), the existing knowledge of alliances and the global entrepreneur is very thin and uncoordinated. This then leads to where a future research agenda begins.

If alliance scholars in the global entrepreneurship area are to be genuinely helpful to practitioners and benefit from, and avoid some of the pitfalls of, the extant alliance literature, a variety of steps can be considered:

1. Don't mix alliance types. There are benefits in examining each type (whether vertical or horizontal, highly cooperative or less so, start-ups or existing ventures) and acknowledging that each may have both overlapping and unique characteristics. There is too much unsubstantiated generalization already. As research plans are developed, consider the use of a research instrument which would allow for comparisons between forms. A common research protocol would be ideal so that eventually the issues to all alliance types could be identified with confidence.

2. Carefully catalogue what has gone before, especially with respect to the nonequity forms. This will require going well beyond a single functional literature, and include consideration of both the practitioner literature, and published case studies.

3. Consider preparing a series of relevant case studies. Great insight into best (and worst) practice can be gained through the preparation of teaching cases, and corresponding teaching notes.

4. In questionnaires, be comprehensive with respect to including some reference to most of the possible explanations for success. One of our objectives must be to be able to tell global entrepreneurs which elements in the alliance process require particular attention.

5. Stay with the subject long enough. Consider developing a program of research—rather than conducting a one-off study—in order to be cutting edge.

As Figure 9 suggests, new challenges await alliance researchers. Of particular relevance here is the need to understand some of the emerging forms of nonequity alliances, and to find better and faster mechanisms for the entrepreneurial firm to work in conjunction with large enterprises in the international arena. Entrepreneurism, internationalization, and alliance usage are all permanent realities. The successful manager and firm will be the one able to combine all three.

ACKNOWLEDGMENT

Comments from Charles Dhanaraj, Charlene Nicholls-Nixon, Richard Wright, and an anonymous reviewer are gratefully acknowledged.

NOTE

1.   Abstracts (and in some instances, Portable Document Format versions) of Ivey-registered case studies can be accessed by www.ivey.uwo.ca/Ivey Publishing/

REFERENCES

Aldrich, H., and M. C. Fiol. 1994. "Fools Rush In? The Institutional Context of Industry Creation." *Academy of Management Review* 19: 645-670.

Baum, J. A. C., and C. Oliver. 1991. "Institutional Linkages and Organizational Mortality." *Administrative Science Quarterly* 36: 187-218.

Baum, J. A. C. 1996. "Organizational Ecology." Pp. 175-190 in *Handbook of Organizational Studies* edited by S. R. Clegg, Cynthia Hardy, and W. R. Nord. London: Sage.

Baum, J. A.C., T. Calabrese, and B. Silverman. 1998. "Don't Go It Alone: Alliance Networks and Startups' Performance in Canadian Biotechnology." Mimeo, University of Toronto, September.

Beamish, P. W., and A. Delios. 1997. "Improving Joint Venture Performance Through Congruent Measures of Success." Pp. 103-127 in *Cooperative Strategies: European Perspectives,* edited by P. W. Beamish and J. P. Killing. San Francisco: The New Lexington Press.

Beamish, P. W., and P. Killing. 1997. *Cooperative Strategies,* 3 vols. San Francisco: The New Lexington Press.

_____. 1999. "Global Strategic Alliances." Pp. 164-182 in *The International Encyclopedia of Business and Management Handbook of International Business,* edited by R. Tung. London, International Thompson Business Press.

Beamish, P. W. 1990. "The Internationalization Process for Smaller Ontario Firms: A Research Agenda." Pp. 77-92 *Research in Global Strategic Management: A Canadian Perspective,* Vol.1, edited by A. M. Rugman. Greenwich, CT: JAI Press.

Calof, J., and P. W. Beamish. 1994. "The Right Attitude for International Success." *Business Quarterly* 59(1/Autumn): 105-110.

_____. 1995. "Adapting to Foreign Markets: Explaining Internationalization." *International Business Review* 4(2): 115-131.

Carroll, G. R., and J. Delacroix. 1982. "Organizational Mortality in the Newspaper Industries of Argentina and Ireland: An Ecological Approach." *Administrative Science Quarterly* 27: 169-198.

Coviello, N., and H. Munro. 1997. "Network Relationships and the Internationalization Process of Small Software Firms." *International Business Review* 6(4): 361-386.

Delios, A., and P. W. Beamish. 1999. "Geographic Scope, Product Diversification and the Corporate Performance of Japanese Firms." *Strategic Management Journal* (In press).

Dunning, J. H. 1995. "Reappraising the Eclectic Paradigm in an Age of Alliance Capitalism." *Journal of International Business Studies*, 26(3): 461-492.

Geringer, M. J., P. W. Beamish, and R. daCosta. 1989. "Diversification Strategy and Internationalization: Implications for MNE Performance." *Strategic Management Journal* 10(2/Mar-Apr): 109-119.

Hannan, M. T., and J. Freeman. 1989. *Organizational Ecology.* Cambridge, MA: Harvard University Press.

Hymer, S. H. 1960. *The International Operations of National Firms: A Study of Direct Foreign Investment.* Cambridge, MA: MIT Press.

Johanson, J., and J.-E. Vahlne. 1977. "The Internationalization Process of the Firm—A Model of Knowledge Development and Increasing Foreign Market Commitment." *Journal of International Business Studies* (Spring-Summer): 23-32.

Mitchell, W., M. Shaver, and B. Yeung. 1994. "Foreign Entrant Survival and Foreign Market Share: Canadian Companies' Experience in United States Medical Sector Markets." *Strategic Management Journal* 28(4): 647-669.

Nelson, R. R., and S. G. Winter. 1994. *An Evolutionary Theory of Economic Change.* Cambridge, MA: Harvard University Press.

Newbould, G. D., P. J. Buckley, and J. Thurlwell. 1988. *Going International: The Experience of Smaller Companies Overseas.* London: The MacMillan Press Ltd.

Oliver, C. 1990. "Determinants of Interorganizational Relationships: Integration and Future Directions." *Academy of Management Review* 15(2): 241-265.

Oviatt, B. M., and P. P. McDougall. 1994. "Toward a Theory of International New Ventures." *Journal of International Business Studies* 25(1): 45-64.

Ranger-Moore, J. 1997. "Bigger May Be Better But is Older Wiser? Organizational Age and Size in the New York Life Insurance Industry." *American Sociological Review* 62(December): 903-920.

Reuber, A. R., and E. Fischer. 1997. "The Influence of the Management Team's International Experience on the Internationalisation Behaviour of SMEs." *Journal of International Business Studies* 28(4): 807-825.

Roy, P. 1998. "Business Networks for SMEs: Powerful Synergy for Growth in the Emerging Global Market Place." Mimeo, September.

Stinchcombe, A. L. 1965. "Social Structure and Organizations." Pp. 153-193 in *Handbook of Organizations* edited by J. G. March. Chicago: Rand McNally.

Timmons J. 1994. *New Venture Creation*, 4th ed. Burr Ridge: Irwin.

Woo, C.Y, U. Daellenback, and C. N. Nicholls-Nixon. 1994. "Theory Building in the Presence of 'Randomness': The Case of Venture, Creation and Performance." *Journal of Management Studies* 31(4): 507-524.

Woodcock, C. P., P. W. Beamish, and S. Makino. 1994. "Ownership Entry Mode Strategies and Performance." *Journal of International Business Studies* 25(2): 253-273.

BROKERING NETWORKS OF SMALL FIRMS TO GENERATE SOCIAL CAPITAL FOR GROWTH AND INTERNATIONALIZATION

Rod B. McNaughton and James D. Bell

I. INTRODUCTION

The potential advantages that firms can derive from a network of relationships have attracted the attention of public agencies charged with helping small- and medium-sized enterprises (SMEs) to grow and internationalize. Several countries including the authors' home country, New Zealand, have made government funding available for relationship brokers to encourage networks (Harper 1993). The role of government agencies and business associations in promoting networks is highlighted in studies of successful regional economies (e.g., Cooke and Morgan 1993, 1994). However, there has been limited discussion of the potential for publicly funded relationship brokers to stimulate firm growth or promote exporting (Field, Goldfinsh, and Perry 1994, p. 4). The primary exception are post hoc evaluations of the impacts of established programs, for example, Welch and col-

Research in Global Strategic Management, Volume 7, pages 63-82.
Copyright © 1999 by JAI Press Inc.
All rights of reproduction in any form reserved.
ISBN: 0-7623-0458-8

leagues (forthcoming) analysis of the Australian Joint Action Group assistance scheme, Lindsay and colleagues (1998) evaluation of the New Zealand Hard Business Networks Scheme, Rosenfeld's (1996) analysis of programs in Oregon and the Pacific Northwest, and analyses of the Danish network program by Gelsing (1992), Nielsen (1994), Martinusson (1994), and Steeman (1994).

The tendency of firms to under-invest in cooperative relationships has been documented (e.g., Curran et al. 1993; Benson-Rea and Wilson 1994; Human and Provan 1997), and some authors have begun to search for theory to explain this phenomenon. Most notably, game theory, in particular the prisoners' dilemma, has been used to provide insight into the failure of the market for relationships (e.g., Jarillo 1988; White, Gorton, and Chaston 1996). However, sound theoretical reasoning for public funding of network brokers, or the welfare benefits of brokering programs is notably absent from the extant literature. Policy implementation is ahead of a clear understanding of how networks help SMEs to grow and internationalize, and how public benefits are derived from brokering network formation.

This chapter contributes to the discussion of public promotion of networks by synthesizing the literature on networks, firm growth, and internationalization to create a theoretical underpinning for network brokering programs. The first section reviews the literature on network formation to explain why they are important to both firm growth and internationalization. In the second section networks are characterized as a form of social capital. This perspective provides a basis for understanding the public welfare benefits of networks, and for discussing programs that facilitate network formation. It also provides a rich metaphor that easily communicates many network concepts. The third section describes the typical structure of such programs, focusing on New Zealand's Hard Business Network Program as an example. A final section discusses the implications of the network model as a strategic framework, and identifies potential problems that need to be mitigated by program design or managerial action.

II. THE RELATIONSHIP BETWEEN LOCAL NETWORKS, FIRM GROWTH, AND INTERNATIONALIZATION

The starting point for both this discussion and network programs is the renewed focus on SMEs. While small firms first attracted the attention of policymakers because of their contribution to employment, recent interest has focused more on the ability of small firms to provide the economic "flexibility" required by changes in the technology and organization of production (Grotz and Braun 1993, pp. 149-151; Malecki and Veldhoen 1993, p. 131). The basic flexibility argument is that the forces of globalization, rapidly changing consumer preferences, and greater division of labor create an environment where the ability to quickly adjust to changing consumer preferences, and produce specialized and customized products is an advantage (Malecki and Veldhoen 1993). While the importance of flexibility is a matter of debate (Amin 1993; Amin and Robins 1991, 1990; Praat 1991; Perrow 1992, pp. 451-453), many policymakers focus on SMEs as a vehicle for delivering on the promise of flexible production.

SMEs, however, are notoriously volatile with a few experiencing exceptional growth rates while many fail. Further, smaller firms under-perform in international markets, accounting for a much smaller proportion of exports than would be expected from their number and employment contribution. In New Zealand, for example, only 200 exporting companies account for over 90 percent of exports (Barber 1996, p. 48). In the EC, SMEs with less than 500 employees account for 70 percent of private non-primary employment, but only 10 percent of exports (European Observatory for SMEs 1993, p. 14). Similar ratios characterize SME activity in most developed countries. As a consequence, policymakers are interested in stimulating SME growth and in encouraging SMEs to export (Rosson and Seringhaus 1991). Network strategies have attracted interest partly because they have the potential to address not only issues of endogenous growth, but of internationalization as well.

A focus on *local* networks comes from at least two influential bodies of research (Sillars 1995, p. 3). The first is Porter's (1990) work which postulates that competitive advantage is created and sustained through a highly localized process in which differences in national economic structures, values, cultures, institutions, and histories contribute to competitive success. In particular, Porter promotes the idea of "clustering" in which related groups of successful firms and industries emerge to gain leading positions in the international market. These clusters function through "coopetition," a complex mix of cooperation, competition, and emulation. As Crocombe, Enright, and Porter (1991, p. 30) describe it: "The complex web of interactions within these clusters can provide a major source of competitive advantage throughout the entire economic system. Often such clusters are geographically concentrated, making the interactions closer and more dynamic."

Porter's views have significantly influenced the development of industry and export promotion programs in a number of countries, including New Zealand. For example, the Porter Project on New Zealand's competitiveness recommended stronger clusters of linked activities and a broader skill base to support export expansion and competitiveness (Cromcombe, Enwright, and Porter 1991). In response, the Trade Development Board (Trade New Zealand, formerly TRA-DENZ) initiated a program of soft networks called Joint Action Groups (sector specific associations that work to foster export interests), the Hard Business Network Program, and an industry "clusters" program to promote local networks in targeted industries (see Perry 1995 and Lindsay 1998, pp. 5-10 for a description of these programs).

The second body of literature concerns the concept of *milieu*, which was introduced by the international research group GREMI (Groupe de Recherche

Européen sur les Milieux Innovateurs). A local *milieu* is "...the set, or the complex network of mainly informal social relationships on a limited geographical area, often determining a specific external 'image' and a specific internal 'representation' and a sense of belonging, which enhances the local innovative capability through synergetic and collective learning processes" (Camagni 1991, p. 3). This concept is related to, but not synonymous with, that of "industrial districts" which are special largely extra-metropolitan areas in which certain types of firms cluster to gain advantage through cooperation, and economies of scale and scope (Camagni 1991).

Recent research has also stressed the role of locally specific knowledge and learning, which is facilitated by the individual contact networks of firm principles and agents (Malmberg 1997). This literature stresses the importance of spatial proximity in the formation of relationships to minimize costs, and because common history and culture facilitates information exchange (Sabel 1989). A large number of studies have documented the advantages borne of specific locational milieu, the most frequently cited European examples being the Prato district in Tuscany, the Herning-Ikast area in Denmark, and Baden-Wurttemberg in Germany (Grotz and Braun 1993). The primary U.S. examples are Silicon Valley (Saxenian 1990, 1992), and Route 128 in Boston (Todtling 1994).

These bodies of literature have fostered a model for development policies that is rooted in the notion of location specific development trajectories for SMEs (e.g., Albrechts et al. 1989; Bassand et al. 1986; Coffey and Polese 1985; Stohr 1990; Storper and Walker 1989). These trajectories are unique to the milieu of entrepreneurs and their networks operating in a particular location, making development success difficult to replicate in, for example, a science park (Maillat 1990). Essentially, this view of firm growth argues that entrepreneurs learn to leverage their competencies by establishing dynamic linkages to other firms in their local production environment.

Internationalization can be seen as a specific form of firm growth, and a number of network researchers have commented that leveraging networks is a particularly useful route to internationalization for SMEs (e.g., Axelsson and Johanson 1992; Forsgren 1989; Bridgewater 1992). The network perspective addresses internationalization as the entire process by which firms enter foreign markets, and does not focus on the entry decision and entry mode, as does much of the traditional internationalization literature. This broader perspective sees current and developing relationships in the domestic, third country, and foreign markets as the key to internationalization (Axelsson and Johanson 1992). Networks enable firms to extend themselves from the domestic to international markets, and international success is often related to the ability to find suitable partners in the immediate environment (Johanson and Vahlne 1992). A recent study by Coviello (1994) of the internationalization of New Zealand software developers provides a good empirical example. Coviello found that linkages with partners were often formed to outsource market-related activities, allowing software firms to achieve interna-

Table 1.   Combining Internal and External Resources in Networks of SMEs

SME Exporters' Internal Resources and Competence		Low	High
Cooperative environment in the local area	Strong	• Potential depends on the ability of the firm to direct and coordinate resources	• Favourable locational conditions, with mutual enforcement of the firms' internationalization
	Weak	• Internationalization of the firm tends to be blocked	• Internationalization of the firm independent of its local environment

Source: Adapted from Vatne (1995, p. 68) and Christensen and Lindmark (1993, p. 145).

tional growth without a well-developed in-house marketing function. In a similar vein, Bell (1995) offers a network interpretation of his finding that European software firms initiate exporting in part because of domestic linkages (especially with clients, i.e., "followership"), and sectoral targeting.

Vatne (1995, pp. 66-70) provides a model that nicely summarizes the relationship between networks and SME internationalization. This model sees internationalization as an entrepreneurial process that is embedded in an institutional and social web that supports the firm in terms of access to information, human capital, finance, and so on. Entrepreneurs use their personal contact networks to gain knowledge, and seek out and mobilize new partnerships that help the firm to grow and expand into foreign markets. A corollary of the importance of social exchange in accessing and coordinating resources is that since face-to-face interaction, and social, cultural and geographic proximity foster the trust needed to facilitate social exchange relationships, the local resource endowment is also important.

If a firm is located in a region that is critically short of an important factor, or is populated by non-dynamic firms that are weak in terms of internationalization, local networking will not in itself overcome these limitations. However, in some industries there is little need for local support, and some small firms have specialized internal resources that make them almost independent of their local environment. This explains why some small firms grow and internationalize even when those around them are not similarly successful. Table 1 summarizes this argument. Internationalization is most likely when there is mutual reinforcement through local cooperative networking, and high internal resources and competencies. On the other hand, internationalization is blocked when there is weak cooperation, and low internal resources and competencies (Christensen and Linkmark 1993, p. 145).

III. LOCAL NETWORKS AS SOCIAL CAPITAL

When viewed at the aggregate level of a local economy, the networks that entrepreneurs develop can be described as the social capital of a business community. The concept of social capital is attributable to the work of Coleman (1990) and Putnam (1993), although both build on earlier work in economic and structural sociology. It is recognized that capital has nonphysical forms, and it is common to refer to both human (Becker 1964) and technological capital (Romer 1990). In a similar vein, the concept of social capital refers to the social structure that facilitates coordination and cooperation (Putnam 1993), which in turn are important to the feasibility and productivity of economic activity (Coleman 1990). Social capital consists of obligations, expectations and trust, information, and sanctions; all of which assist economic exchange by mitigating contracting (or transaction) costs (Routledge and von Amsberg 1996, p. 1).

Social capital is distinct from other forms of capital in that it is intangible, potentially volatile, and highly idiosyncratic. Social capital is created when positive relationships are formed, and it appreciates by repeated interactions that help to build trust. Since relationships are affected by each transaction, social capital can quickly appreciate or depreciate (either by being reinforced by good relationships or destroyed by bad ones). Further, when an entrepreneur makes use of social capital to facilitate an exchange, a debt is incurred in the form of expected reciprocity. Most important, social capital exists as the goodwill between individuals and firms. It is idiosyncratic and not easily transferred. Therefore, individual ownership can not appropriate its benefits. The result is that individual entrepreneurs and firms have little incentive to invest in social capital as it is essentially a public good (Coleman 1990).[1]

The difficulty firms have in appropriating benefits from investments in social capital, along with a shortage of network management skills, leads to frequent under-investment in relationship development. Curran and colleagues (1993), for example, found that small firms shunned "voluntary relationships," and made little use of networking even to overcome problems that threatened the survival of the firm. Curran and colleagues suggest this is because of the independent attitude of entrepreneurs, coupled with the time constraints created by having to deal with many day-to-day management problems. In addition, entrepreneurs are sometimes fearful of "outside" interference, loss of control, and the potential for local competitors to gain inside knowledge. Human and Provan (1997) compared firms in two relatively large networks with a control sample of "market firms," and found that market firms made only minimal use of inter-firm relationships. Managers explained this in terms of limited time, no perceived need, and fear of losing proprietary information.

Another barrier to the formation of inter-firm relationships is a belief among many managers and policymakers that networks are "anti-competitive" or "collusive" (Harper 1993; Benson-Rea and Wilson 1994). This view is fostered by government emphasis on the benefits of competition in moves toward deregulation, and enforcement of anti-competition laws. In most cases networks are not anti-competitive, but do require a change in business culture, from being competitive as individual firms, to being competitive collectively (Martinusson 1994). Fukuyama (1995) suggests that cultural differences influence social capital, and that high trust societies tend to view competition collectively and have an advantage in the formation of social capital.

Beyond the mere formation of relationships and networks is the issue of their planning and governance. Strategic systems of network relationships involving coordination and a clear strategic intent are relatively rare (Benson-Rea and Wilson 1994, pp. 25-27). In a study of the networks of 18 manufacturing firms in New Zealand, Benson-Rea and Wilson (1994) identified only two firms involved in a "strategic system" of relationships. Similarly, Field, Goldfinch, and Perry (1994) found little evidence of strategic networking activity by firms in a sample of small business in the Canterbury region of New Zealand. Even in regions such as Silicon Valley, where networking has made an acknowledged contribution to economic growth, the lack of "administrative coordination" can make the network vulnerable to environmental changes over time (Saxenian 1990, p. 105). In fact, the primary examples of organic networks that exhibit strong coordination and strategic direction are those formed around a large focal firm, and are often based on subcontracting relationships.

The lack of strategic direction and coordination in many organic networks impacts the stock and usefulness of social capital. Social capital in the broader community is often associated with organizations such as the Rotary Club, religious groups, and other community and cultural associations (Fukuyama, 1995). In the business community the equivalents are trade associations, federations, commissions, chambers of commerce, and the like. These associations are hierarchical interorganizational systems that arise in an effort to reduce the transaction costs associated with idiosyncratic investments in relationships, and environmental uncertainty (Alexander 1992, p. 194). Formal associations, and their governance structure of positions, committees, and task forces, help to foster and appreciate social capital by mitigating transaction costs, and directing its use toward common goals. This is analogous to the way in which social capital can be harnessed within the hierarchical structure of large organizations (Lipnack and Stamps 1994).

Networks of relationships between firms require strategic and coordinative planning. Exchanges in a network are not organized by market forces, rather they are structured by patterns of trust and opportunity. When the transaction costs of informal relations and spontaneous adjustment to environmental changes are low, a "feudal" form of interorganizational governance characterized by limited interaction between firms, and bilateral information coordination is often sufficient. Chisholm (1988) refers to this as "coordination without hierarchy." However, when firms in a network constitute a value chain or a "flexible production system," the relationships between them are more frequent, complex, and interdependent. They may also require more idiosyncratic investments, which increases transaction costs. The result is a need for interorganizational hierarchical governance and coordinative planning to "...design strategies for deploying the relevant organizational resources ensuring the commitment of each to its assigned role in the common undertaking. This can involve sanctions, monitoring and control" (Alexander 1992, p. 195). Here again, however, the same considerations that inhibit network formation mitigate against the development of mechanisms for coordination within networks. Namely, the benefits of coordination are difficult for an individual firm to appropriate, and to collectively achieve benefits, firms must give up some autonomy and call on uncommon managerial skills (i.e., managing between firms rather than within them). This is particularly difficult for SMEs which typically have few slack resources, and whose managers may have limited experience outside their own firm.

IV. NETWORK BROKERING PROGRAMS

Given evidence that networks can contribute to firm growth and internationalization, but that there are barriers to the spontaneous creation of this organizational form, there is considerable interest in public policies that foster networks (Andrez 1993; Field, Goldfinsch, and Perry 1994). The Danish Technological Institute developed the archetype network promotion program, which was launched in 1989. This program was based on the external facilitation of networks by trained brokers who identified prospective networks and guided their formation. Brokers were usually independent management consultants who receive program specific training. The Danish program was subsequently adopted and adapted by a number of countries including Norway, Finland, several U.S. states and Canadian provinces (Hill 1992; Bosworth 1993; Lichtenstein 1993; Ferland et al. 1994), Brazil (Cavagnoli and Santos 1993), Australia (Mitchell 1994; Commonwealth of Australia 1994), New Zealand, and several EC member countries including Portugal (Santana 1992), Spain, and Britain. In most of these countries a multi-pronged industrial development strategy is used in which cooperation between firms is also promoted through soft networks of trade associations, and promotion of strategic clusters of firms in the same sector. In New Zealand these programs are called joint action groups, and cluster musters.

Network brokering programs typically promote the formation of networks of three to 15 firms. The firms are usually within the same region, but could be located nationally within a sector. A few programs, notably those implemented in Australia, encourage inclusion of overseas firms in networks. Programs typically divide the network formation process into three or four stages. The New Zealand Hard Business Networks Program followed the four stages of the original Norwegian model[2]: exploration, feasibility, business planning, and implementation (Cragg and Vargo 1995). This model emphasizes the formation of networks, rather than their ongoing operation, and involves brokers early in the process. The exploration phase includes raising awareness of the network paradigm, searching for and assessing potential participants, and interviewing potential participant firms. Participants are often identified through "multipliers" which are institutions such as trade associations, and professional service firms that see the benefits of networks, and "spotters" who are individuals within multiplier organizations that become aware of opportunities through their regular contact with business. Like brokers, multipliers and spotters are interested third parties. The exploration phase typically takes from two to four months.

The feasibility stage involves assembling network members, formally investigating whether a network is practical, identifying various network alternatives, and establishing a commitment between firms to develop a network "blueprint." This stage also takes two to four months. During the next stage a business analysis is conducted that results in a formal cooperation agreement and a comprehensive strategic plan for the network. This may take a further six to nine months. The final stage is the establishment of operations by which time each of the firms should be firmly committed to the network, and coordination procedures should be worked out so that the broker's role diminishes. Thus, the overall network formation process usually takes between 12 and 18 months.

The costs of using a broker are typically shared between the sponsoring government program, and the firms in the network. The original Danish program funded 100 percent of the first two stages, 50 percent of the third stage, and a third of the final stage, although programs in other countries have varied this weighting. In New Zealand grants of up to $NZ20,000 to employ a broker, $NZ10,000 for R&D, $NZ5,000 for market intelligence, and $NZ7,500 to attend an overseas trade fair were made available through local Business Development Boards. All funding was on a matching basis of up to 50 percent of actual expenditures. Funding was not linked to stages of network formation as in the Danish program. The Business Development Board grant scheme was discontinued in November 1997 leaving the Hard Business Networks program effectively unfunded. Trade New Zealand continues to promote the concept of "Export Networks" as part of its portfolio of services. Basically, Trade New Zealand provides information on networking, and refers companies to independent management consultants with experience as brokers (many of whom participated in the original broker training arranged as part of the Hard Business Networks program).

Network brokering programs emphasize the importance of partner selection, and the mix of skills and resources within networks. White, Gorton, and Chaston

(1996, p. 39) explain that the right mix of partners is crucial to network success. A cohesive, yet heterogeneous mix is required because "…through the co-operation of heterogeneous entrepreneurs, small businesses will be able to overcome their individual weaknesses by co-operating with those that possess the skills they need, but lack, for producing goods and services for the market place." They further argue that while networks may arise organically, "…without intervention from outside the market place, the level of co-operation may be socially sub-optimum due to asymmetrical information and risks within the market" (p. 42). Thus, neutral brokers that facilitate network formation (preferably through public sector employment) are advocated as a means of overcoming the failure of the market for social capital.

Evaluating the success of brokers at correcting market imperfections is difficult, as the expected outcomes of increased cooperation are varied, and the real outcomes are often serendipitous. As a result there is little hard evidence, and considerable debate about the effectiveness of government programs that facilitate cooperation (Rosenfeld 1996). Program evaluation, when conducted, is usually based on a combination of qualitative and quantitative approaches, including written reports from brokers, surveys of participating firms, and interviews with multipliers and spotters (e.g., Gelsing 1992; Nescheim 1994; Shapiro 1992). Such evaluation is particularly important since most business network programs are designed with termination in mind.

The Danish program led to the formation of over 500 networks. Many observers credit these networks with a significant role in the recovery of the Danish economy, especially in transforming a 25-year negative balance of trade into the highest per capita balance of trade surplus in the OECD (Nielsen 1994; Martinusson 1994; Steeman 1994). With regard to the specific benefits for participating firms, Gelsing (1992) reported that in a sample of 520 Danish SMEs participating in 82 business networks, 19 percent had reduced costs, 42 percent had increased sales, 72 percent had accelerated innovation, 75 percent had strengthened their international position, and 82 percent had increased employment. Two more recent studies (Amphion 1996; Neergaard and Nielsen 1997) are less positive about the outcomes of the program. In particular, Amphion found that three-quarters of the networks formed did not survive, and that large proportions of program funds were either not spent, or went to projects that no longer exist. Inadequate implementation and lack of defined expectations for outcomes hampered the use of other measures of success. Both Amphion and Neergarrd and Nielsen down play the role of the program in addressing the structural problems of the Danish economy.

The New Zealand Hard Business Networks program has not had a formal evaluation per se, although regular reports on broker activities have been obtained.[3] However, a pilot project operated in the Canterbury region during 1994 and 1995 was evaluated in some detail. This trial produced 11 trained brokers who worked to develop 25 networks involving 150 firms. Examples of the networks formed include those between six furniture manufacturers who export to Australia, four agricultural equipment manufacturers who export to the United States, six building products manufacturers who jointly promote their products to architects, and eight tourism companies (Ffowcs Williams 1996, p. 36). A study of the 150 firms found a significant change in awareness of the benefits of networking, and enthusiasm for the network strategy (Cragg and Vargo 1995). The majority of the networks were involved in joint marketing (89%), followed by R&D (44%), and joint manufacturing (37%). The most important benefits identified by participants were entering new markets, increased market share, and increased overseas sales. The funding provided by the Business Development Boards was a major incentive to participation in the program for more than half of the firms.

Lindsay and colleagues (1998) recently conducted qualitative interviews with 10 brokers who between them helped to form over 40 networks as part of New Zealand's Hard Business Networks program. A number of themes emerged from these interviews. The first was that there is considerable variability in the network formation process, and brokers capitalized on the flexibility of the New Zealand program. Second, variability in the approach pursued by brokers is influenced by two "contingency variables": the presence of a predetermined idea or project, and the degree of convergence in the goals of the firms. The fastest forming and most successful networks are those with a predetermined idea and a high degree of convergence. Third, successful brokers have either significant industry knowledge or knowledge of value systems, are successful business consultants, and are highly committed. Fourth, geographic proximity is helpful, but is not a necessary factor for network success. Finally, the presence of a lead firm, and participants that are top performers with resources, skills, and a positive attitude toward risk are important factors in the success of a network.

Despite a paucity of thorough assessments of the outcomes of brokering programs, the facilitation of networking remains a popular policy tool. A number of countries, including South Africa, which is using a consultant from New Zealand, are in the process of establishing a program. Brokering programs have attractive characteristics, even if it is difficult to demonstrate that they contribute to the achievement of specific goals for growth or export expansion. The funds provided to hire a broker help several firms, some of which may even be competitors. Thus, governments concerned about creating a "level playing field" are not seen to be using public funds to assist one firm over another. Further, they have a clear exit path, with a specified lifetime in the span of three to five years. Networking programs are essentially educational programs, with brokers helping managers to learn about networking concepts, and to learn from each other. They also operate at several levels, from that of the individual manager or owner, to the firm, sector, or even whole community. Finally, Perrow (1992, pp. 461-463) argues that networks of small firms contribute to a more equitable distribution of income, sharing of power, greater community involvement, and generally more civil society.

Thus, there is potential for significant welfare outcomes in addition to those realized directly through improved firm performance.

Network brokering programs can be relatively inexpensive, especially in comparison with export promotion programs based on tax or other financial incentives.[4] The success of New Zealand's new approach, in which networks are promoted without financial assistance to hire brokers, will be interesting to follow. Tourism New Zealand has also initiated a program that has little funding to facilitate networks between firms in the tourism sector. The results of the Canterbury pilot program, which found that the availability of funding was a major incentive for more than half of the firms, suggests that the participation rate is likely to be low. However, others argue that networks are easily self-funding from cost savings and revenue growth, and that the numbers of firms pursuing networking strategies will increase once the advantages become better known (Roy 1998). As one U.S. consultant who helps design work groups and organizational networks commented: "Fund them too much, and you'll start to want deliverables. It won't work. You'll get what the community wants to deliver" (quoted in Stewart and Brown 1996, p. 3).

V. IMPLICATIONS FOR ENTREPRENEURS

Networking offers managers of SMEs an alternative to internally oriented strategies for growth and internationalization. Like any new management approach, the potential benefits of networking should be appraised within the context of individual firms. Brokers involved in the pilot of New Zealand's Hard Business Networks program commented "a network should not be seen as a quick fix," and "networks must be seen in context, as part of a firm's strategic planning, not just another idea" (Cragg and Vargo 1995, p. 13). One of the long-term goals of the New Zealand HBN program is simply to shift the traditional entrepreneurial model of "going it alone," toward one in which cooperative action is considered as a strategic option.

Many entrepreneurs confuse networking strategies with their personal contact networks, and respond to approaches by brokers by saying "we already do networking" (Cragg and Vargo 1995, p. 13). While personal contact networks are an important source of support for entrepreneurs, they lack the focus and strategic intent of a hard business network. Personal ties can be important in network formation, but are not a substitute for more formal coordination processes. For example, Birley (1985) in studying the role of networks in the entrepreneurial process of firms in Indiana concluded that too much emphasis was placed on "informal" networks, and too little on "formal" ones. The implication is that entrepreneurs should look at their social ties to see how they can be levered into more formal strategic arrangements, and how those arrangements can be actively managed to provide stability and strategic direction.

Cooperation and networking will be a more appealing strategy to some entrepreneurs than to others. White, Gorton, and Chaston (1996, pp. 38-40) argue that there are a number of key skills required for successful entrepreneurship, and that it is important that entrepreneurs be generalists with adequate proficiency in all key skills. White and colleagues call entrepreneurs who have such proficiencies (or who think they do) "individualists," and those who perceive that they lack one or more important skills "suboptimal realists." Suboptimal realists are more likely to be receptive to networking as a way of overcoming individual weaknesses. By bringing together heterogeneous skills in a network, each cooperating firm can both fill gaps in competencies, and learn skills required for long-term development.

Successful networks require participants to exercise managerial skills that may be unfamiliar to entrepreneurs used to managing within the environment of their own firm. These skills relate to the need to share decision making, be cooperative, achieve consensus, maintain commitment, adapt to the style and systems of other firms, coordinate, and be organized (McCormack 1993). Mazzonis (1993) identifies eight core elements for sustainable networks: objectives, function, structure, process, context, catalyst, participants, and resources. Sillars (1995, p. 12) expands on these, identifying numerous success factors including:

- A clear vision with explicit commercial objectives and priorities that can be easily communicated between firms.
- Defined responsibilities and timetables, and an implementation strategy or business plan.
- A relatively small number of participants with a common business culture.
- Exclusion of poorly performing firms.
- Time spent identifying commonalties, exchanging information, and generally building trust.
- Development of a common image and external profile for the network.
- Willingness of network participants to change the way they operate, openly show their commitment, and treat other network partners as equals.
- Adequate resources for network management and coordination.

Brokers can help to facilitate some of these success factors, and to develop network management skills among participants. However, as brokering programs generally focus on the formation stage, there may be a need for additional training or management intermediaries to assist entrepreneurs with the management of mature networks.

Entrepreneurs also need to be aware that there are potential costs of network involvement beyond those of formation and coordination. The most commonly cited is the potential for loss of autonomy (e.g., Barley, Freeman, and Hybels 1992), which seems to be a particular concern of those entrepreneurs who place greater emphasis on autonomy than on profits (Kets de Vries 1985). However, entrepreneurs concerned with independence often fail to consider that no firm is an island, and that networking is an opportunity to better influence the firm's environment through choice of dependencies. Other problems include the potential for unplanned loss of knowledge, and the transaction costs of allocating resources, integrating procedures, quality control, and conflict resolution (Biemans 1992; Wissema and Evser 1991; Nueno and Oosterveld 1988). These costs must be evaluated when determining if a network strategy is appropriate, and firms in networks must manage their relationships to minimize these costs. As existing brokering programs focus on the initial stages of partner selection and network formation, they are of little help in this regard, except to the extent that good partner selection mitigates transaction costs.

The social capital literature suggests some general problems that may accompany network strategies (Portes and Landolt 1996). The first is that strong ties between members of a network can be used to exclude outsiders. In some cases this might constitute a barrier to start-up firms by preventing access to an important resource controlled by the network. A second problem is that membership in a network brings demands for conformity that may limit creativity and stifle the entrepreneurial spirit. Third, network membership may reinforce poor management practices if they are also used by other members (more generally, social capital does not necessarily increase human capital). Fourth, networks may limit the extent to which firms have the time or inclination to search further afield to acquire resources. Thus, they may fail to identify important new suppliers and customers, or to import new technologies. Finally, network strategies are limited in extent as the transaction costs within networks increase sharply as members are added and more resources must be devoted to measurement and enforcement (North 1991, p. 99).

VI. CONCLUSION

A vision of firm growth and increased international activity achieved through cooperative action in small dense networks is replacing the traditional picture of internally driven firm growth spurred by independent entrepreneurial action. A considerable literature has developed that shows SMEs can successfully use network strategies to access needed resources and lever competencies to increase returns, access new markets, and be more innovative. This is particularly so of networks that have a clear strategic intent. However, entrepreneurs also tend to under invest in cooperative relationships because of concerns about loss of autonomy, and because the benefits of cooperation are difficult for any one firm to appropriate.

The contribution of SMEs to employment, and their potential to provide the flexibility required in global markets, has attracted the attention of policymakers. Network brokering programs have been developed to help SMEs to overcome their constraints of size and volatility. The rationale for such programs is the observed link between networking activity and firm success in a number of specific locales. This paper argues that viewing networks as a form of social capital provides an understanding of the potential for public involvement in brokering networks of SMEs. In particular, networks are a public good and brokers act to correct imperfections in the market for relationships thus improving the welfare outcomes of SME activity. Research specifically designed to estimate the nature and magnitude of these outcomes would be a welcome addition to the academic consideration of the role of networks in firm growth, and to the assessment mechanisms used by policymakers. Comparison of matched samples of "market" versus "networked" firms such as that conducted by Human and Provan (1997) may be one way of providing this evidence.

Most brokering programs are based on a model developed by the Danish Technological Institute. This model breaks down the network formation process into stages that emphasize the early activities of network creation, rather than the operation of mature networks. Public funds are provided to employ a professional broker to help find and screen partners, and to develop a strategic plan. This model has been modified in different countries by changing the amount and timing of funds available, the source of brokers, and even whether networks include international partners. An evaluation of these different modifications and their outcomes would be valuable to program decision makers.

Finally, there are a number of implications of network strategies for entrepreneurs. The first is that brokering programs attempt to create positive attitudes toward cooperation, and promote the use of network strategies. SME owners and managers should be receptive to these initiatives, but also need to evaluate network strategies in the context of their own firm, and relative to their personal orientation and skills. Some firms, for example, may have such unique and specialized internal resources that they are almost independent of their local environment (Christensen and Linkmark 1993). For such firms, the costs of network membership, including the potential for unplanned loss of information, may be too high. Others might find working in a network very difficult because they are "individualists" (as described by White et al. 1996). A second consideration is that entrepreneurs who choose to work in a network need to develop management skills that emphasize shared decision making, consensus, flexibility, and so on. Managers whose experience is within the context of their own firm where they have sole control may not have developed these skills. Finally, network participants should be aware of the potential down side of network strategies, and manage their network to minimize the potential costs. All of these implications suggest that individual entrepreneurs and their "mental models" play a significant role in the formation and success of networks. Relatively little research has focused on this aspect of networks, and more needs to be learned about the process of partner selection, and how to determine the best mix of skills and resources within networks.

NOTES

1. Some authors such as Chirinko (1990) argue that social capital influences the relative bargaining strength between altruistic and egoistic tendencies in decision making, and can lead to the private provision of public goods. However, Routlege and von Amsberg (1996) argue that social capital can be modeled using only reference to self-interest, consistent with the assumption of most economic theory.

2. The Norwegian program now only has three stages: feasibility, planning, and running.

3. One Trade New Zealand official suggested in an interview that a formal evaluation was not conducted because the cost of the program did not justify the expenditure.

4. The Danish program likely involved the largest investment made by any single country in networking to date, costing approximately $US25 million over its three-year life span (Rosenfeld 1996, p. 251). Most programs have invested only a fraction of this amount.

REFERENCES

Albrechts, L., F. Moulaert, P. Roberts, and E. Swyngedouw, eds. 1989. *Regional Policy at the Crossroads.* New York: Jessica Kingsley.

Alexander, E. R. 1992. "A Transaction Cost Theory of Planning." *Journal of the American Planning Association* 58(2): 190-200.

Amin, A. 1993. "The Globalization of the Economy, an Erosion of Regional Networks." Pp. 278-295 in *The Embedded Firm: On the Socioeconomics of Industrial Networks*, edited by G. Grabher. London.

Amin, A., and K. Robins. 1990. "The Re-Emergence of Regional Economies? The Mythical Geography of Flexible Accumulation." *Environment and Planning D: Society and Space* 8: 7-34.

_____. 1991. "These are not Marchallian Times." Pp. 105-118 in *Innovation Networks: Spatial Perspectives*, edited by R. Camagni. London: Belhaven Press.

Amphion. 1996. *Evaluation of the "Network Co-operation Program" 1989-1992.* Denmark: Agency for Development of Trade and Industry, February.

Andrez, J. 1993. "Workshop Summary Theme A—Programs and Mechanisms to Stimulate Interfirm Cooperation." Pp. 91-102 in *Cooperation and Competitiveness. Interfirm Cooperation—A Means Towards SME Competitiveness, International Conference Proceedings.* Lisbon: Programa Especifico de Desenvolvimento do Industria Portuguesa.

Axelsson, B., and J. Johanson. 1992. "Foreign Market Entry—the Textbook View vs. the Network View." Pp. 218-234 in *Industrial Networks: A New View of Reality*, edited by B. Axelsson and G. Easton. London: Routledge.

Barber, D. 1996. "Business Networks Aim to Widen Export Base." *The National Business Review* (March 29): 48.

Barley, S. R., J. Freeman, and R. C. Hybels. 1992. "Strategic Alliances in Commercial Biotechnology." In *Networks and Organisations - Structure, Form and Action*, edited by N. Nohria and R.G. Eccles. Boston: Harvard Business School Press.

Bassand, M., E. A. Brugger, J. M. Bryden, J. Friedman, and B. Stuckey, eds. 1986. *Self-Reliant Development in Europe.* Aldershot: Gower.

Becker, G. S. 1964. *Human Capital.* New York: Columbia University Press.

Bell, J. 1995. "The Internationalization of Small Computer Software Firms: A Further Challenge to Stage Theories." *European Journal of Marketing* 29(8): 60-75.

Benson-Rea, M., and H. I. M. Wilson. 1994. *Networks in New Zealand,* Final Report to the Ministry of Commerce. Auckland: University of Auckland.

Biemans, W. G. 1992. *Managing Innovation within Networks.* London: Routledge.

Birley, S. 1985. "The Role of Networks in the Entrepreneurial Process." *Journal of Business Venturing* 1: 107-117.

Bosworth, B. 1993. "Building Learning Networks: Emerging Experiences in the United States." Pp. 123-130 in *Cooperation and Competitiveness. Interfirm Cooperation—A Means Toward SME Competitiveness, International Conference Proceedings.* Lisbon: Promgrama Especifico de Desenvolvimento da industria Portguguesa.

Bridgewater, S. 1992. *Informal Networks as a Vehicle of International Market Entry: Future Research Directions,* Warwick Business School Research Paper No. 54. Warwick: University of Warwick.

Camagni, R. 1991. *Innovation Networks.* London: Belhaven Press.

Cavagnoli, I., and S. A. Santos. 1993. "The Brazilian Experience with Horizontal Networks of Cooperation Amongst Small Businesses: Project Polo, Mechanisms and Results." Pp. 131-160 in *Cooperation and Competitiveness. Interfirm Cooperation – A Means Toward SME Competitiveness, International Conference Proceedings,* Lisbon: Promgrama Especifico de Desenvolvimento da industria Portguguesa.

Chirinko, R. S. 1990. "Altruism, Egoism, and the Role of Social Capital in the Private Provision of Public Goods." *Economics and Politics* 2: 275-290.

Chisholm, D. 1988. *Coordination Without Hierarchy: Informal Structures in Multiorganisational Systems.* Berkeley: University of California Press.

Christensen, P. R., and L. Lindmark. 1993. "Location and Internationalization of Small Firms." Pp. 131-152 in *Visions and Strategies in European Integration: A North European Perspective,* edited by L. Lundqvist and L.O. Persson. Berlin: Springer.

Coffey, W. J., and M. Polese. 1985. "Local Development: Conceptual Bases and Policy Implications." *Regional Studies* 19: 85-93.

Coleman, J. S. 1990. *Foundations of Social Theory.* Cambridge, MA: The Belknap Press of Harvard University.

Commonwealth Government of Australia. 1994. *Working Nation—Policies and Programmes.* White Paper, Canberra.

Cooke, P., and K. Morgan. 1993. "The Network Paradigm: New Departures in Corporate and Regional Development." *Environment and Planning D: Society and Space* 11: 543-564.

———. 1994. "The Regional Innovation Center in Baden-Wurttemberg." *International Journal of Technology Management* 9 (3/4): 394-429.

Coviello, N. 1994. "Internationalizing the Entrepreneurial High Technology, Knowledge-Intensive Firm." Unpublished Ph.D. Dissertation. Auckland: Department of Marketing, University of Auckland.

Cragg, P., and J. Vargo. 1995. *Hard Business Networks in New Zealand: An Early Evaluation of the Canterbury Pilot.* Christchurch: University of Canterbury.

Crocombe, G. T., M. J. Enright, and M. E. Porter. 1991. *Upgrading New Zealand's Competitive Advantage: The Porter Project on New Zealand.* Auckland: Oxford University Press.

Curran, J., R. Jarvis, R. Blackburn, and S. Black. 1993. "Networks and Small Firms: Constructs Methodological Strategies and Some Findings." *International Journal of Small Business* 11 (2): 13-25.

European Observatory for SMEs. 1993. *First Annual Report.* Report submitted to Directorate-General XXIII (Enterprise Policy, Distributive Trades, Tourism and Cooperatives) of the European Commission.

Ferland, M., B. Montreuil, D. Poulin, and S. Gauvin. 1994. *Quebec's Strategy to Foster Value-Adding Interfirm Cooperation: A Dual Focus on Clustering and Networking.* Quebec: Universite Laval.

Ffowcs Williams, I. 1996. "Hard and Soft Networks: Helping Firms Co-operate for Export Growth." *New Zealand Strategic Management* (Summer): 30-36.

Field, A., S. Goldfinch, and M. Perry. 1994. *Promoting Small Business Networking: An Agency Comparison*, Research Report # 2. Christchurch: Social Research and Development.

Forsgren, M. 1989. *Managing the Internationalization Process: The Swedish Case.* London: Routledge.

Fukuyama, F. 1995. "Social Capital and the Global Economy." *Foreign Affairs* 74 (5): 89-103.

Gelsing, L. 1992. "Evaluating Programs Promoting Networks—Measures of Success and Evaluation Methods." Pp. 19-23 in *Significant Others: Exploring the Potential of Manufacturing Networks.* Aspen: The Aspen Institute, Regional Technology Strategies Inc, July.

Grotz, R., and B. Braun. 1993. "Networks, Milieux and Individual Firm Strategies: Empirical Evidence of an Innovative SME Environment." *Geografiska Annaler B* 75 (3): 149-162.

Harper, D. 1993. *An Analysis of Interfirm Networks.* Report prepared for the New Zealand Ministry of Commerce, Contract No. 584, New Zealand Institute of Economic Research, July.

Hill, K. S. 1992. *Flexible Networks in Theory and Practice: How and Why to Set Up Flexible Networks in British Columbia.* Vancouver: Trade Development Corporation.

Human, S. E., and K. G. Provan. 1997. "An Emergent Theory of Structure and Outcomes in Small-Firm Strategic Manufacturing Networks." *Academy of Management Journal* 40 (2): 368-403.

Jarillo, J.C. 1988. "On Strategic Networks." *Strategic Management Journal* 9: 31-41.

Johanson, J., and J. Vahlne. 1992. "Management of Foreign Market Entry." *Scandinavian International Business Review* 1 (3): 9-27.

Kets de Vries, M. F. R. 1985. "The Dark Side of Entrepreneurship." *Harvard Business Review* (November/December).

Lichtenstein, G. A. 1993. "A Strategic Typology of Network Approaches." In *Cooperation and Competitiveness. Interfirm Cooperation—A Means Toward SME Competitiveness, International Conference Proceedings.* Lisbon: Promgrama Especifico de Desenvolvimento da industria Portguguesa.

Lindsay, V. J., R. Brookes, I. Ffowcs Williams, and P. Healy. 1998. *Hard Business Networks: The New Zealand Experience.* Auckland: Department of International Business, University of Auckland.

Lipnack, J., and J. Stamps. 1994. *The Age of the Network: Organizing Principles for the 21st Century.* Essex Junction, Vermont: Omneo/Oliver Wright Publications.

Maillat, D. 1990. "SMEs, Innovation and Territorial Development." Pp. 331-351 in *Technological Developments at the Local Level*, edited by R. Cappelin and P. Mijkamp. Aldershot: Avebury.

Malecki, E. J., and M. E. Veldhoen. 1993. "Network Activities, Information and Competitiveness in Small Firms." *Geograpfiska Annaler B* 75 (3): 131-147.

Malmberg, A. 1997. "Industrial Geography: Location and Learning." *Progress in Human Geography* 21(4): 573-582.

Martinusson, J. 1994. "More then an End in Itself, The Export Network as a Stepping Stone." *Firm Connections* (May/June).

Mazzonis, D. 1993. "Workshop Summary Theme C—Types and Aspects of interfirm Cooperation." Pp. 105-108 in *Cooperation and Competitiveness. Interfirm Cooperation—A Means Towards SME Competitiveness, International Conference Proceedings.* Lisbon: Programa Especifico de Desenvolvimento da Industria Portuguesa.

McCormack, J. 1993. "Selling Tassie Tourism." Pp. 131-132 in *Proceedings, National Seminar for Networkers.* Adelaide: South Australia Centre for Manufacturing.

Mitchell, S. 1994. "Good Result for the Right SMEs." *The Australian Financial Review* (May 5): A8.

Neergaard, H., and K. Nielsen. 1997. "Competence Building or Destruction in Small Business Networks." Paper Presented at the Strategic Management Society's 17th Annual Conference, Barcelona, Spain, October.

Nescheim, T. 1994. *The Norweigan Business Network Program: Content, Context and Output.*

Nielsen, N. C. 1994. "Letter from Denmark, The Network Program Concludes." *Firm Connections* (May/June).

North, D. C. 1991. "Institutions." *Journal of Economic Perspectives* 5 (1): 97-112.

Nueno, P., and J. Oosterveld. 1988. "Managing Technological Alliances." *Long Range Planning* 21 (3).

Perrow, C. 1992. "Small-Firm Networks." Pp. 445-470 in *Networks and Organizations; Structure, Form, and Action,* edited by N. Nohria and R. G. Eccles. London: Harvard Business School Press.

Perry, M. 1995. "Industry Structures, Networks and Joint Action Groups" *Regional Studies* 29(2): 208-217.

Porter, M. E. 1990. *The Competitive Advantage of Nations.* London: MacMillan Press.

Portes, A., and P. Landolt. 1996. "The Downside of Social Capital." *The American Prospect* 26: 18-21, 94. (http://epnorg/propsect/26/26-cent2).

Praat, H. 1991. "Principles of Networking." In *Complexes, Formations and Networks,* edited by M.D.E. Smidt and E. Wever. *Nederlandse Geografische Studies* 132: 93-102.

Putnam, R. D. 1993. "The Prosperous Community: Social Capital and Public Life." *American Prospect* (Spring): 35-42.

Romer, P. M. 1990. "Endogenous Technical Change." *Journal of Political Economy* 98: 71-102.

Rosenfeld, S. A. 1996. "Does Cooperation Enhance Competitiveness? Assessing the Impacts of Inter-firm Collaboration." *Research Policy* 25: 247-263.

Rosson, P. J., and F. H. R. Seringhaus. 1991. "Export Promotion and Public Organisations: Present and Future Research." Pp. 319-339 in *Export Development and Promotion: The Role of Public Organisations,* edited by F. H. R. Seringhaus and P. J. Rosson. Boston: Kluer.

Routledge, B. R., and J. Von Amsberg. 1996. "Endogenous Social Capital." Mimeograph.

Roy, P. 1998. "Business Networks for SMEs: Powerful Synergy for Growth in the Emerging Global Market Place." Presented at a conference on *Globalization and Emerging Businesses: Strategies for the Twenty-first Century.* Montreal, Canada, September 26-28.

Sabel, C. 1989. "Flexible Specialisation and the Reemergence of Regional Economies." Pp. 17-70 in *Reversing Industrial Decline? Industrial Structure and Policy in Britain and Her Competitors,* edited by P. Hirst. and J. Zeitlin. Oxford: Berg.

Santana, A. 1992. "Cooperation Networks in Portugal: The Importance of the Broker." In *Significant Others: Exploring the Potential of Manufacturing Networks.* Aspen: The Aspen Institute, Regional Technology Strategies Inc., July, 24-28.

Saxenian, A. 1990. "Regional Networks and the Resurgence of Silicon Valley." *California Management Review* 33(1): 89-112.

_____. 1992. "The Origins and Dynamics of Production Networks in Silicon Valley." *Research Policy* 20: 423-437.

Shapiro, P. 1992. "What is 'Success' and How Can Progress be Measured?" In *Significant Others: Exploring the Potential of Manufacturing Networks.* Aspen: The Aspen Institute, Regional Technology Strategies Inc., July.

Sillars, K. J. 1995. *Business Use of Interfirm Networks in New Zealand: A Study of the Business Links Used by Some Tourism Businesses in the Nelson Region.* Palmerston North: Master of Business project, Massey University.

Steeman, M. 1994. "Hard Networks Critical for Future Growth." *Export News,* October 17.

Stewart, T. A., and V. Brown. 1996. "The Invisible Key to Success," *Fortune,* August 5, (http://pathfinder.com/@@Xu4wowQA4...une/magazine/1996/960 805/edg.html).

Stohr, W. B. 1990. *Global Challenge and Local Response: Initiatives for Economic Regeneration in Contemporary Europe.* London: Mansell.

Storper, M., and R. Walker. 1989. *The Capitalist Imperative: Territory, Technology, and Industrial Growth,* Oxford: Basil Blackwell.

Todtling, F. 1994. "Regional Networks of High-Technology Firms—The Case of the Greater Boston Region." *Technovation* 14 (5): 323-343.

Vatne, E. 1995. "Local Resource Mobilization and Internationalization Strategies in Small and Medium Sized Enterprises." *Environment and Planning A* 27: 63-80.

Welch, D. E., L. S. Welch, I. F. Wilkinson, and L. C. Young. forthcoming. "The Importance of Networks in Export Promotion: Policy Issues." *Journal of International Marketing*.

White, J. E., M. J. Gorton, and I. Chaston. 1996. "Facilitating Co-operative Networks of High-Technology Small Firms: Problems and Strategies." *Small Business and Enterprise Development* 3: 34-47.

Wissema, J. G., and L. Euser. 1991. "Successful Innovation Through Inter-Company Networks." *Long Range Planning* 24(6).

PART III

EMPIRICAL STUDIES

DOMESTIC MARKET SIZE, COMPETENCES, AND THE INTERNATIONALIZATION OF SMALL- AND MEDIUM-SIZED ENTERPRISES

A. Rebecca Reuber and Eileen Fischer

I. INTRODUCTION

"How much does industry matter?" asks a recent paper examining the importance of different factors on the profitability of U.S. corporations (McGahan and Porter 1997). The findings of that paper, as well as an enormous body of economics and strategy literature, indicate that industry effects are often consequential to a wide variety of outcomes. In the entrepreneurship literature, industry effects have been found to explain outcomes such as firm performance (McDougall, Covin, Robinson, and Herron 1994; McDougall, Robinson, and DeNisi 1992; Sandberg and Hofer 1987), strategies followed by emerging ventures (Carter, Stearns, Reynolds, and Miller 1994; Covin, Slevin, and Covin 1990), and job creation by small

Research in Global Strategic Management, Volume 7, pages 85-100.
Copyright © 1999 by JAI Press Inc.
All rights of reproduction in any form reserved.
ISBN: 0-7623-0458-8

businesses (Picot, Baldwin, and Dupuy 1995; Reuber and Fischer 1998; West head and Birley 1995).

In studies of the internationalization of emerging (new and/or small) firms however, industry effects have not been much examined. Indeed, many studies focus on one industry in order to control for industry differences (Leonidou and Katsikeas 1996). One distinction that has been made is whether or not the industry is service-based (e.g., Erramilli 1991; Erramilli and D'Souza 1993); another is whether an industry is technology-intensive (e.g., Boter and Holmquist 1996). In none of these studies, though, have industry effects been the primary focus though Boter and Holmquist (1996, p. 484) conclude their study of various factors influencing the internationalization of small firms by noting that the "concept of industry" is among the *most* important to consider.

A central issue in any research program designed to build our knowledge of the internationalization of emerging firms, then, should be to increase our under standing of industry as a concept. This paper takes up this challenge by conceptu alizing and exploring the implications of one particular industry characteristic domestic market size. This industry characteristic is an important one to consider for a number of reasons.

First, domestic market size represents a unidimensional, objective demand-side versus a supply-side industry variable (Arora and Gambardella 1997). The major ity of work considering industry effects in entrepreneurship generally, and the internationalization of emerging firms in particular, has been concerned exclu sively with supply-side variables such as the nature of the technology employed in the industry (e.g., Boter and Holmquist 1996; Erramilli 1991; Erramilli and D'Souza 1993) or with subjective assessments of multidimensional environmen tal characteristics such as dynamism, hostility, and heterogeneity (e.g., Zahra Neubaum, and Huse 1997). Focusing on a single, objective, demand-side industry variable that is knowable at start-up helps extend the conceptual repertoire of entrepreneurship research.

A second reason domestic market size is important to consider is that it is a fac tor that can vary between firms in a single industry based in different countries thus helping to explain differences between nations in the ways comparable firms will compete internationally. Arora and Gambardella (1997) have followed this line of inquiry. They compare U.S., European, and Japanese engineering firms and find support for their argument that the larger domestic market faced by U.S firms resulted in U.S.-based firms having greater efficiency than those from Europe and Japan, particularly for activities involving product-specific versus generic management competences. It must be noted that Arora and Gambardella' study was concerned with an industry composed mostly of older firms, formed before World War II. Their analysis is based on the assumptions that firms operate initially in a domestic market and can survive in that domestic market, assump tions that are not unreasonable for an industry that had little global activity when most of the firms in the sample were started. As such, however, their study may have limited applicability for emerging firms in particular industries today. McDougall and Oviatt (McDougall, Shane, and Oviatt 1994; Oviatt and McDougall 1994) have brought to attention the phenomenon of international new ventures—ventures that are international from birth. Their insight raises awareness that today it is not necessarily the case that firms can or will grow in their domestic markets prior to internationalizing. Thus between-nation comparisons which assume that firms are likely to operate domestically prior to internationalization may be less compelling than between-industry comparisons which make no such assumption. This leads to the third reason why domestic market size is an important industry-level variable to consider.

Domestic market size is a factor that can vary between firms operating in different industries within a nation, thus providing insights on how a single nation may require differing strategies to support internationalization in different industries. It is this within-nation, between-industry perspective that motivates this paper. We examine differences *between* SMEs that operate in small domestic markets (SDMs) and those from the same country that operate in large domestic markets (LDMs). Drawing on resource theory we argue that, compared with SMEs in LDMs, SMEs in SDMs from the same country of origin develop greater international business competency and innovation competency but less product-specific competences.

This chapter also conceptualizes the factors related to market size which are and are not likely to account for within-industry, between-firm differences in performance with respect to internationalization. Drawing on institutional theory, we posit that international business competences, but not innovative capabilities or product-specific competences, are associated with SMEs' overall degree of internationalization *within* particular industries. The chapter proceeds from a conceptual discussion of domestic market size to a report on an empirical study of Canadian SMEs from the software products industry (SDM) and the food and beverage industry (LDM) and concludes by discussing the implications for practice, public policy, and further research.

II. THE CONCEPT OF DOMESTIC MARKET SIZE

At a very basic level, the size of the domestic market a firm faces is expected to effect the internationalization patterns of emerging firms simply because the impetus for internationalization is very strong if the local market is not big enough to support a sufficient level of sales (Bonaccorsi 1992; Reuber and Fischer 1997). This basic insight can be further refined and developed to offer insight into the differences in the competences that firms facing small versus large domestic markets are likely to develop.

A resource-based perspective views firms as bundles of resources and competences (e.g., Barney 1991; Penrose 1971; Peteraf 1993; Wernerfelt 1984). These competences and resources, if they are distinctive or superior relative to those of competing firms, constitute firm-specific assets that are a basis of competitive advantage. The usefulness of a resource-based view of firms for understanding ventures that are international from birth was proposed by McDougall, Shane, and Oviatt (1994, p. 479). The value of the perspective for the internationalization of emerging firms was reinforced by Bloodgood, Sapienza, and Almeida (1996) who drew upon it to study the internationalization of firms at the time of IPO issuance.

An assumption underlying the resource-based perspective is that initial differences in firm competences exist, and tend to persist over time (Dierickx and Cool 1989; Teece, Pisano, and Shuen 1997). Arora and Gambardella (1997) adopt and build on this argument to suggest that, even though any firm may contemplate selling to foreign markets eventually, the size of the domestic market at the time of founding shapes the decision such that the competences that firm founders consider relevant when deciding to enter an industry will be influenced by the size of the domestic market.

What differences in competences, then, might we expect to find in SMEs founded in an industry with a relatively large domestic market versus those founded in an industry with a relatively smaller one?

One source of insight on firms founded in small domestic markets comes from studies of international new ventures and early exporters (McDougall, Shane, and Oviatt 1994; Oviatt and McDougall 1994; Reuber and Fischer 1997). These studies have focused on technology-based firms. McDougall and Oviatt (1996) point out that technology-based firms often have specialized, global market niches and high R&D costs that require a level of sales above that which a domestic market will support. They identify three resources—founders with global vision, international business competences, and an established international network—which enable these firms to sell beyond their domestic market immediately. Building on this work, Reuber and Fischer (1997) found evidence that these concepts can be extended to small- and medium-sized enterprises (SMEs) that internationalize early, rather than necessarily at start-up.

Given the assumption that market size at founding will influence the competences both in place at founding and persisting through the life of the firm, of these three resources, the one most likely to vary at the industry level, as well as the firm level, is international business competency. In particular, it is expected that international business competence will be more characteristic of firms in SDMs than those is LDMs. This leads to the between-industry hypothesis with respect to international business competency:

Hypothesis 1.   SMEs in SDM industries will have greater international business competency than do SMEs in LDM industries.

An additional type of competency that is likely to differ between SMEs in SDMs and SMEs in LDMs is innovation competency. Considerable research has shown that ventures that must seek foreign markets in order to survive are likely to exhibit a high degree of product-based innovation in very specialized niches (e.g., Baldwin 1994; Beamish, Craig, and McLellan 1993; Bloodgood, Sapienza, and Almeida 1996; Boter and Holmquist 1996; Cavusgil, Zou, and Naidu 1993). This finding has been popularized in the business press that targets the owners of SMEs and in the information that resource providers (e.g., banks and governments) provide to their clients (e.g., Baldwin 1994). It is reasonable to expect that SMEs founded and grown in SDMs will have placed a greater emphasis on innovative capabilities than those founded in LDMs. Further, to the extent that innovative competency is associated with survival in an SDM, we expect that those firms which continue to exist in an SDM, compared with those which are able to survive in an LDM, will have a higher average level of innovative competence. This leads to our second hypothesis:

Hypothesis 2. SMEs in SDM industries will have greater innovative competences than do SMEs in LDM industries.

The third and final type of resource to be discussed here borrows its logic from Arora and Gambardella (1997) who noted that firms that are founded and that survive in large domestic markets are particularly likely to develop product-specific competences. Start-up ventures in LDMs not only face a greater potential demand from customers, but also a greater potential level of competition from other firms attracted to the same market opportunity. As Arora and Gambardella note, firms that survive are likely to have an efficiency advantage that is particularly marked in the case of product-specific competences. This gives rise to the third hypothesis:

Hypothesis 3. SMEs in LDM industries have greater product-specific competences than those in SDM industries.

Having considered the competences that are expected to differ between firms in SDMs and LDMs, within-industry hypotheses can be developed. The issue to be addressed is whether the factors which are expected to differ *between* SMEs in SDMs and SMEs in LDMs are related to variance in international performance *within* particular industries. In other words, if firms in SDMs and in LDMs are developing differential capabilities over time, at least partially in response to the size of their domestic markets, then are intra-industry differences in these capabilities related to how well SMEs within each industry do in foreign markets? The existence of such a relationship will depend on whether or not behavior with respect to a particular factor increases the heterogeneity among firms. The heterogeneity associated with effective strategy can create competitive advantage, but if institutional norms are so prevalent that there are unlikely to be consequential within-industry differences, then there may not be an impact on performance (Oliver 1996).

The evidence from the international business and entrepreneurship literatures is that market entries are difficult and costly, and that internationally experienced founders and management teams are likely to have a greater degree of international business competency (e.g., McDougall, Shane, and Oviatt 1994; Oviatt and McDougall 1994; Reuber and Fischer 1997). Further, it is expected that these managerial resources will be scarce and inimitable and likely to lead to sustained advantage. Thus, in both of the industries examined, regardless of the size of the domestic market, international business competency will be related to an SME's international performance. This leads to the following within-industry hypothesis:

Hypothesis 4.   For SMEs in both an SDM and an LDM, international business competency is related positively and significantly with SMEs' international performance

On the other hand, research findings suggest that the nature of industrial innovation is a function of institutional norms within particular industries (e.g., Abrahamson and Fombrun 1994; Cavusgil and Zou 1994), and so is unlikely to be related to SMEs' international performance within particular industries. This leads to the following within-industry hypothesis:

Hypothesis 5.   For SMEs in both an SDM and an LDM, innovation competence is not related to SMEs' international performance.

In the case of product-specific competences, it can be argued that firms which survive must all reach a high level of such competences. If there is little within-industry variation in such competences, then we should not expect to find a relationship between these competences and internationalization. Thus the final within-industry hypothesis is:

Hypothesis 6.   For SMEs in both an SDM and an LDM, the firms' degree of product-specific competence is not related to SMEs' international performance.

III.   RESEARCH METHOD

A. Sample

Two Canadian industries were selected: the software products industry (SDM) and the food and beverage industry (LDM). We selected two industries in order to control for different competitive contexts (cf. Keeley and Roure 1990; McDougall, Covin, Robinson, and Herron 1994; McDougall, Robinson, and DeNisis 1992; McGahan and Porter 1997; Roure and Keeley 1990; Sandberg and Hofer 1987). Statistics Canada data reported in 1998[1] indicates that the Canadian food and beverage industry has a domestic market which is roughly 328 times that of the Canadian software products industry. The size of the domestic market for food and beverage firms in 1996 was roughly $1,752.40 billion, while that of the software products industry in 1996 was roughly $5.348 billion (calculated as industry GDP minus exports).

Despite the wide discrepancy in size of the their domestic markets, the two industries are quite comparable in terms of their share of world markets and international growth potential. Canadian food and beverage firms have just over 3 percent of the global market, and Canadian software product firms have between 2 and 3 percent of the global market. Exports in both sectors increased over the 1995-1996 period (the last period reported); roughly 13 percent for the food and beverage sector and 13 to 14 percent for the software products sector. Thus, there is strong and comparable potential for international growth in both industries.[2]

Firms were selected in order to obtain a sample which varied in size and age, but which retained the focus on SMEs. Therefore, only firms that had 200 or fewer employees, which were not subsidiaries of other firms, and which were headquartered in Canada were considered eligible for inclusion. In the software products industry, only those firms deriving 50 percent or more of their revenue from software products (versus hardware or computing services) were eligible. In the food and beverages industry, all agricultural producers and all pure distributors were excluded, ensuring that the firm derived some portion of its revenue from processing of raw materials. The majority of the firms in both samples were located in the Greater Toronto Area region, which has the largest concentration of both households and businesses in the country, in order to reduce any systematic variation due to the size of local markets.

Several sources were used to identify firms in both industries. The primary sources for identifying software product firms were the Branham 400 database (version 2.4) and the Canadian government's BOSS Directory of Computer Software and Services. The primary sources for identifying food and beverage firms were the Ontario Agri-Food Source Guide and the Canadian government's Canadian Food and Beverage Exporters Directory. After examining all sources and conducting short telephone interviews to screen firms based on the listed criteria, a list of potential candidates in each industry was identified. Of the 202 firms in the software products industry that were contacted and eligible, 98 agreed to participate and provided usable data, for a response rate of 49 percent. Of the 149 firms in the food and beverages industry that were contacted, 48 agreed to participate and provided usable data, for a response rate of 32 percent.

These response rates are respectable relative to those often obtained in studies of entrepreneurial firms, and reflect the personalized method of obtaining data. The questionnaires were administered to the firms' CEO or to a member of the firms' top management team by trained research assistants. The research assistants contacted the firms by telephone to arrange an interview, faxed to confirm the interview, traveled to each respondent's office to give them the questionnaire, and sat with the respondent while the questionnaire was being completed. The research assistants were trained to clarify the nature of the questions and to explain their rationale, in order to enhance the completeness and accuracy of the data collected. They also noted any difficulties in answering the questions or in interpreting the answers, and these were followed up and clarified through subsequent communication with the respondent. Data collection took place between June of 1996 and December of 1997.

The software product firms in the sample were significantly younger than the food and beverage firms (a mean age of 10 years versus a mean age of 19 years; $t = -4.15$, $p = .000$) and somewhat, but not significantly, smaller in terms of number of employees (a mean of 35 full time employees versus a mean of 47 full time employees; $t = -1.65$, $p = .100$).

B. Measures

FSTS. Firms' international performance, the dependent variable, was measured using foreign sales as a percentage of total sales. Although more complex measures of international performance are available (Ramaswamy, Kroeck, and Renforth 1996; Sullivan 1994), including DOI_{SME}, a degree of internationalization measure specifically developed for SMEs (Reuber and Fischer 1997), FSTS remains a standard measure of international performance for emerging firms, which reflects the extent to which foreign sales contributes to a firm's success (Zahra, Neubaum, and Huse 1997). Its use is attractive here because it is independent of firms' structure and activities (which can be industry-related), and so it facilitates between- and within-industry comparisons.

For software product firms, the FSTS mean was 46.6 percent (s.d. is 37.1; range is 0 to 100) whereas for food and beverage firms, the mean was 28.3 percent (s.d. is 30.2; range is 0 to 100). A t-test indicated a significant difference between the means for the two industries, with software product firms having a significantly higher level of foreign sales ($t = 4.01$; $p = .000$).

For both of the industries, and consistent with the hypotheses and the literature on international new ventures (McDougall, Shane, and Oviatt 1994; Oviatt and McDougall 1994), neither firm age nor firm size were positively and significantly correlated with FSTS, and so they were not used as control variables in the regressions.

INTCOMP. International business competency for SMEs is reflected by two interrelated factors. The first factor is the ability to enter foreign markets quickly at, or after, start-up. What is of interest is not for how *long* a firm has been selling in foreign markets, but rather, for how long the firm delayed after start-up *before* selling in foreign markets.

The second related factor of international business competency is the ability to enter multiple foreign markets. While selling beyond the domestic market early *allows* for multiple country entry, not all SMEs are equally able to deal with the complexities of multiple local markets (Preece, Miles, and Baetz 1998). Those that can, arguably, demonstrate a second facet of international business competency. Firms that not only face small domestic markets, but also small markets in other countries they enter, are systematically more likely to have developed this second facet of international business competency.

Therefore, INTCOMP is conceptualized as a variable reflected by these two interrelated indicators of international business competence, both of which measure achieved (rather than attempted) international competence. Since the two measures are correlated for both sectors (see Table 2), it is not only logical but also justifiable to combine them into one measure. So that each element constitutes the same proportion of the composite variable, INTCOMP is calculated as the sum of the z-scores of DELAY and MARKETS (with the sign of DELAY's z-score reversed in order to take into account its opposite expected impact on the dependent variable FSTS).

INNOVATE. Competence in innovation was measured in terms of both product/service and production process innovation, consistent with OECD guidelines (OECD 1992). In order to ensure that the measure addressed achieved (rather than attempted) innovation, the questions focused on actual innovation rather than on input factors, such as R&D spending. Respondents were asked whether, in the past two fiscal years, more than half of their (a) product lines; (b) services; and (c) system development processes (for software firms) or production processes (for food and beverage firms) were new. With a "yes" (1) or "no" (0) response for each, INNOVATE can vary from 0 to 3. The scale had a Cronbach's alpha of .73 for the software product firms and .80 for the food and beverage firms, indicating acceptable reliability.

PRODUCT. Product specific competences are those that cannot be applied across a wide variety of products or activities; they involve expertise and/or efficiency in the production of a specific good or service. Arora and Gambardella, in measuring this construct for specialized engineering firms, concentrated on the range of proprietary process licences that were held by firms. An analogous measure of product specific competence for the industries studied here was developed by asking the respondents "How many distinct products does your company offer?"

IV. FINDINGS

Table 1 presents the mean, standard deviation, and range for each of the variables involved in the between-industry hypotheses, H1, H2, and H3. It also shows the results of the *t*-tests, comparing the means of these variables for the software prod-

Table 1.   Descriptive Statistics and *T*-tests

	Software Products Firms			Food and Beverage Firms			t-value
	Mean	S.D.	Range	Mean	S.D.	Range	
DELAY (years)	4.1	4.0	0 to 18	8.6	11.0	0 to 38	2.42*
MARKETS (no./age)	1.5	4.3	.04 to 37.3	0.4	6.8	.03 to 4	2.37*
INNOVATE (scale)	1.3	1.2	0 to 3	0.5	1.0	0 to 3	4.01***
PRODUCT (number)	1.0	1.5	.06-9.00	4.4	9.2	.03 to 50	−2.38*

Note: $*p < .05;$ $**p < .01;$ $***p < .001.$

Table 2.   Zero-Order Correlations Among Research Variables

	Software Products Firms			Food and Beverage Firms		
	2	3	4	2	3	4
1 INTVAR	.27	.03	.43**	.18	.15	.49**
2 INNOVATE		.09	−.15		−.11	.20
3 PRODUCT			.07			−.22
4 FSTS						

Note: $*p < .05;$ $**p < .01;$ $***p < .001.$

Table 3.   Regression Results

	Software Products Firms		Food and Beverage Firms	
Dependent variable:	FSTS		FSTS	
INTCOMP	8.18**	(2.96)	8.74**	(2.82)
INNOVATE	.32	(5.30)	6.74	(4.57)
PRODUCT	−1.14	(0.98)	−0.11*	(0.05)
Intercept	44.13	(12.39)	33.65	(5.50)
Adjusted R^2	.15		.29	
F	3.21*		6.20**	

Notes: Standard errors are in parentheses.
$*p < .05;$ $**p < .01;$ $***p < .001.$

ucts industry with the means for the food and beverage industry. As can be seen from the table, the means for each variable are significantly different between the two industries. Consistent with the three hypotheses, SMEs in the software products sample, compared with those in the food and beverage sample, exhibited: more international business competence (i.e., entered foreign markets earlier and entered more foreign markets), more innovation competence, and less product-specific competence. Thus, the three between-industry hypotheses cannot be rejected.

Table 2 presents the zero-order correlations among the variables, for each industry separately. For both industries, only INTCOMP is significantly related to the dependent variable, FSTS, and there is no multicollinearity among the independent variables.

Table 3 presents the results of the multiple regressions used to test the three within-industry hypotheses H4, H5, and H6. The results shown in Table 3 indicate that H4 and H5 cannot be rejected. Within both industries, firms' proportion of sales from foreign markets was significantly and positively related to the measure of international business competency. Thus, consistent with resource theory, the competence reflected in the ability to get into multiple markets and/or the ability to achieve international sales early is a differentiating advantage enjoyed by some SMEs within each industry, that is positively related to international performance. On the other hand, innovative competence—the development of new products, and services and/or processes—is not significantly related to international performance within either industry. This suggests that the importance of innovativeness as a factor in the internationalization of SMEs has greater explanatory power between industries than within industries, arguably because the degree of innovativeness among firms is strongly influenced by institutional norms.

The results for H6 are supportive in the software industry but are somewhat puzzling for the food and beverage industry. Although product-specific competence is not significantly related to international performance for the software product firms, it is significantly and *negatively* related for the food and beverage firms. Since the food and beverage firms have a broader product offering, this finding suggests that firms may substitute product-specific competence for international business competence in LDMs and, by extension, that product diversification can be a viable substitute growth strategy for firms in LDMs, as suggested by Bonaccorsi (1992).

Finally, it is worth noting that less of the variance in FSTS is explained by the three independent variables for the software product firms than for the food and beverage firms (15 versus 29%, respectively). This difference could be a result of the fact that the overall level of international business competency is lower in the food and beverage firms than in the software product firms, and so an increase in competency makes a bigger competitive difference to a firm in the former industry.

V. DISCUSSION AND CONCLUSIONS

This chapter has examined the consequences of domestic market size for the internationalization of small- and medium-sized enterprises (SMEs). The findings are similar to those of Arora and Gambardella (1997), who found that domestic market size made a difference to the competences developed, in their study of a single industry that developed nearly a century ago in each of three national economies. Because emerging firms in the twenty-first century are going to be founded under conditions of increasing globalization, many will start out as niche players in small domestic markets. Thus, in examining the impact of industry characteristics, we compared an industry with a small domestic market (software product firms) and an industry with a large domestic market (food and beverage firms), in the same national economy, and showed that SMEs in the small domestic market demonstrate greater international business competency, greater innovative competence, and less product-specific competence. Only one of these factors—international business competency—is positively related to SMEs' international performance in a within-industry analysis. Thus, firms that need to survive in a small domestic market are more likely to develop the international business competences that are related to international performance.

Before discussing the implications of these findings for practice or for future research, it is necessary to acknowledge the limitations associated with both the sample and the methodology employed. The sample was limited in that only two industries were compared, and in that these two industries may have differed not only in terms of market size, but also in terms of other characteristics (such as the technology employed). While we have attempted to anticipate and mitigate the possibility that factors other than market size account for some of the between-industry variance, it is possible that industry variables which co-vary with market size did play a contributing role in the pattern of findings observed. This limitation of the study can best be addressed by future research that examines other industries, and other industry characteristics, in order to determine the links between industry-level variables and entrepreneurial firm behavior and performance variables, including internationalization.

With regard to the methodology employed, the measures used, while all consistent with those developed elsewhere, are doubtless subject to some measurement error. The measures, which are all simple in nature, have obvious face validity. The relative simplicity and objectivity of the measures also suggests that their reliability should be high. The measures may, however, underrepresent the domains of the constructs in question, in that they do not capture all possible variance in the constructs, in particular the competence constructs. To the extent that the measures underrepresent variance in the constructs, they yield a conservative test of the hypotheses. Nevertheless, given the limitations of both the measures and the sample used, the results of this study should be regarded as preliminary and caution should be exercised in generalizing from them.

Turning to the implications of this paper with these limitations in view, an initial reply to the question posed at the beginning of the paper can be offered. It appears that industry *does* matter to the internationalization of SMEs. This study adds to a growing body of research cautioning against the over-generalization of understandings that have been gleaned from particular industries or from particular national patterns of internationalization. Industry characteristics in place when the firm is founded and as it grows will impact the competences that firms develop, and will therefore influence the nature of SME internationalization.

Future research should examine in more detail the influence of industry characteristics on the internationalization of SMEs. Software product firms and food and beverage firms are admittedly very different, and there is heterogeneity within each industry. One next step is to examine the relationship between domestic market size and internationalization patterns in a more detailed fashion, by considering more similar and more narrowly defined industries. Another useful extension of the current work would be to examine a wider range of domestic market sizes in order to examine "how large is large," or in other words, what size of domestic market is sufficiently large that firms founded in it are less likely to have the impetus to develop international business competences. A further step is to examine other industry characteristics which might constitute founding conditions, influencing the nature of competences developed in new firms, such as industry dynamics and the extent or severity of legal and regulatory barriers. Another logical extension of the current work would be to examine the emergent firms in the same industry from different nations with differing domestic market sizes. For instance, while the software industry is a globalized one, with *relatively* small domestic markets in every national economy, the *absolute* size of the domestic market in two countries such as Canada versus the United States is quite different. Would this mean that we should expect different levels of international business competence in firms from one nation compared with those from the other? This is a question only future research can answer.

The strong between-industry differences highlight the importance of institutional norms in SME behavior. Along these lines, the study indicates that SME owners and managers may not have broad discretion over certain decision areas. For example, owners of Canadian software products firms are likely to experience less discretion than food and beverage firm owners over a commitment to innovativeness. This is likely to have implications for the type and level of planning done in the firm. Because of their relatively narrow, specialized niches, software products firms may be better able to respond quickly to unanticipated international opportunities, such as an unsolicited order from a customer in a new foreign market. Food and beverage firms, on the other hand, appear to need to become product specialists in order to survive in their more intensively competitive industry. Since the development of this competence is likely to be time-consuming and costly, SMEs in this industry will have fewer resources left to internationalize effectively. They will need to plan foreign market entries more carefully, and be more cautious of responding to unanticipated opportunities. Managers in such industries might even consider that, despite the encouragement of government or industry groups, internationalization might *not* be a rational route to growth and profitability.

The study also supports the path dependency arguments of resource theory. Consistent with the findings of McDougall, Shane, and Oviatt (1994), software products SMEs enter foreign markets earlier, and therefore can develop a culture and organizational processes that are able to support internationalization. On the other hand, food and beverage SMEs enter foreign markets later, after having tailored their products and services to the domestic market. In this industry the product-specific competencies are high, which appears to be an impediment to foreign market entry. From the perspective of resource providers to emerging firms, such as governments, lenders, or investors, these results indicate that customization is required. Different industry conditions lead to different service and program requirements. In particular, the findings here are somewhat paradoxical for those public policy programs, investors and lenders who prefer to see a domestic track record before providing support to the internationalization of an SME. In the case of technology-based firms in small domestic markets, a domestic track record may not be possible because of there being so few potential customers. In the case of firms in large domestic markets, a domestic track record may even be dysfunctional if it increases the product diversification that must be managed while the firm is attempting foreign market entries. It is important to be aware of industry differences and their implications for the internationalization of SMEs, because "one size fits all" policies are unlikely to be effective. One interesting possibility this study raises is that internationalization may not be something that should be equally encouraged or comparably supported in all industries.

ACKNOWLEDGMENTS

The authors gratefully acknowledge the comments and suggestions of seminar participants at the International Conference on Globalization and Emerging Businesses, held at McGill University in September 1998, the research assistance of Hayley Osher, Rob Gosse, and Paul Smith, and the financial support of the Rotman School of Management's Centre for International Business and the Social Science and Humanities Research Council of Canada.

NOTES

1. Industry data are reported on Internet (e.g., Web) sites managed by Industry Canada and by Agriculture and Agri-Food Canada.

2. It might be argued that the software industry differs from the food and beverage industry not only in terms of domestic market size, but also in terms of the relative ease of exporting in one versus the other. This argument is supported by the view that product standardization (in the global software industry) might facilitate exporting while differentiation (in market preferences for food and beverage products) and government barriers (to the export of food and beverage products) might inhibit exporting. The counterargument can be made, however, that the perceived ease or difficulty of exporting is not as salient as the size of the domestic market in determining which types of competencies are likely to develop at an industry level. Without a sufficiently large domestic markets, firms in industries that pose greater challenges to exporting would have no choice but to develop the competence to do business in international markets. Further, if doing business in foreign markets were truly much less feasible for food and beverage than for software firms, we would not expect to see that Canadian firms in both industries have roughly the same (3%) share of global markets.

REFERENCES

Abrahamson, E., and C. Fombrun. 1994. "Macrocultures: Determinants and Consequences." *Academy of Management Review* 19(4):728-755.

Arora, A., and A.Gambardella. 1997. "Domestic Markets and International Competitiveness: Generic and Product-Specific Competencies in the Engineering Sector." *Strategic Management Journal* 18 (Summer Special Issue):53-74.

Baldwin, J. 1994. *Strategies for Success: A Profile of Growing Small and Medium-Sized Enterprises (GSMEs) in Canada.* Ottawa, Canada: Statistics Canada.

Barney, J. 1991. "Firm Resources and Sustained Competitive Advantage." *Journal of Management* 17 (1):99-120.

Beamish, P. W., R. Craig, and K. McLellan. 1993. "The Performance Characteristics of Canadian versus U.K. Exporters in Small and Medium Sized Firms." *Management International Review* 33 (2): 121-137.

Bloodgood, J. M., H. J. Sapienza, and J. G. Almeida. 1996. The Internationalization of New High-Potential U.S. Ventures: Antecedents and Outcomes. *Entrepreneurship Theory and Practice* 2 (4): 61-76.

Bonaccorsi, A. 1992. On the Relationship Between Firm Size and Export Intensity. *Journal of International Business Studies* 23 (4): 605-635.

Boter, H., and C. Holmquist. 1996. "Industry Characteristics and Internationalization Processes in Small Firms." *Journal of Business Venturing* 11: 471-487.

Calof, J. L., and P. W. Beamish. 1994. "The Right Attitude for International Success." *Business Quarterly* (Autumn): 105-110.

Carter, N. M, T. M. Stearns, P. D. Reynolds, and B. A. Miller. 1994. "New Venture Strategies: Theory Development with an Empirical Base." *Strategic Management Journal* 15 (1): 21-41.

Cavusgil, S. T., and S. Zou. 1994. "Marketing Strategy-Performance Relationship: An Investigation of the Empirical Link in Export Market Ventures. *Journal of Marketing* 58 (1): 1-21.

Cavusgil, S. T., S. Zou, and G. M. Naidu. 1993. "Product and Promotion Adaptation in Export Ventures: An Empirical Investigation." *Journal of International Business Studies* 24 (3): 479-506.

Covin, J. G., D. P. Slevin, and T. J. Covin. 1990. "Content and Performance of Growth-Seeking Strategies: A Comparison of Small Firms in High- and Low-Technology Industries." *Journal of Business Venturing* 5: 391-412.

Dierickx, I., and K. Cool. 1989. "Asset Stock Accumulation and Sustainability of Competitive Advantage." *Management Science* 35 (12): 1504-1511.

Erramilli, M. K. 1991. "The Experience Factor in Foreign Markets Entry Behaviour of Service Firms." *Journal of International Business Studies* 22 (3): 479-501.

Erramilli, M. K. and D. E. D'Souza. 1993. "Venturing Into Foreign Markets: The Case of the Small Service Firm." *Entrepreneurship Theory and Practice* 17 (4): 29-41.

Keeley, R. H., and J. B. Roure. 1990. "Management, Strategy and Industry Structure as Influences on the Success of New Firms: A Structural Model." *Management Science* 36 (10): 1256-1267.

Leonidou, L. C., and C. S. Katsikeas. 1996. "The Export Development Process: An Integrative Review of Empirical Models." *Journal of International Business Studies* 27 (3): 517-551.

McDougall, P. P., J. G. Covin, R. B. Robinson, and L. Herron. 1994. "The Effects of Industry Growth and Strategic Breadth on New Venture Performance and Strategy Content." *Strategic Management Journal* 15: 537-554.

McDougall, P. P., and B. M. Oviatt. 1996. "New Venture Internationalization, Strategic Change, and Performance: A Follow-Up Study." *Journal of Business Venturing* 11 (1): 23-40.

McDougall, P. P., R. B. Robinson, and A. S. DeNisi. 1992. "Modeling New Venture Performance: An Analysis of New Venture Strategy, Industry Structure, and Venture Origin." *Journal of Business Venturing* 7 (4): 267-289.

McDougall, P. P., S. Shane, and B. M. Oviatt. 1994. "Explaining the Formation of International New Ventures: The Limits of Theories from International Business Research." *Journal of Business Venturing* 9: 469-487.

McGahan, A. M., and M. E. Porter. 1997. "How Much Does Industry Matter, Really?" *Strategic Management Journal* 18 (Summer Special Issue): 15-30.

OECD. 1992. *Oslo Manual: OECD Proposed Guidelines for Collecting and Interpreting Technological Innovation Data*. Paris: Organisation for Economic Co-operation and Development.

Oliver, C. 1996. "The Institutional Embeddedness of Economic Activity." Pp. 163-186 in *Advances in Strategic Management* 13, edited by J. A. C. Baum and J. E. Dutton. Greenwich, CT: JAI Press.

Oviatt, B. M., and P. P. McDougall. 1994. "Toward a Theory of International New Ventures." *Journal of International Business Studies* 25 (1): 45-64.

Penrose, E. 1971. *The Growth of Firms: Middle East Oil, and Other Essays*. London: Frank Cass and Co. Ltd.

Peteraf, M. 1993. "The Cornerstones of Competitive Advantage: A Resource-Based View." *Strategic Management Journal* 14: 179-191.

Picot, G., J. Baldwin, and R. Dupuy. 1995. "Small Firms And Job Creation—A Reassessment." *Canadian Economic Observer* (January): 3.1-3.18.

Preece, S. B., G. Miles, and M. C. Baetz. 1998. "Explaining the International Intensity and Global Diversity of Early-Stage Technology-Based Firms." *Journal of Business Venturing* 14 (3): 259-281.

Ramaswamy, K. K., G. Kroeck, and W. Renforth. 1996. "Measuring the Degree of Internationalization of a Firm: A Comment." *Journal of International Business Studies* 26 (1): 167-177.

Reuber, A. R., and E. Fischer. 1997. "The Influence of the Management Team's International Experience on the Internationalization Behavior Of SMEs." *Journal of International Business Studies* 28 (4): 807-825.

_____. 1998. "The Impact of Social Capital on Employment Patterns in Higher and Lower Growth Industries." *Frontiers of Entrepreneurship Research:* 414-425.

Roure, J. B., and R. H. Keeley. 1990. "Predictors of Success in New Technology Based Ventures." *Journal of Business Venturing* 5 (4): 201-220.

Sandberg, W. R., and C. W. Hofer. 1987. "Improving New Venture Performance: The Role of Strategy, Industry Structure, and the Entrepreneur." *Journal of Business Venturing* 2: 5-28.

Sullivan, D. 1994. "Measuring the Degree of Internationalization of a Firm." *Journal of International Business Studies* 25 (2): 325-342.

Teece, D. J., G. Pisano, and A. Shuen. 1997. "Dynamic Capabilities and Strategic Management." *Strategic Management Journal* 18 (7):509-533.

Wernerfelt, B. 1984. "A Resource-Based View of the Firm." Strategic Management Journal, 5: 171-180.

Westhead, P., and S. Birley. 1995. "Employment Growth in New Independent Owner-Managed Firms in Great Britain." *International Small Business Journal* 51 (April-June): 10-33.

Zahra, S. A., D. O. Neubeum, and M. Huse. 1997. "The Effect of the Environment on Export Performance among Telecommunications New Ventures." *Entrepreneurship Theory and Practice* 22 (1): 25-46.

BUSINESS STRATEGY IN TRANSITIONAL INDUSTRIES

ENTREPRENEURIAL RESPONSE TO THE GLOBALIZATION OF A FRAGMENTED INDUSTRY

Odd-Jarl Borch

I. INTRODUCTION

Global competition is becoming the characteristic feature of today's business environment. Increased globalization has appeared because of the removal of trade barriers between countries, technological gains, and revolutionary changes in cross-regional communication and transportation infrastructure. Globalization is defined as a process whereby the competitive position of a firm in one country is affected by actions of competitors in another country (Porter 1986).

In spite of these global integration trends, some industries are still characterized by regional dispersion and limited cross-national activity. These sectors often have a large number of small- and medium-sized enterprises (SMEs), each having a small share of the regional market. Government subsidies and import barriers,

Research in Global Strategic Management, Volume 7, pages 101-129.
Copyright © 1999 by JAI Press Inc.
All rights of reproduction in any form reserved.
ISBN: 0-7623-0458-8

for example, protect the food industry in several countries from the distorting competition of global markets. There are also geographical and cultural barriers that cause imperfect competition.

A fragmented environment creates a specific competitive setting because of the absence of market leaders to shape the working conditions within an industry (Porter 1980). While trade barriers continue to be reduced, successful firms in this environment must be prepared to manage the challenges of the removal of the barriers, as well as the increase in cross-border competition. They also have to be ready to reap the benefits of the emerging international markets. Firms in a regional, fragmented industry risk being "stuck in the middle" in the transition process and losing ground to large international enterprises (Harrison 1997; Porter 1980).

This chapter focuses on the ability of corporate entrepreneurs to develop new strategies to meet globalization. Entrepreneurship is defined as the degree of a firm's risk-taking propensity, its tendency to act in a competitively aggressive, proactive manner, and its reliance on "frequent and extensive strategic innovation" (Covin and Slevin 1991, p. 7).

Only a few studies have so far centered on the business-strategy patterns of fragmented and regionally dispersed industries. The main focus of strategy research during the 1980s and 1990s has been the strategic action of firms that have expanded into international markets (McDougall et al. 1994) or firms that have been "global born" (Knight and Cavusgil 1996). In particular, the global strategies of multinational corporations (MNCs) have been reviewed in detail (Dess and Davis 1984; Hambrick 1983a; Kim and Lim 1988; Morrison and Roth 1992).

This study advances the knowledge of business strategies in a fragmented regional-based industry on the threshold of internationalization. Efforts are made, on empirical grounds, to broaden the concept of business strategy to fit into this setting. First, a business strategy taxonomy is developed that provides stringent guidelines for studying a fragmented environment containing mostly small- and medium-sized enterprises. Second, outcomes associated with the specific business strategies of firms facing increased international competition are discussed. Finally, future implications of trade-integration efforts for SMEs and for government policy are presented.

II. THEORETICAL BACKGROUND

A. The Fragmented Industry

A fragmented industry is defined as a business environment with a majority of small, geographically dispersed firms. There are no market leaders, nor is there a firm that has the power to shape industry events (Porter 1980, p. 191). Government regulations are among the most important barriers to today's markets. These regulations, such as industry subsidies, import quotas, and market monopolies, limit the flow of goods across borders, as well as the exploitation of scale and scope advantages. In a fragmented industry imperfect competition is a result of such barriers. Other factors causing fragmentation are: low overall entry barriers; a lack of economies of scale or scope within logistics, production or distribution; diverse market needs; and high exit barriers.

Several countries, however, are striving to reduce trade barriers and to increase market competition. They are also entering or applying for membership in trade blocs, such as the European Union and NAFTA, which share the objectives of removing all trade barriers. The World Trade Organization (WTO) as well has increased power to improve cross-border trade in industries earlier protected by parochial regulations. Thus, the competitive forces of the global markets are now so strong that, unless strategic adjustments are made, firms in a traditionally fragmented setting may be devastated (Dunning 1992).

B. Business Strategy Approaches

Strategy researchers have made significant efforts in categorizing strategic adaptation in different industrial settings. In particular, the development of the strategy-structure-performance perspective has provided an understanding of how firms adjust to environmental challenges (Ansoff 1971; Hofer 1975; Hofer and Schendel 1978; Porter 1980; Ginsberg and Venkatraman 1985). This study adds to this tradition by analyzing the strategic features of firms competing within a fragmented industry. It presents industry-specific strategic instruments. The general complexity and turbulence of the market stated within economics and strategy research adds to the importance of building more adequate models of market behavior. It is also necessary to connect the context of the market to the choice of strategy at the company level (Rumelt et al. 1991; Porter 1991). The strategic adaptability of small firms in particular will depend on the resources developed in their present industrial setting.

In spite of significant contributions, generic strategy research is still criticized for presenting typologies which are too broad (Hill 1988; Miller 1992); which lack contingency emphasis on different market environments (Dess et al. 1990; Hambrick and Lei 1985; Murray 1988); and which are too simply constructed or one-dimensional (Day and Wensley 1988; Morrison and Roth 1992; Spender 1993). Another criticism has been its bias toward the life-cycle phases of industries with large-scale characteristics, such as emerging industries (Aaker and Day 1986; Kim and Lim 1988; Yip 1982), mature industries (Hambrick 1983b; Harrigan 1982), and declining industries (Harrigan 1980). In particular, there are an increasing number of studies oriented toward multinationals (Ghosal 1987; Kogut 1989; Mitchell 1992; Morrison 1990; Roth 1992).

However, research on the strategic behavior of companies in fragmented environments has been largely ignored. According to the contingency theory, these markets make unique demands on how a firm adapts its business strategy to changing conditions (Carpano et al. 1994). Also, as market integration continues with the removal of trade barriers, further information is needed about the strategic capability of these firms to predict the consequences of increased cross-border competition. Knowledge of their strategy response to new market conditions is particularly important when analyzing their capability to meet international competition and to enter international markets (Bijmolt et al. 1994). With less access to risk capital than their larger counterparts, smaller firms may get stuck more easily in a static or given strategic pattern (Harrison 1997; OECD 1997).

To improve both the rigor and relevance of the strategy construct, several authors contend that business strategy should be conceptualized according to substrategies at the level of the business unit. This approach would facilitate the study of strategy from a managerial perspective, and would reduce the risk of creating models which are too simplistic (Chrisman et al. 1988; Hofer and Schendel 1978; Morrison 1990). The substrategy approach may also provide a general manager with a more useful set of tools with which to make the strategic decisions.

A broad business-strategy model was implemented in this study to include the many expected strategic approaches within SMEs. Earlier studies of integrated and global industries have been limited to competitive positioning. But limiting the study to positioning could prove insufficient in fragmented markets. Smaller firms may have less freedom to develop substrategies that match their ideal competitive position. Consequently, SMEs will need a greater diversity of strategic tools, or different managerial combinations, to survive. Also, as opportunities in the global market open, new modes of adaptation may develop that are beneficial for small business firms.

Hofer and Schendel (1978) stated that a business strategy should include at least three interrelated substrategies; competitive positioning, organizational, and political. Reve (1990) emphasized the need for an integrated model, which included both competitive positioning and strategies for the organization of the unique resources within a firm. Day and Wensley (1988) and Spender (1993) criticized strategy research for not sufficiently addressing the conversion of organizational skills and resources into positional advantages in the market. Including the resource-based dimensions of competence, routines, and working culture may accentuate the intra-organizational premises for achievement and maintenance of competitive advantage (Barney 1991; Black and Boal 1994; Leonard-Barton 1992).

A further complicating factor of fragmented industries is that they often owe their unique characteristics to government regulations, such as taxes and import and trade barriers. Even though the political economy may play a less influential role in more integrated markets (Oviatt and McDougall 1998), we still find that governments will actively interact with firms to improve their capabilities and global competitiveness (Porter 1990). We should, therefore, include political substrategy dimensions in the range of possible strategic instruments (Dunning 1992; Mintzberg 1988). The empirical challenge is then manifest when trying to build classifications based on multiple substrategies. Unfortunately there are few empirical studies available to suggest the position of each substrategy (Chrisman et al. 1988) or to define their various components. This study used the following defined substrategies.

1. *The competitive positioning substrategy.* A competitive positioning substrategy is the implementation of tools that relate the firm to customers in the market and restrict competition through the creation of entry barriers (Porter 1980; 1985). It includes finding the geographic setting of the firm's products, deciding whether to compete on price or customer differentiation, and the degree of product innovation.

2. *Organizational substrategy.* Building on Reve (1990), organizational substrategy is the structural configuration of the value-chain owned or influenced by the firm. The organizational substrategy may include both functional parts within the firm, as well as parts of the value chain controlled through cooperative relations with other organizations, that facilitate the development of mutual resources across organizational borders to create scale and scope advantages. The organizational substrategy determines the size and the functions of the value chain and the couplings and directions of the cooperative efforts.

3. *The resource base substrategy.* According to Bartlett and Ghosal (1991), resource base substrategy is defined as the immaterial quality of an organization in terms of competence, routines, personal commitments and working culture. The resource base is the core of the organizational structure.

4. *Investment substrategy.* Investment substrategy is the amount of new capital directed toward a firm's activity and the specific location of these investments. The investment substrategy also determines the age of the technology and other physical resources found within the firm.

5. *Political substrategy.* Political substrategy concerns the efforts of shaping the working environment of a firm through the active influence of political decisions and policy. It also includes public policies (Mintzberg 1988). A firm may direct its efforts toward improved working conditions through legislation, subsidies, and other intervention schemes. In some economies, a firm may have a delegated government authority to ensure their implementation.

III. METHODOLOGY

A. Research Design

This study focused on the strategic business unit (SBU), or a firm's activities within a single, industrial environment (Morrison 1990). This focus is appropriate when studying a fragmented environment with several small- and medium-sized firms. In such environments diagonal integration is rare and the lack of strategic diversification reduces the need for studies at the corporate level. It is also important to understand strategic behavior at the business level when studying corporate strategies (Porter 1991).

An exploratory approach was implemented to identify strategic factors appearing within an agro-food industry with fragmented characteristics. Firm-level case studies were conducted over six years to examine changes in strategic posture. In addition, a survey was organized in the middle of this period to determine the strategic patterns of the whole industry. The results of the survey are presented with supplementary information from the case studies.

B. Research Setting

The investigation of business strategy was based on a sample of independent businesses in the meat-processing industry in Norway. This industry was selected because of its fragmented and geographically dispersed characteristics. It was also on the threshold of global competition. The food industry has a legislated protected status in several countries, as well as enjoying the protection of distance and local taste and consumption patterns. For these reasons, this heretofore isolated industry is well suited for a study of emerging global entrepreneurship.

The competitive forces of this specific setting were weakened through (1) farmers' subsidies which reduced the suppliers' use of negotiation power, (2) import barriers and geographical distances which minimized the threat of new entrants, and (3) subsidies on agricultural products which limited the competition from substitutes.

In 1993 the market share of the four largest processors in this study was 25 percent, significantly below the level of 40 percent mentioned by Porter (1980) as typical of a fragmented industry. Therefore the concentration rate for this industry was at the level of the U.S. meat-packing industry 20 years ago (Porter 1980). The ratio between the national price level and world market prices was 3:1. Norway was rated among the top nations in the world when it came to agricultural protectionism and subsidies (Koester 1991).

The protected status of the agriculture sector was at the time of this study in the process of being dramatically changed. Even larger changes were expected at the millennium as the European Economic Agreement (EEA) gradually integrates most European economies into the market system of the European Union, thus exposing the markets and industries of both Western and Eastern Europe to severe competition. (A similar development can be found within NAFTA and its expansion towards South America.) The new round of WTO negotiations will probably result also in a removal on a global scale of trade barriers for agricultural products. Coupled with these developments is increased consumer awareness. Consumers, discontented with the price differences of goods among countries, encouraged an increased, partly illegal, trade of food products with the neighboring nations. Finally, wholesaler chains systematically started to integrate and to build alliances towards European and globally integrated wholesaler associations to increase their negotiation power.

C. Sample and Data Collection

To ensure focus on the market level most likely to influence the firms' business-level strategy, we identified companies at the four-digit, industry code level (Carpano et al. 1994; Dess 1987; Porter 1980). The industries were similar to the U.S. SIC codes: 2011, meat-packaging plants; 2013, companies manufacturing sausages and other prepared meat; and 2015, poultry processing. The collection of data started with in-depth pilot studies of (a) the biggest wholesaler/retailer group which served as customers for the meat industry, (b) a private manufacturing enterprise and (c) a large farmers' cooperative. The main goal of this phase was to develop instruments for the study of a broad range of substrategies. Macro-environment data was collected using governmental statistics (SSB), OECD statistics, reports on agricultural outlooks and national policy white papers.

In the second phase, a survey was conducted among all firms within the industry with more than five employees. Because of the expected high variance in strategic behavior, data collection instruments were selected that gave as large a sample as possible within the financial limitations of the study. The structured questionnaire was aimed at the managing director (CEO), and distributed by post to all firms within the study area. Two separate mailings resulted in 46 useful cases, a 55 percent response rate.

The sample represented not only 55 percent of the total number of companies, but also 62 percent of the sales within the meat industry and 74 percent of the workforce. All the SIC codes presented above were included. These replies are significantly above the median of a 33 percent response rate for samples of smaller firms (Alpar and Spitzer 1989). Eight out of nine farmers' cooperatives were included. There was also an over-representation of medium-sized and larger firms, and an under-representation of the largest group in the population, those companies with less than 10 employees.

For the qualitative analysis, additional data were collected from the firms through documentary studies, such as newspaper and magazine articles and annual reports, over a period of six years. Eventually, this qualitative, research phase provided a data base with archival information from 80 percent of the firms in the survey.

D. Measures

The questionnaire was developed through the selection of items and factors used in earlier strategy studies, if they matched the theoretical definition of each substrategy. The factors used in earlier studies are reviewed above. New items were added as a result of the case studies. Finally, we tested the measures chosen through discussions with some of the managing directors.

Seeking an exhaustive list of attributes for the foundation of business typologies (Rich 1992), a total of 70 items were finally included in the questionnaire. We asked the respondents to indicate whether they agreed with the statements in the questionnaire using a 5-point Likert-type, response scale ranging from Totally Disagree to Totally Agree.

E. Analysis

The analysis of data was conducted in several steps using the SPSS PC+ version 4.0. First, descriptive analysis mapped the overall features of the firms' adaptation. In this process, we chose to eliminate two *outlier* cases. To achieve a more aggregated and theory-related set of substrategy factors, we refined the constructs through principal component analysis (PCA). The factors were independently derived from the items chosen for each of the five substrategy dimensions (Kim and Muller 1978) through PCA with VARIMAX rotation. In accordance with Kim and Muller, factor loadings higher than .50 were accepted. From the initial 70 items included in the questionnaire, 17 strategy factors, building on 48 items, were developed. The eigenvalues for all the factors were well above one. Within each substrategy, the factors' accumulated explained variance beyond 60 percent. The following are the items included and the factors developed through the principal component analysis.

1. *Competitive positioning substrategy.* Several empirical studies have developed tools for the study of business substrategies. In particular there is a broad selection of competitive positioning scales. Dess and Davis (1984) used 16 variables in identifying four distinct strategic factors: efficiency, service, product innovation, and brand/channel influence. On the basis of 27 variables, Davis (1986) revealed six strategic factors: production efficiency, differentiation, degree of specialty production, research intensity, geographic concentration, and cost consciousness. In one of the few studies of a fragmented industry, Johnson and Thomas (1987) gathered data from the UK brewing industry. They emphasized geographical scope among the

Table 1.　Principal Component Analysis of
Competitive Positioning Substrategy Items

Competitive positioning substrategy items:	Factor 1: Marketing Leadership (Alpha= .76)	Factor 2: Innovation leadership (Alpha= .74)	Factor 3: Cost leadership (Alpha= .73)	Factor 4: Geographic scope Alpha= .52)	Factor 5: Product quality (Alpha= .58)
Brand names adapted to different customer groups	**.656**	.335	.196	−.280	−.165
Aggresive new marketing efforts	**.791**	−.035	.011	.315	.187
Money on advertising	**.828**	.020	−.038	−.021	.187
Knowledge about customer needs	**.739**	.099	−.172	.286	.140
New products or product improvement	.049	**.672**	−.158	.111	.349
Research on new trends	.096	**.501**	−.131	.512	.032
Products developed toward specific customer groups	.053	**.785**	−.216	−.088	.025
Marketing developed toward specific customer groups	.085	**.883**	.134	−.062	.084
Not high priced products	−.169	−.086	**.789**	−.017	−.208
As low prices as possible to be competitive	.107	−.108	**.895**	.128	−.011
Expanding geographical market	.033	−.148	.006	**.802**	−.150
Geographical range	.242	.079	.293	**.681**	.241
Emphasize on product quality	.109	.103	−.015	−.065	**.882**
Resources on developing high reputation	.251	.203	−.265	.094	**.649**
Eigenvalue	3.631	2.213	1.575	1.371	1.035
Cumulative percentage of explained variance	25.9	41.8	53	62.8	70.2

Table 2. Principal Component Analysis of Resource-Base Substrategy Items

	Factor 1: Organizational efficiency (Alpha=.75)	Factor 2: Organizational competence (Alpha=.68)	Factor 3: Organizational flexibility (Alpha=.68)	Factor 4: Organization improvement routines (Alpha=.57)
Resource-base substrategy items:				
Emphasizes winning culture	.201	.172	.170	**.655**
Resources used in increasing productivity	.244	163	.073	**.690**
Routines for management control	.200	.154	−.109	**.795**
Emphasizes flexibility in manufacturing	.099	.047	**.797**	.286
Emphasizes employees' flexibility	.103	−.058	**.843**	−.094
Routines for improved customer adaptation	.119	.447	**.598**	−.278
Competence development	.411	**.560**	.263	.150
High formal education	−.190	**.7729**	−.029	.351
Routines for long-range planning	.241	**.623**	.017	.351
Just-in-time principles in the value chain	**.578**	.234	.101	.200
Several shifts in production	**.685**	.082	−.456	.145
High productivity goals	**.773**	−.174	.272	.261
Emphasizes high capacity utilization	**.767**	.196	.093	.364
Employees loyal to rationalization to improve competitive ability	**.701**	.208	.136	−.007
Eigenvalues	4.806	2.037	1.525	1.231
Cumulative percentage of explained variance	32	45.6	55.8	64

Table 3.   Principal Component Analysis of Organizational Substrategy Items.

Organizational substrategy items:	Factor 1: Horizontal cooperation (Alpha=.84)	Factor 2: Upstream cooperation/ integration (Alpha=.52)	Factor 3: Downstream integration (Alpha=.82)	Factor 4: Downstream cooperation
Cooperation with distributors	−.007	−.134	−.119	**.949**
Dependency on distributors	−.001	−.032	**.928**	.018
Ruled by the distributors as to transport	−.052	−.085	**.913**	.108
Cooperation with other processors on distribution	.735	.406	−.115	.253
Cooperation with other processors to increase negotiation power towards customers	**.916**	.097	.0123	.010
Cooperation with other processors on marketing	**.882**	.028	−.008	−.279
Cooperation with other processors on value-added production	**.599**	.487	−.032	.261
Cooperation with suppliers	.107	**.849**	−.240	−.148
Including upstream functions	.180	**.812**	.081	−.064
Eigenvalue	3.282	1.855	1.146	1.041
Cumulative percentage of explained variance	36.5	57.1	69.8	81.4

competitive positioning factors. Table 1 shows the principal component analysis for the competitive positioning items.

The PCA showed that the competitive positioning factors accounted for 70.2 percent of the variance within this group. The analysis expanded the previous set of factors within this field. Porter's differentiation strategy split into three factors: product quality (alpha=.58); marketing leadership (alpha=.76); and, innovation differentiation (alpha=.74). These findings confirmed the earlier criticism of the Porter dimensions because they

Table 4.   Principal Component Analysis of Investment Substrategy Items

Investment substrategy items:	Factor 1: Investment localization (Alpha=.50)	Factor 2: Investment level (Alpha=.50)
Relations with investors to secure investment capital	.513	.273
Invests in regions with low manufacturing costs	.865	−.273
Locates plants in areas with high-competence levels	.739	.198
High investment level to improve competitiveness	.114	**.831**
High-equity capital financing	.038	**.739**
Eigenvalue	1.689	1.312
Cumulative percentage of explained variance	33.8	60

lacked empirical accuracy (Kim and Lim 1988; Miller and Dess 1993). Only one factor reflected Porter's (1980) overall cost leadership (alpha=.73). We also used one factor for the focus dimension (geographical scope) (alpha=.52).

2. *Organization substrategy.* Table 2 shows the principal component analysis for the organizational items. The PCA gave a fine-grained set of factors adding to the instruments of, among others, Morrison and Roth (1992). We developed the factors of downstream integration (alpha=.82), upstream integration/cooperation (alpha=.52), and horizontal cooperation (alpha=.84). The four organizational substrategy factors accounted for 81.3 percent of the total variance among the organization-related items included in the questionnaire.

3. *Resource-base substrategy.* Because of the lack of previous empirical research focusing on immaterial, internal resources, the resource-base scales were developed mainly from the in-depth case studies and the documentary studies. Table 3 shows the principal component analysis for the resource base items. This analysis yielded a set of four resource-base substrategy factors: organizational efficiency routines (alpha=.75), flexibility routines (alpha=.68), competence (alpha=.68), and organizational improvement routines (alpha=.57). It was one of the first efforts to include

Table 5.   Principal Component Analysis of Political Substrategy Items

Political substrategy items:	Factor 1: Political influence (Alpha=.81)	Factor 2 Political cooperation Alpha=.84)
Frequent contact with public authorities	**.810**	.211
Involvement in policy activities to mprove working conditions	**.929**	.0497
Gives advice to authorities as to government regulations	**.797**	.227
Responsible for market regulations	.205	**.905**
Responsible for public R&D	.133	**.931**
Eigenvalue	2.738	1.265
Cumulative percentage of explained variance	54.8	80.1

a separate set of the resource-base dimensions in an empirical, business strategy study. The factors accounted for 64 percent of the variance among the resource items.

4. *Investment substrategy.* Table 4 illustrates the principal component analysis for the investment items. The investment substrategy scales of Morrison (1990) were complemented with two factors: investment level (alpha=.50), and investment localization (alpha=.50). These two factors accounted for 60 percent of the variance among the items included.

5. *Political substrategy.* The political substrategy concentrated on items that covered the frequency of contact with public authorities; involvement in policy activities to improve working conditions; advice to authorities regarding government regulations; responsibility for market regulations; and government-funded research and development (R&D). Table 5 depicts the results of the principal component analysis for the items related to polit-ical substrategy. The two emerging factors, political influence (alpha=.81) and political cooperation (alpha=.84), accounted for 80.1 percent of the variance in this group of items.

6. *Performance.* The measurement of performance of SMEs is a challenging task in strategy studies. First, there is less public access to financial data. Second, small business managers are often either not capable or are reluc-tant to provide objective, interpretable, or comparable data for research purposes (Miller and Toulouse 1986; Olsen and Kolvereid 1994; Sapienza et al. 1988). For strategy purposes, accounting measures may also reflect

only the short-term economic performance of the firm. They do not include the broad range of goals and strategies found within SMEs.

Because of the low availability of accurate, financial-performance data, subjective performance measures were used in this study (Sapienza et al. 1988). Performance was measured through the following four indices: the three-year average of (1) after-tax return on investment, (2) change in market share, (3) change in sales volume, and (4) a self-report of the manager's ranking of the company's profitability compared with the rest of the industry. As the foreign activity was indirect and focused on input factors, international-performance measures were not included.

Building on the 17 strategy factors developed above, the firms were classified according to similarity along strategic dimensions by hierarchical cluster analysis. To determine the final cluster solution, experiments with two-, three-, four- and five-cluster solutions were conducted. A five-cluster solution gave a classification showing differences in implemented strategy of interest from both a theoretical and practical standpoint (Hambrick 1984). The results differed along the main constructs presented in the theory section on size, geographical range and different combinations of substrategies. The five clusters were ultimately selected instead of four, because of the smallest firms in the sample, "The Local Niche Servants." This group represented a large number of underrepresented firms in the sample. Multivariate analysis (MANOVA) showed that the five clusters were significantly different from each other ($F=165.73, p < 0.001$). Thus, the cluster analysis managed to develop a meaningful classification of the strategic groups in this sample.

Analysis of variance (ANOVA) was conducted showing high variance in the factor dimensions among the five clusters. This variance implied that the factors presented in the cluster analysis were important in revealing differences in strategic approach among the firms.

Finally, discriminant analysis assessed the stability of the strategy clusters through a pooled-within-group correlation of factors. A weakness of the discriminant analysis results is the small sample, which threatens the statistical validity of the results. However, discriminant analysis is found to be robust to violations on the assumptions such as normal distribution and equal variance structures (Jackson 1983). The results indicated that the factors grouped into two main functions. Function 1 was primarily concerned with the political and the horizontal cooperation factors. Function 2 was mainly focused on the lack of downward integration, marketing differentiation, resource base substrategy factors and investment localization.

The analysis also showed that all the substrategies were represented in the two main discriminant functions. In total, they accounted for 84 percent of the total variance in the sample. This percentage confirms the expectations that political substrategy should be included, as well as cooperative organizational substrategy

studies of fragmented industries, at least where the government plays an impor-
ant role in calibrating the competitive forces.

F. Validity

Face validity of the instruments was tested in two steps. First, five scholars
f strategy research critically evaluated the questionnaire. Second, three experi-
nced executives from the industry reviewed both the content and the layout of
e questionnaire. Only then were test interviews conducted within eight meat-
rocessing firms of differing size, location and product range, which yielded a
ritical opinion from the industry leaders. The respondents were asked to eval-
ate the clarity of the questions, and the degree to which the questionnaire
ncluded the most important variables explaining the differences in strategy.
he managers were also asked for suggested improvements in the overall
esign of the questionnaire.

The use of subjective measures of strategy increases the reliability problems of
e data. In strategy studies there is a risk of subjective judgments biased by selec-
ve perceptions and domination of facts and opinions related to past or current
uccess (Barnes 1984; Day and Wensley 1988). For this reason, multiple mea-
ures were employed to reflect the nature of the construct and to increase validity.

The final version of the questionnaire was posted to the managing directors of
e firms in the study. In SMEs, the manager is often the most knowledgeable
bout strategy within the firm, and the one with largest influence over these deci-
ions (Miller and Toulose 1986). Anonymity was promised. The subsequent cross
hecking of the answers showed they represented a broad cross-section of the
ndustry's geographical and physical profile. Follow-up telephone interviews
ith some of the firms confirmed the managers' involvement in answering the
uestionnaire.

Internal reliability tests performed on the factors showed fairly strong Chron-
ach alphas, confirming the internal consistency of the factors (See Tables 1-5).
lso included are some of the factors showing low alpha values because of their
orth in describing the theory behind the measures developed.

IV. RESULTS

A. The Business Strategy Clusters

Below is a detailed review of the five business-strategy patterns, which
merged from the cluster analyses. Each pattern is given a name reflecting its
ain strategic characteristics. The strategic clusters are: (1) The Regional
rena Protectors; (2) The Quality Innovation Leaders; (3) The Mediocrity;
4) The Local Niche Servants, and (5) The Aggressive Conquerors. Table 6

Table 6. Strategic Clusters (Mean Values)

Sub-Strategy Group :	FACTORS:	Cluster 1 (n=13) The Regional Arena Protectors	Cluster 2 (n=6) The Quality Innovation Leaders	Cluster 3 (n=17) The Mediocrity	Cluster 4 (n=2) The Local-Niche Servants	Cluster 5 (n=6) The Aggressive Conquerors	F value
Competitive positioning	Geographical scope	2.46	3.08	3.03	1.00	3.75	4.91*
	Marketing leadership	3.48	1.87	2.00	1.12	3.50	17.94**
	Low-price eadership	2.34	1.41	2.62	2.00	2.50	1.62
	Innovation leadership	3.36	3.25	3.31	3.37	4.12	1.02
	Product quality/ reputation	4.65	4.58	4.00	4.00	4.67	2.64*
Organizational:	Organizational efficiency	3.95	3.04	3.13	1.75	4.25	9.19**
	Organizational improvement routines	4.15	3.80	3.43	1.83	4.16	12.39**
	Organizational flexibility	4.23	4.27	4.31	4.33	4.94	1.82
	Organizational competence	3.30	3.20	2.94	1.87	4.00	6.38*
	Horizontal cooperation	3.71	2.37	1.76	1.50	2.33	8.19*
	Upstream (slaughter) cooperation/ integration	2.61	.58	.91	1.125	1.58	12.80*
	Downstream (wholesaler/ retailer) cooperation	3.23	4.00	3.88	1.00	4.00	4.03*
	Downstream integration (own distribution)	4.69	1.66	4.47	5.00	2.41	34.91*
Investment	Investment level	3.80	3.58	3.84	2.25	4.66	4.37*
	Investment localization	3.05	1.88	2.14	1.00	3.27	9.70*

(continue

Table 6. (Continued)

Sub-strategy Group :	FACTORS:	Cluster 1 (n=13) The Regional Arena Protectors	Cluster 2 (n=6) The Quality Innovation Leaders	Cluster 3 (n=17) The Mediocrity	Cluster 4 (n=2) The Local-Niche Servants	Cluster 5 (n=6) The Aggressive Conquerors	F value
Political							
	Political influence	3.94	2.38	3.19	1.33	3.66	6.57***
	Political cooperation	4.03	1.16	1.55	1.25	1.66	31.64***
	Aver.. No. of employees	798	23	63	9	138	

Notes: * Significance of difference in strategy means p < 0.10.
      ** Significance of difference in strategy means p < 0.05.
      *** Significance of difference in strategy means p < 0.001.

illustrates the characteristic features of the different clusters based on the 17 classification factors.

Cluster One: The Regional Arena Protectors

In cluster one there were 13 firms with an average of 700 employees. This cluster had the largest firms, dominated by the Farmers' Cooperatives. The Regional Arena Protectors implemented a quality differentiation profile with a broad range of products. These firms used their dominant position in the market to create a vertical, quasi-integration into the retailer system. They had their own merchandisers filling the shelves of the supermarkets. They also scored high on marketing-differentiation tools, such as advertising. The secondary data showed that this group had the strongest brand name in the industry.

The Regional Arena Protectors were restricted to marketing their products within a certain region because of their links to the farmers as suppliers and owners. The market range limitations toward the regional market gave them a clear geographical focus. As for the internal resource base, this cluster scored among the highest on the internal resource-base factors, such as competence and development of procedures for organizational improvement.

This cluster of firms also had the highest degree of vertical integration in the value chain, including both slaughtering houses and distribution systems. The firms were also profiled on close horizontal relations with other processors, especially the other cooperatives in this industry. Cooperative efforts included a joint venture for marketing and a joint organization for political lobbying. With the farmers' associations and others, this organization was fighting against the removal of import barriers.

The high scores on political substrategy factors in this cluster are explained by lobbying activity and, not the least, by the institutional agreements between the government, the farmers' association and the farmers' cooperative processors. These agreements included the role as market regulators and the responsibility for government-supported R&D and the provided restrictions on geographical scope and obligations toward buying the production surplus. However the commitment to purchasing surplus products created problems with over-capacity caused by seasonal variations. The fluctuations in the quality of raw materials also created difficulties.

The volume problems were intensified when the wholesale/retail chains found loopholes in the import-trade protection policies against the importation of low-priced substitutes. Catering firms also started to buy raw materials from African countries using the special quotas for less developed countries. Problems with selling the surplus products were solved by dumping the produce in the world market.

Finally, the Regional Arena Protectors were hampered when it came to the investment substrategy. The farmers wanted a greater share of the profit, as increased payments for their supplies. It was therefore difficult to accumulate sufficient funding for future investments. Also, every change in the location of the plants was controversial, causing delays in the restructuring process of these firms.

Cluster Two: The Quality Innovation Leaders

Cluster two included six firms with an average size of 23 employees. These firms profiled themselves with competitive positioning tools, emphasizing high, customer-oriented quality in the up-market consumer segments. They limited the range of their products to one or two specific groups, for example, sausages. These firms already had a relatively broad geographic scope aimed at the national market and had agreements with retail and catering chains and gasoline companies. They also experimented with selling small quantities abroad. Exporting was achieved by exploiting a government support program and export quotas to EU countries. Through these efforts, these firms achieved a benchmarking of their products, and knowledge of the best-practice marketing mix of potential competitors within the European Union.

The Quality Innovation Leaders emphasized a high quality image in every aspect of production and distribution. Through relational marketing schemes, they interacted with their customers to develop a select quality of products. They thereby built a strong loyalty among customers and a reputation for quality in the market.

Their strong reputation in the market reduced the need for vertical ownership integration. They relied instead on close cooperative relations or relational contracts. Upstream they prospered from agreements with slaughtering houses, receiving select, quality raw material. The downstream distribution was arranged through long term cooperation with chosen retail and catering firms as described above. The investment substrategy of these firms included advanced machinery to achieve high technical quality, and cutting-edge packaging techniques to meet new market trends for fresh food. New technology also facilitated transportion over longer distances.

Cluster Three: The Mediocrity

There were 17 firms with an average of 63 employees in cluster three. These firms were characterized by a rather gray or non-distinct profile. The cluster analysis showed middle values on most competitive dimensions. This cluster had the largest number of firms (approximately 40 percent), several of which were family enterprises. They emphasized business as usual and concentrated on the traditional pattern of operation in their regional market.

The lack of profile for this group of firms may be explained by reduced strategic orientation in industries characterized by regional dispersion. The firms were protected in their region by market barriers such as a fragmented retail system and the high cost of transporting perishable goods. Also, they lived their life as second-brand suppliers, especially of fresh products, behind the Farmers' Cooperatives. As long as the Farmers' Cooperatives followed their Regional Arena Protection strategy of selling produce at the highest price possible at home and dumping their surplus abroad, the cluster three enterprises could concentrate on making the daily operations run smoothly.

Even though this strategy might cause severe challenges in adjusting to new conditions, the focus on keeping the organization reasonably in shape gave the companies a potential for reorientation. However, with a very limited strategic focus and the fast pace of change, they were gradually squeezed out of the number two spot by The Aggressive Conquerors, resulting in a lower volume of sales and reduced prices. Also, in some regions, this group of firms was also vulnerable to volume reduction because of an increase in cross-border trade. They risked being stuck-in-the-middle with no financial or human resources left to adapt a new strategy.

Cluster Four: The Local Niche Servant

Cluster four had two firms with an average of nine employees. Although the background analysis showed that this category of firms represented the dominant group in the whole industry, in our sample, they were underrepresented.

The firms in cluster four were quite similar to those in cluster three. However, the cluster four companies were smaller in size, had a more profiled, local quality image, and also possessed a downstream integration substrategy. They served a local market with their own combined transport staff/sellers, and/or own outlets. They reduced the cost of advertising, relying on word-of-mouth, and concentrated on maintaining customer loyalty at the operational buyer-salesman level in a relationship-marketing pattern similar to cluster two. But they did not have a distinct, product-development focus. The internal resource base was not a priority among these firms. They scored low on resource-base factors such as efficiency, organizational improvement routines, and competence. Most significantly, they scored low on organizational efficiency. The latter could have been the result of the low volume in their markets, which limited production. Finally, the dedication of these firms to the local market, as well as their established relations with customers, seemed to limit their interest in a new investment substrategy. Therefore the capability for strategic reorientation in this cluster seems rather limited.

Cluster Five: The Aggressive Conquerors

In cluster five there were six firms with an average of 138 employees. Cluster five firms were in the process of expanding their geographical market, reducing their range of products, and streamlining their manufacturing towards scale production for cost-efficiency purposes. They emphasized country-wide distribution with a standard range of products and also produced customers' or retailers' brand name goods.

The cluster five firms matched the emerging trend toward a more centralized structure of distribution found in most consumer goods markets, as well of that of producing retailers' own brands. They concentrated on serving the national retail chains through just-in-time delivery systems. Through their cooperative relations, they managed to reach customers nation-wide with a limited sales force. They combined this distribution with marketing leadership efforts that focused on reaching customers through intensive advertising. A strong brand name increased their bargaining position with wholesalers and retailers.

The emphasis on cost-efficient production made cluster five firms competitive on price when necessary, and capable of having the lowest bid when rivals tried to gain access to their customers. These firms implemented a differentiation strategy and prepared for a hybrid differentiation and price-leadership substrategy.

The firms in this cluster also emphasized deliberate investment substrategies. They had the highest investment focus in the sample. They were preparing to locate their plants closer to the consumer and/or distribution centers. Secondly, they invested their profits in the neighboring countries. Through this strategy, they received knowledge about the competition abroad, and also prepared themselves for the day when the import barriers were removed. Through the firms they invested in, they had the opportunity to benchmark, especially when it came to cost efficiency in production and distribution in the international market.

B. Cluster Performance

We compared the emerging clusters along four performance measures. Previus strategy studies have shown that firms with a clear strategic profile and a set ˌf matching strategic tools have the best performance. The worst is the non-posiioned or stuck-in-the-middle group. However, in a fragmented and protected ndustry it was assumed that there would be fewer differences between the clusers when it came to performance.

In addition to returns on investment, we asked the managers to report the averge changes in market share and sales volume for the last three years. We also ncluded a self-reporting performance evaluation of their firm compared with the ˌverage of the industry over the same time period.

The analysis of results indicates that the performance advantage goes to posiioned companies. The organizations in clusters one and five, with a differentiaion positioning substrategy, an active resource base substrategy, and a combined nvestment and organizational substrategy toward larger production volumes, outˌerformed the others. In particular, the Aggressive Conqueror firms, with their ˌtrategy for increased market shares, prospered when it came to return on investnent. The Regional Arena Protectors also traditionally earned a good profit. Iowever, they suffered from over capacity and from the payment demands of the ˌarmers.

The Quality Innovation Leader enterprises also enjoyed a good return on nvestments, but had problems with achieving the same scale of advantages as heir counterparts. They too had high costs, pursuing their customers with a coopˌrative strategy when entering national and partially international markets.

According to previous studies of generic strategies, the in-the-middle firms ˌvere expected to score low on performance. They were number four on both ROI ˌnd change in market share. There was a small but non-significant difference in ˌesults compared with the differentiated clusters. This deviation could reflect the ˌow, internal rivalry of the industry, especially in low-price positioning.

The most dramatic figures were related to cluster four firms, with their ˌtrong emphasis on the local market and their reluctance to change. In much of he strategy literature, a local niche approach was recommended as beneficial ˌor smaller firms. Our findings imply, however, that in a market where geoˌraphical barriers are removed, the probability of existing, scale advantages is ˌigh. The size of the target market and the re-scaling of production may prove ˌritical for the performance.

The superior results of the cluster three Mediocrity firms compared with the Local Niche Servant firms may be explained by differences in geographical scope ˌnd scale. There are also significant variations in investment levels that may ˌxplain the differences between the two clusters with the best performance, and he rest. Clusters one and five firms had the highest investment levels, implying ˌerhaps that the largest firms have better access to investment money. They also prepared themselves for future competitiveness through a planned investment program. Lack of access to such funds could prove a severe handicap for the smaller firms of clusters three and four.

It was also determined that the larger firms of cluster one placed a strong emphasis on political substrategies, which could explain why this cluster had acceptable results in spite of a geographical focus substrategy. The results also showed that cluster five, with Aggressive Conqueror firms, did not abandon the political substrategy dimension. However, they were more targeted toward shaping their environment to support their competitive strategy and investment plans

As an example of their political influence, the firms of cluster one and five managed to receive the bulk of the funding from a government-support scheme founded to prepare the industry for EU membership. This support gave them an advantage both in competence development, and in investment in modern machinery.

V. DISCUSSION AND CONCLUSIONS

A. Competitive Forces

This study presented an industry characterized by a large number of firms, each with a small market share and a high geographical dispersion. Even in an industry protected heavily by government subsidies and import barriers, the force of global markets had an increasing influence on the competitive context, and forced the firms towards extensive corporate entrepreneurship. The global trends hit this industry by:

- The implementation of customers' negotiation-power techniques and logistics, adopted by entering into international wholesaler alliances. The wholesale/retail chains used this knowledge to restructure their delivery systems and to demand a national delivery capacity for their suppliers.
- The customer's import of low-priced substitutes to increase their negotiation power with the processors.
- Investment in advanced production technology from abroad.
- Exploitation of loopholes in the import regulations, export quotas and licenses to gain competitive experience in international markets, together with an increase in direct-consumer traffic across the border to buy products at the lower EU prices.
- Investment abroad to achieve opportunities for international benchmarking and to prepare for new international agreements on lowering trade barriers.

The result of this indirect influence was a swift change of structure toward a national and an international integration of the whole value chain of this industry.

For each firm, not the least the smaller ones, a repositioning of strategy was imperative.

B. The Substrategy Approaches

The results of this study revealed significant differences, at a substrategy level, in the entrepreneurial posture of the different categories of firms in this industry. There were also major differences in the substrategy-mix chosen to meet the new market challenges. The competitive positioning substrategies, along with organizational, resource-base, investment, and political substrategies, created a multitude of strategic patterns.

Firms with a quality-oriented differentiation substrategy that emphasizes internal resource-base development seemed to have the potential for success in a fragmented industry facing global integration challenges. They were prepared for more severe competition, with their emphasis on improved learning capacity among employees, and employee adaptability for frequent changes in technology and working routines. Hambrick and Lei (1985), among others, predicted this pattern, stating that in a fragmented market structure with emerging growth, firms should turn toward a more customer-oriented differentiation substrategy. Within the manufacturing of consumer goods, differentiation based on intensive advertising has been found to affect product prices positively (Wills 1983). The results also indicated that an even more successful combination would be to develop a resource base with efficiency routine instruments that prepared for a combination of differentiation and price leadership. These results confirm earlier studies that a differentiation and price leadership strategy is the most successful combination across industries (Miller and Dess 1993).

In this industry, however, we found that the limited, internal rivalry, caused by trade protectionism and government market-intervention, reduced the need for the firms to increase their efficiency through a low-price leadership positioning. This finding contradicts previous studies, for example, that of service industries where there is a majority of small and medium-sized firms (Cappel et al. 1992), and more general investigations of small manufacturing firms and new ventures (Olsen and Kolvereid 1994). Murray (1988) argues that the structural characteristics of the industry form the necessary preconditions for a price-leadership strategy. The protected features of the meat processing industry, and the large number of firms with geographic focus, may lower the internal rivalry within the industry and confirm earlier postulates about the importance of control-of-industry effects in strategic management research (Dess et al. 1990). Instead of a competitive-positioning profile on low price leadership, the entrepreneurial firms in this study implemented an active investment substrategy, investing heavily in more efficient, strategically located plants and in companies abroad, to gain experience, to prepare for new opportunities, and also, to test sales abroad.

The study illustrates how political substrategies contribute to different strategic patterns. The results revealed problems when strong bonds to government institutions exist (Mintzberg 1988), although close cooperative relations to political bodies for investment in job creation, innovation and export sales may prove beneficial. However, political substrategies which reduce the ability to choose supplier relations, market range and investment patterns may cause severe problems in a transitional industry, such as the exploitation of scale economies through expanding markets and the adaptation to the international wholesaler systems.

C. Large- versus Small-Firm Strategies

The largest firms in this study belonged to the strategic clusters titled the Regional Arena Protectors and the Aggressive Conquerors. Both groups had a broad, differentiated product range and strong brand names. They emphasized improved internal routines and learning abilities that supported their competitive tools. The Aggressive Conquerors concentrated on geographical expansion and the achievement of scale advantages through an active investment substrategy. While the Regional Arena Protectors followed similar substrategies, their geographical scope, strong organizational ties to suppliers and political substrategies hampered them. They therefore faced the risk of being unable to accumulate investment capital and to develop knowledge on the efficient use of production capacity to prepare for price competition. Earlier studies indicate that the cross-national integration of markets forces successful businesses to adapt both differentiation and cost efficiency strategies (Hill 1988; Jones and Butler 1988). Alternatively, they should at least be able to make timely shifts between differentiation and cost leadership (Gilbert and Strebel 1987).

It can be inferred from this study that finding the right level of activity is important in transitional industries. Larger firms, with their ambitions of becoming full assortment processors, have to accumulate investment capital, find the right technology, and scale up their production plants to meet higher volume demands. For smaller firms, a matching geographical scope is important (Johnson and Thomas 1987). They either have to upscale their activity to be able to fight their larger counterparts, or to implement more segmented tools that may protect them from damaging price competition. The results of this study indicate a strong position among the Quality Innovation Leaders, a category of firms which seems to prosper in most markets (Douglas and Ree 1989). However, these companies are also vulnerable to price competition and to the more aggressive marketing efforts of larger competitors, which are able to seek cost advantages through the use of flexible production technology and to secure a technical quality. Continuous innovation, a superior, internal resource-base of product and production technique development, as well as close customer relations, are all critical substrategies for success within this group.

The larger group of small firms in this industry was only, to a limited extent, prepared for the changes in competitive forces. Among these enterprises, a non-profiled and in-the-middle strategy dominated. The lack of strategic profile could be explained both by stable, local relationships embedded in social relations and traditions, and by the limited strategic focus of smaller firms. In these firms, the managers are busy on several levels and within several functions. They lack the time and competence necessary for analyzing and deciding on the strategic situation of the firm. In addition, as these companies are often family-owned, there usually is no active board of directors to contribute to strategic decisions (Borch and Huse 1993). Consequently, there can be a critical time lag and mismatch between the strategic decision-making of the small firm and the changes in the market. It has been found in numerous studies that this category of firms has the worst performance across industries (Douglas and Ree 1989; Kim and Lim 1988; White 1986).

However, several entrepreneurial measures are at hand. The Mediocrity Firms may implement horizontal integration substrategies to exploit larger geographical markets through strategic alliances with other firms in this group, or by ownership integration. Thus they can more rapidly improve their capacity, and achieve scale advantages without having the resources necessary for a full scale, investment strategy. These efforts also imply difficult and conflicting decisions as to owner-ship, in particular for family-owned firms.

The same strategy may also prove beneficial for The Local Niche Servant. However, they have even more limited resources, and are less attractive to poten-tial alliance partners. One solution may be to develop specialty products that would be of interest to narrow segments in the national and international markets. For example, the international trend toward such items as original food, special tastes, food culture, ecological products, small scale, home made production, could create a potential for the smallest category of firms. However, the distribu-tion challenges are quite large for this type of company. An increased focus on cooperative relations and especially joint-sales ventures with other firms and organization may prove crucial to their eventual well being.

D. Governmental Implications

The firms of an industry in transition from a fragmented structure to global inte-gration have to make significant adjustments in their business strategy to survive such a transition. Therefore there are significant challenges for the governments involved in the restructuring process. In particular, governments of nations with strong protective schemes should be aware of the dramatic changes taking place in the competitive forces, and their attendant negative effects on small and regional-based firms. Nations with a small-scale structure may even face a loss of a significant part of "the underbrush" of small and medium-sized firms. Programs are necessary to improve the resource base of this category of firms and to support the restructuring of the industry through investment funding and support for organizational cooperation and integration. During a transitional phase, joint business-government alliances can evolve to improve industrial capability (Porter 1990). Such alliances could help to keep the home industry intact, and to increase the opportunity for exploitation of new potentials in the international market place.

E. Implications for Future Research

With more industries being exposed to international competition, the focus must continue on the strategic adjustments to market integration at the firm level. The results of this study confirmed the importance of control for industry structure in such studies (Dess et al. 1990). An increased emphasis on industry characteristics may, for example, explain the different patterns of internationalization found within small business research (Oviatt and McDougall 1997).

This study had its empirical shortcomings in a cross-sectional design, one single industry and nation, and a relatively small sample size. When it comes to future research in this area, longitudinal studies, comparing different countries and industries, are needed. Time series analyses to show the effects of changes in market structure are also recommended. Such an approach could reveal the critical strategic decisions effective over time in meeting changes in environmental conditions (Douglas and Rhee 1989). It could also provide a more in-depth picture of the complicated, dynamic relationships between strategy and performance (Mosakowski 1993). In this type of research, a broad conceptual set of business substrategy factors should be instrumental in finding patterns unique to industries in transition toward global integration.

More explorative research is also needed on the managerial processes involved in adopting a new business strategy. In particular, one should elaborate on the development of internal resources, such as learning capabilities, and also the human aspects of building cooperative relations to achieve competitive strength. To achieve these ends, more qualitative and even action-oriented research approaches must be implemented.

REFERENCES

Aaker, D., and G. Day. 1986. "The Perils of High Growth Markets." *Strategic Management Journal* 7: 409-421.

Alpar, P., and D. Spitzer. 1989. "Response Behavior of Entrepreneurs in a Mail Survey." *Entrepreneurship Theory and Practice* 14 (2):31-44.

Ansoff, H. I. 1971. *Business Strategy*. Bungay: Penguin Books.

Barnes, J. H. 1984. "Cognitive Biases and Their Impact on Strategic Planning." *Strategic Management Journal:* 129-138.

Barney, J. B. 1991. "Firm Resources and Sustained Competitive Advantage." *Journal of Management* 17:99-120.

Bartlett, C. A., and S. Ghosal. 1991. "Global Strategic Management: Impact on the New Frontiers of Strategy Research." *Strategic Management Journal* 12: 5-16.

Bijmolt, T. H. A., and P. S. Zwart. 1994. "The Impact of Internal Factors on the Export Success of Dutch Small and Medium-sized Firms." *Journal of Small Business Management* 32 (2): 535-557.

Black, J. A., and K. B. Boal. 1994. "Strategic Resources: Traits, Configurations and Paths to Sustainable Competitive Advantage." *Strategic Management Journal* 15 (Special issue, Summer): 131-148.

Borch, O. J., and M. Huse. 1993. "Informal Strategic Networks and the Board of Directors." *Entrepreneurship Theory and Practice* 18 (1): 23-36.

Cappel, S., P. Wright, M. Kroll, and D. Wyld. 1992. "Competitive Strategies and Business Performance. An Empirical Study of Select Service Businesses." *International Journal of Management* 9 (1): 1-11.

Carpano, C., J. J. Chrisman, and K. Roth. 1994. "International Strategy and Environment: An Assessment of the Performance Relationship." *Journal of International Business* 25 (3): 639-656.

Chrisman, J., W. Boulton, and C. Hofer. 1988. "Toward a System for Classifying Business Strategies." *Academy of Management Review* 13: 413-428.

Covin, J. G., and D. P. Slevin. 1991. "A Conceptual Model of Entrepreneurship As Firm Behavior." *Entrepreneurship Theory and Practice* 16 (1): 7-25

Davis, P. S., and P. L. Schul. 1993. "Addressing the Contingent Effects of Business Unit Strategic Orientation on Relationships Between Organizational Context and Business Unit Performance." *Journal of Business Research* 27: 183-200.

Day, G. S., and R. Wensley. 1988. "Assessing Advantage: A Framework for Diagnosing Competitive Superiority." *Journal of Marketing* 52: 17.

Dess, G. G. 1987. "Consensus on Strategy Formulation and Organizational Performance: Competitors in a Fragmented Industry." *Strategic Management Journal* 8 (3): 259-277.

Dess, G. G., and P. S. Davis. 1984. "Porter's Generic Strategies as Determinants of Strategic Group Membership and Organizational Performance." *Academy of Management Journal* 27 (3): 467-488.

Dess, G. G., R. D. Ireland, and M. A. Hitt. 1990. "Industry Effects and Strategic Management Research." *Journal of Management* 16: 7-27.

Douglas, S. P., and D. K. Rhee. 1989. "Examining Generic Competitive Strategy Types in the U.S. and European Markets." *Journal of International Business Studies* 20: 437-463.

Dunning, J. H. 1992. *Multinational Enterprises and the Global Economy*. Reading, MA: Addison-Wesley Publishing Company.

Gilbert, X., and P. Strebel. 1987. "Developing Competitive Advantage." In *The Strategy Process*, edited by H. Mintzberg. Prentice-Hall.

Ginsberg, A., and N. Venkatraman. 1985. "Contingency Perspective of Organizational Strategy: A Critical Review of the Empirical Research." *Academy of Management Review* 10: 421-434.

Ghosal, S. 1987. "Global Strategy: An Organizing Framework." *Strategic Management Journal*: 425-440.

Hambrick, D. C. 1983a. "Some Tests of Effectiveness and Fictional Attributes of Miles and Snow's Strategic Types." *Academy of Management Journal* 26 (1):5-26.

———. 1983b. "High Profit Strategies in Mature Capital Goods Industries: A Contingency Approach." *Academy of Management Journal* 26 (4): 687-707.

———. 1984. "Taxonomic Approaches to Studying Strategy: Some Conceptual and Methodological Issues." *Journal of Management* 10 (1): 27-41.

Hambrick, D. C., and D. Lei. 1985. "Toward an Empirical Prioritization of Contingency Variables for Business Strategy." *Academy of Management Journal* 28:763-788.

Harrigan, K. R. 1980. *Strategies for Declining Industries*. Lexington, MA: Lexington Books.

———. 1982. "Exit Decisions in Mature Industries." *Academy of Management Journal* 25: 707-732.

Harrison, B. 1997. *Lean and Mean: The Changing Landscape of Corporate Power in the Age of Flexibility*. New York: Guilford Press.

Hill, C. W. L. 1988. "Differentiation versus Low Cost or Differentiation and Low Cost: A Contingency Framework." *Academy of Management Review* 13 (3): 401-412.

Hofer, C. W. 1975. "Toward a Contingency Theory of Business Strategy." *Academy of Management Journal* 18: 784-810.

Hofer, C. W., and D. Schendel. 1978. *Strategy Formulation: Analytical Concepts*. St. Paul, MN: West Publishing.

Jackson, B. B. 1983. *Multivariate Data Analysis*. Homewood, IL: Richard D. Irwin, Inc.

Johnson, G., and H. Thomas. 1987. "The Industry Context of Strategy, Structure and Performance: The UK Brewing Industry." *Strategic Management Journal* 8: 343-361.

Jones, G. R., and J. E. Butler. 1988. "Costs, Revenue, and Business-level Strategy." *Academy of Management Review* 13 (2): 202-213.

Kim, J., and C. Mueller. 1978. *Factor Analysis*. Beverly Hills, CA: Sage Publications.

Kim, L., and Y. Lim. 1988. "Environment, Generic Strategies, and Performance in a Rapidly Developing Country: A Taxonomic Approach." *Academy of Management Journal* 31 (4): 802-827.

Knight, G. A., and S. T. Cavusgil. 1996. "The Born Global Firm: A Challenge to Traditional Internationalizatin Theory." In *Advances in International Marketing, Vol. 8*, edited by S. T. Cavusgil and T. K. Madsen. Greenwich, CT: JAI Press.

Koester, U. 1991. "The Experience with Liberalization Policies. The Case of the Agricultural Sector." *European Economic Review* 35: 562-570.

Kogut, B. 1989. "A Note on Global Strategies." *Strategic Management Journal* 10: 393-389.

Leonard-Barton, D. 1992. "Core Capabilities and Core Rigidities: A Paradox in Managing New Product Development." *Strategic Management Journal* 13: 111-125.

McDougall, P. P., S. Shane, and B. M. Oviatt. 1994. "Explaining the Formation of International New Ventures: The Limits of Theories from International Business Research." *Journal of Business Venturing* 9: 469-487.

Miller, A., and G. G. Dess. 1993. "Assessing Porter's (1980) Model in Terms of Its Generalizability, Accuracy and Simplicity." *Journal of Management Studies* 30 (4): 553-585.

Miller, D. 1992. "The Generic Strategy Trap." *The Journal of Business Strategy* (Jan/Feb): 37-41.

Miller, D., and J. M. Toulose. 1986. "Chief Executive Personality and Corporate Strategy and Structure in Small Firms." *Management Science* 32: 1389-1409.

Mintzberg, H. 1988. "Politics and the Political Organization." In *The Strategy Process—Concepts, Contexts and Cases*, edited by H. Mintzberg and J. B. Quinn. Englewood Cliffs, NJ: Prentice-Hall International.

Mitchell, W. 1992. "Getting There in a Global Industry: Impacts on Performance of Changing International Presence." *Strategic Management Journal* 13 (6): 419-432.

Morrison, A. J. 1990. *Strategies in Global Industries. How U.S. Businesses Compete*. Westport, CT: Quorum Books.

Morrison, A. J., and K. Roth. 1992. "A Taxonomy of Business-level Strategies in Global Industries." *Strategic Management Journal* 13 (6): 399-418.

Mosakowski, E. 1993. "A Resource-based Perspective on the Dynamic Strategy-Performance Relationship: An Empirical Examination of the Focus and Differentiation Strategies in Entrepreneurial firms." *Journal of Management* 19 (4): 819-839.

Murray, A. I. 1988. "A Contingency View of Porter's 'Generic Strategies'." *The Academy of Management Review* 13 (3): 390-400.

OECD. 1997. *Globalization and Small and Medium Enterprises*. Paris: OECD.

Olsen, B., and L. Kolvereid. 1994. "Development of New Ventures Over Time: Strategy, Profitability and Growth in New Scandinavian Firms." *Entrepreneurship and Regional Development* 6: 357-370.

Oviatt, B. M., and P. P. McDougall. 1997. "Challenges for Internationalization Process Theory: The Case of International New Ventures." *Management International Review* (Special Issue) 2: 85-99.

———. 1998. "Accelerated Internationalization: Why are New and Small Ventures Internationalizing in Greater Numbers and with Increasing Speed?" In *Proceedings from the Workshop "The International Conference on Globalization and Emerging Businesses-Strategies for the 21st Century."* McGill University, Montreal, Canada, September 26-28.

Porter, M. E. 1980 *Competitive Strategy*. New York: The Free Press.

———. 1985. *Competitive Advantage*. New York: The Free Press.

———. 1986. "Competition in Global Industries: A Conceptual Framework." In *Competition in Global Industries*, edited by M. E. Porter. Boston: Harvard Business Press.

———. 1990. *The Competitive Advantage of Nations*. London: The Macmillan Press.

———. 1991. "Towards a Dynamic Theory of Strategy." *Strategic Management Journal* 12 (Special Issue): 95-117.

Reve, T. 1990. "The Firm as a Nexus of Internal and External Contracts." In *The Firm as a Nexus of Treaties*, edited by M. Aoki, B. Gustavsson, and O. E. Williamson. London: Sage Publishing Ltd.

Rich, P. 1992. "The Organizational Taxonomy: Definition and Design." *Academy of Management Review* 17(4): 758-781.

Roth, K. 1992. "International Configuration and Coordination Archetypes for Medium-sized Firms in Global Industries." *Journal of International Business Studies* 23 (3): 533-549.

Rumelt, R. P., D. Schendel, and D. J. Teece. 1991. "Strategic Management and Economics." *Strategic Management Journal* 12 (Special Issue): 5-29.

Sapienza, H. J., K. G. Smith, and M. J. Gannon. 1988. "Using Subjective Evaluations of Organizational Performance in Small Business Research." *American Journal of Small Business* 3: 45-53.

Spender, J. C. 1993. "Business Policy and Strategy: An Occasion for Despair, a Retreat to Disciplinary Specialization, or for New Excitement." *Academy of Management Best Paper Proceedings* 42-46.

Venkatraman, N., and J. H. Grant. 1986. "Construct Measurement in Organizational Strategy Research: A Critique and Proposal." *The Academy of Management Review* 11 (1): 71-87.

White, R. E. 1986. "Generic Business Strategies. Organizational Context and Performance: An Empirical Investigation." *Strategic Management Journal* 7: 217-231.

Wills, R. 1983. "The Impact of Market Structure and Advertising on Brand Pricing in Processed Food Products." Doctoral dissertation, University of Wisconsin, Madison.

Yip, G. 1982. "Gateways to Entry." *Harvard Business Review* (Sept-Oct.): 85-92.

AN ENTREPRENEURIAL MODEL OF SME INTERNATIONALIZATION

EVIDENCE FROM SIX CASES

James H. Tiessen and Bill Merrilees

I. INTRODUCTION

Small and medium enterprises account for more than half the employment and value-added in most countries (UNCTAD 1993). Yet they have not contributed proportionately to export trade (UNCTAD 1993). In Canada for example, small and medium firms accounted for 64 percent of employment, but made only 9 percent of the country's foreign sales (Industry Canada 1996). As trade and investment barriers continue to drop, and communication and transportation technologies facilitate global approaches, SMEs will become more international to sustain their vitality (UNCTAD 1993). SME owners and managers, policymakers and researchers therefore have an interest in understanding how SMEs internationalize.

This chapter develops an entrepreneurial model of SME internationalization by analyzing how this process unfolded for six Canadian firms which vary widely in terms of age, size, industry and export performance. We begin by reviewing the

Research in Global Strategic Management, Volume 7, pages 131-154.
Copyright © 1999 by JAI Press Inc.
All rights of reproduction in any form reserved.
ISBN: 0-7623-0458-8

core findings and theories produced by research in the fields of SME exporting and entrepreneurship. Next, we introduce the firms studied and outline how they internationalized. This is followed by a description of our model, developed by integrating the case data with extant research. We conclude with discussions on the model dynamics, managerial implications and future research directions.

II. BACKGROUND: RESEARCH ON SME EXPORTING AND ENTREPRENEURSHIP

Researchers have focused on two related aspects of SME exporting: the links between firm and management characteristics and export performance, and the stages of export involvement. Both streams highlight the importance of the entrepreneurial behavior of the SME owner or manager who spearheads foreign market involvement.

A. SME Management and Firm Characteristics

A broad body of research has studied factors associated with exporting and/or export performance. This work generally shares the key finding that manager characteristics are related to both the proclivity to export and its success. Companies run by people who are internationally oriented, competent, and positively oriented towards risk are more likely to export, and export successfully (Bilkey 1978; Aaby and Slater 1989; Holzmüller and Kasper 1991; Beamish, Craig, and McLellan 1993; Leonidou and Katsikeas 1996).

Studies have also found that company features associated positively with exporting and export performance are commitment to foreign markets and the uniqueness of the product offered (Bilkey 1976; Aaby and Slater 1989; Beamish, Craig, and McLellan 1993; Cavusgil and Kirpalani 1993). There is evidence that firm size is positively linked to exporting, but the relationship is not strong (Calof 1994). Successful firms also typically execute formal export policies and build strong relationships with distributors in other markets (Aaby and Slater 1989).

B. Stage Models

Research on firm internationalization has provided fairly consistent descriptions of firms at different levels of export involvement. This work has identified at least three and as many as nine levels of increasing firm involvement in exporting (Bilkey 1978; Cavusgil 1984; Leonidou and Katsikeas 1996). For example, Cavusgil's (1984, p. 207) interviews with 71 U.S. companies revealed three broad categories: "Experimental," "Active," and "Committed." Wiedersheim-Paul, Olson, and Welch (1978) describe a pre-export stage, which can lead to involvement in foreign markets. Promotion through these stages is accomplished through experience which builds capabilities and demonstrates the benefits of exporting (Johanson and Vahlne 1977, 1990; Bilkey 1978; Cavusgil 1984). Higher stage exporting tends to be associated with "unique" products (Cavusgil and Nevin 1981; Cavusgil 1984).

Recent research has found that not all firms progress through these stages. McDougall, Shane, and Oviatt (1994) and McDougall and Oviatt (1996) identified the instant international firm. Brush's (1995) work, which explicitly recognizes the relevance of entrepreneurship theory to SME internationalization, led her to focus on the serendipitous nature of this process. She found that firms do not rationally plan their level of export commitment, so they do not progress through stages in an orderly fashion.

C. Entrepreneurial Behavior

The factors associated with exporting and export performance are, not suprisingly, the same orientations and behaviors identified more generally with "entrepreneurship." Miller (1983, p. 771), for example, defines an entrepreneurial firm as one that "engages in product-market-innovation, undertakes somewhat risky ventures, and is *first* to come up with 'proactive' innovations." Amit, Glosten, and Muller (1993, p. 816) similarly define entrepreneurship as a "process of extracting profits from new, unique, and valuable combinations of resources in an uncertain and ambiguous environment." These writers also stress the importance of a growth orientation implicit in such an approach to business.

Entrepreneurial behavior comprises two core ingredients: an economic opportunity, and resources (Kilby 1971; Stevenson and Gumpert 1985; Tiessen 1997). The opportunity arises from innovation, typically through making Schumpeter's (1968) famed "new combinations." The opportunity or innovation alone though is necessary, but not sufficient. Entrepreneurial firms perceive the real opportunity in the firm-environment nexus and gain the use of resources needed to exploit it. As Schumpeter (1968, p. 116) wrote, "Capital is nothing but the lever by which the entrepreneur subjects to his control the concrete goods which he needs, nothing but a means of diverting the factors of production to new uses, or of dictating a new direction to production." We label the processes of developing opportunities "variety generation," and the marshaling of the means to pursue them, "leveraging resources" (Tiessen 1997). Both are described in greater detail when we present the model.

Entrepreneurial behavior is not unique to small firms (e.g., Stevenson and Jarillo 1990). Carland and colleagues (1984) specifically differentiate between "entrepreneurial" and "small business" ventures. The former are characterized by innovation, profitability, and growth. Small business ventures, in contrast, are typically owner-operated, "not dominant in [their] field" and less innovative (Carland et al. 1984, p. 358). The firms studied here are all entrepreneurial by definition, because they have sought growth by operating in somewhat risky overseas

Table 1.   Characteristics of Case Study Firms

Company	Main Business	Date of Establishment	No. Employees	Overseas Exports as % of Revenues[1]
Sunset Neon	custom signs	1982	18	0[2]
Canadiana Homes	pre-engineered housing	1985	25	90
Fjord Pacific	processed seafood	1963	50	55
Protexion Products	sporting goods	1901	250	10
Bartek Ingredients	food additives	1969	135	45
CRS Robotics	robots	1981	85	45

Notes: 1. Overseas exports for these Canadian companies are all non-US exports.
               2. 1998 figure. In 1995 overseas exports were 10% of revenues.

markets. However, they differ in the degree of entrepreneurship practiced. In most of the cases presented here, the small nature of the firms means this behavior is conducted by the founders who still control their enterprises.

III.   METHOD

We developed our model by conducting 12 long interviews of key informants from Canadian SMEs who have done business with Japan. We were guided by Eisenhardt's (1989) advice that we select cases purposefully and use semi-structured interview protocols. Japan-experienced firms were selected because they are unequivocally exporters. This cannot be said of companies whose export sales have been limited to the United States, which of course shares both a similar culture and market under the NAFTA. Also, Japan is Canada's second largest export destination. The selected firms were chosen from a list of Canadian companies compiled by the Canada-Japan Trade Council. Because this research was exploratory we sought to look at a broad range of firm types.

The interviews, which ran from one and a half to three hours, were semi-structured and conducted with two researchers present. Ten took place at the firm sites and the other two were done by conference call. In all cases the research notes were written up within 24 hours of the interview. Written case summaries were sent back to the informants for their review.

Our approach has limitations. Neither the six cases reported here, nor the full set of 12, represent a population of SME exporters. Further, reliance on key informants for information could have introduced a bias. That said, the method was appropriate for an exploratory study because it revealed a rich, longitudinal analysis of a complex topic. With respect to bias, we believed the knowledge of the informants added credibility to the information provided because, for all but one of our cases, they were directly involved in exporting. Further, the majority of our informants are thoughtful owner-managers accountable only to themselves, not an official company line.

IV. THE SIX CASES

Though our model emerged from our study of 12 cases, here we illustrate it using six representative firms: Sunset Neon, Canadiana Homes, Fjord Pacific, Protexion Products, Bartek Ingredients and CRS Robotics (Computing Resources Services). As seen in Table 1 these firms vary widely in terms of age, size, industry, and the percentage of revenues accounted for by sales outside of Canada and the United States.

A. Sunset Neon

Sunset Neon of southern Ontario designs, manufactures, and installs custom signs for customers such as major retailers, gas stations, and shopping malls. Sunset was founded in 1982 and has 18 employees. The company works closely with customers throughout all phases of sign building. Sunset does most of its business in Canada, though recently U.S. sales have made up as much as 40 percent of their revenues.

Sunset sold only in Canada until 1989 when they made a sale to nearby New York State. In many respects their markets are bound geographically because shipping and post-installation service costs can be substantial. Signs are bulky and it can be expensive to dispatch staff to make minor repairs on signs still under warranty.

In late 1994 Sunset was offered the chance to do its first overseas job. They were approached by Toronto firm Cricket Design to join them in a bid to provide signs for an entertainment complex near Nagoya, Japan. Cricket themselves were part of a Tokyo consortium led by International Leisure Systems, which has UK roots. International Leisure was linked to Toronto through its director of development, Robert Harrison, who has a home near the city.

Sunset's founder and president Dave Carley went to Japan in early 1995 to make a formal presentation to the Japanese customer. Carley's task was made more difficult when his airline sent his portfolio and presentation materials through to Jamaica rather than Japan. After a long day of discussions and negotiations though, he won the contract. A key reason for the Japanese buyer's preference for Sunset, over Japanese competitors, was that they wanted an "American" atmosphere in the complex. Further, the Toronto and UK firms in the consortium lent Sunset legitimacy. Finally, Sunset offered a good price and had significant experience doing similar work in North America.

Sunset Neon made the signs in Canada and sent two staff to Japan for a week to install them. There were some minor shipping and customs delays, but nothing out of the ordinary. Sunset completed the work as scheduled in only nine weeks. Soon after the signs were up, Sunset was asked for replacement parts as part of the warranty agreement. Fortunately for Sunset, they did not need to send staff to complete this work. This sale made up 10 percent of Sunset's 1995 billings.

Sunset has not done any more overseas work, though they have retained low-key contact with both their partners on the Japanese job. They have channeled most of their efforts recently to making further inroads in the U.S. market. There are three reasons for this emphasis. First, the U.S. economy's robustness has offered sufficient opportunities for a firm of Sunset's size. As well, the cultural similarity means business practices are similar to those in Canada. And, as mentioned above, on-site installation and servicing do not incur significant costs in the closer market.

Carley does say though that his firm's Japanese experience has supported their North American sales two ways. First, the Nagoya job raised their Canadian profile when it attracted coverage in the business press. Second, Carley cites that sale in contract bids as evidence of their design ability. This is because Japan is renowned for its creative and high quality graphic design and neon signs.

B. Canadiana Homes

Canadiana Homes, like Sunset Neon, is a small Ontario company which does project-based work. They make and sell wooden pre-engineered homes. The business, run by founder/owner Joe Mayer, depends on overseas markets for about 90% of its revenues.

Mayer founded his original company in 1985 to serve Canada's market. A key resource he developed was the ability to execute all stages of construction. Canadiana works with customers to design buildings and then makes wood panels and frames, procures windows and fixtures from other suppliers, and then sends technicians to building sites.

Mayer took deliberate steps to develop foreign sales. In 1992 he established his own export company, Canadiana Homes, as an extension of his first business. He had concluded he could profit more in overseas markets than in Canada and the United States, which are more competitive and were in recession at the time.

The same year Mayer also became a founding member of the Manufactured Housing Association of Canada (MHAC). This association pools the financial and information resources of small and medium firms facing the same constraints as Mayer. MHAC member Mark Ando, a Japanese Canadian who works with Douglas Homes of BC, was an important source of Japanese market knowledge, especially building standards. The association and the government's Department of Foreign Affairs and International Trade contributed equally to produce a directory which was distributed to Canada's embassies and consulates around the world.

Canadiana decided to pay most attention to inquiries from where they saw their most promising markets—Germany, Japan and Spain. Their first substantial contact came, via the directory, from a Japanese shipping company, CHMC. CHMC shipped Japanese autos to Canada and wanted product to fill the empty containers returned to Japan. After one and a half years of "toing and froing" a deal was made, with CHMC acting as an agent. This relationship continued for two years until CHMC set up its own competitive business. Canadiana now sells to several other agents who have contacted him as a result of the MHAC directory.

Mayer acts to make sure he can adapt to his international markets. In 1994, he attended an exporter education program in Japan sponsored by the Japan External Trade Organization (JETRO). He also makes substantial changes in his designs to account for Japanese differences in physical stature (e.g., lower counters) and house styles (e.g., *tatami* rooms).

Canadiana made a sale to its second overseas customer, in Germany, while the first Japanese transaction was being negotiated and completed. The German deal took considerable effort because of that country's very rigorous building codes. Mayer, though Canadian, is of German ancestry and speaks the language. This helped him cope with red tape. Being able to build to such strict standards however now enables Canadiana to take on any market because, as Mayer said, "It's like Frank Sinatra sang. If you can make it there, you can make it anywhere." Both Japan and Germany continue to be Canadiana's key markets. They account for about 23 percent and 45 percent of Mayer's overall sales, respectively. Mayer visits these markets regularly, and takes part in trade shows in order to sustain a visible presence.

C. Fjord Pacific

Fjord Pacific of Vancouver, founded in 1963, produces value-added seafood products such as smoked salmon and pickled herring. Their major competitors in world markets for their most important product, smoked salmon, are the low cost fish farming operations of Chile and Norway.

Fjord sources its raw material from the British Columbia fishery. Though they sell over half of their output overseas to Europe, Australia, and Japan, Fjord tends to act as an "active," rather than "committed" exporter. This is because Fjord's primary focus is on making quality standard products, rather than searching and tailoring their output for foreign markets. As a company representative said, "We've never really chosen a country before."

Fjord supplied seafood to the U.S. market from the early 1970s. By the 1990s they had built a major business selling directly to a restaurant chain. However, the chain went out of business in the late 1990s, reducing the U.S. component of Fjord's sales to only 5 percent.

Fjord's first overseas exports were to Australia, in 1978. They had been contacted by an Australian distributor, Europa. This relationship has continued for 20 years, and now that country accounts for 20 percent of Fjord's total sales. Their second major overseas foray was around 1983. An Italian distributor came to Fjord looking for smoked salmon to sell in Europe. This firm later requested, and was awarded, exclusive rights for Fjord's smoked products in Europe. This was a good opportunity for Fjord, because most of the foreign seafood in that market is processed in Europe. Fjord has expressed concern with their Italian agent's level of activity, and the European Union now makes up only 6 percent of Fjord's revenues.

Also around 1983, Fjord made trial shipments to Japan through a Japanese trading company. Sporadic spot orders followed for about 10 years. However, in the past few years the same trading company's Vancouver office arranged sales contracts for salted salmon and canned smoked salmon for Japan's market.

Since 1996, Fjord has taken a more market specific approach to exporting. They found a Hong Kong agent and were making inquiries into Taiwan's market. In both cases, they have worked with the Canadian government's trade offices to identify potential importers. They will continue to use agents in these markets because, as the Fjord representative said, "They know what consumers want."

D. Protexion Products

Protexion Products of Ontario, recently taken over by Montreal's Saputo Group, is the oldest of the companies studied. They invented and patented the athletic supporter, or "jock strap" more than 60 years ago. They serve world markets through their ability to design and produce sewn equipment and work closely with their customers. Protexion now produces a full line of Protex sports training products, NHL-quality hockey equipment, personal floatation devices (life jackets) as well as grass catchers for lawn mowers.

Protexion licensed their first invention internationally before World War II. This was a sensible option in the days when trade barriers were higher. They did though start selling offshore during the 1950s when they entered the UK and then other European markets. Through this experience they learned how to produce for and serve markets overseas.

Protexion works to sustain high quality and excellent service to their dealers; they otherwise could not survive with a product that is, according to their current sales and marketing director Terry Ackerman, "just pieces of cloth and elastic sewn together." While athletic supporters are basically the same, Protexion make sure they adjust their products to suit the sports and consumers in each country.

Protexion diversified both into other countries and markets through the 1960s and 1970s. In the late 1960s the firm's former owner Hugh Kent sought entry into Japan. Ackerman says Kent was interested in Japan's market at least partly because he was adventurous and "wanted to go to Japan." Kent lined up his Japanese distributor through his European contacts, with whom he had built strong working ties.

During this period Protexion also entered the North American markets for high quality hockey pants and other equipment. These markets require expertise and distribution channel contact similar to those needed in the athletic supporter trade. For example, Protexion now has a dominant share of Canadian life jacket sales. This opportunity was created when they combined their design and production capability with a gap in the market. They saw a demand for a range of jackets, in different colors and styles. At the time, most of the available product was bulky and orange. They plan to enter more markets, confident that Canada's strict safety standards will ease approval processes in other countries.

Protexion continues its drive to learn and innovate. They worked closely with their Japanese distributor to develop hockey equipment to suit the smaller frames of most Japanese players. In that market as well, they take special steps to efficiently ship the small lots needed by Japan's space-limited retailers. Both in Canada and the United States, they have expanded their Protex line to offer a range of branded products, some produced by other suppliers. Wal-Mart has become a major conduit for Protex goods. Protexion monitors and replenishes its stock directly store-by-store by connecting to the retailer's information system. This is not a great stretch for a firm accustomed to shipping small lots overseas.

E. Bartek Ingredients

Bartek started as a chemical distributor in 1969. About 10 years later they became a manufacturer first of malic, and later fumaric, acid which are common food additives. These two product markets were attractive to a small producer because neither offer the economies of scale large makers depend on. Malic and fumaric acids, though demanded by many customers, are only used in small lots. As well their chemical production processes are temperamental and take considerable effort to learn.

The founding partners took about four years to learn how to make the additives. They started working in a "hole in our backyard," recalls one founding partner. Between 1979 and 1981, Bartek had to rebuild its plant three times. Their intention from the start was to go international, because they knew Canadian demand would soon be filled.

Their first foreign step was not to sell in the United States, but rather to Europe. This move was aimed at developing their exporting competence in a market with smaller stakes. They did not want to risk their reputation as a reliable supplier in the United States. Once they became experienced selling abroad, and confident in their ability to consistently supply high quality product, they went into the United States, which now takes nearly half of Bartek's output. Fortuitously for them, just as they made forays into the United States, a main competitor's factory "blew up," and another one closed, leaving U.S. food processors desperate for product.

Bartek's activities in Japan show the firm's strategic international motives. The company was interested in Japan because it is home to its largest world competitor. Bartek wanted to learn, on the ground, how this competitor operated domestically, so they could understand them better in third markets. So, one of the firm partners, Mr. Joop den Baars met his competitors during his initial visit to that country in 1985. Bartek first worked with a large general trading company.

Four years after entering Japan, Bartek sought another agent who would take a longer view of the market. After a nearly year-long search, Bartek began working with a Japanese manufacturer. Three years later, a chemical trading company 75 percent owned by the same manufacturer took responsibility for distributing Bartek's additives in Japan.

Bartek is a committed exporter, serving a niche market in more than 30 countries. One of the partners drove the export process, though recently Bartek hired a full time person to work on foreign market development. Distributors are critical to Bartek. This shown by the representative's comment, "I want distributors, not traders. Distributors are interested in market share and other long run issues. Traders only look at the deal." Bartek selects, through interviews, only people who are nationals in the markets served. This reduces conflicts across markets and motivates distributors to focus on building their own markets.

F. CRS Robotics

CRS Robotics originated at McMaster University's (Ontario) engineering school in 1981. Three of CRS's founders had developed a low cost small robot for student use. When CRS was formed with the fourth partner, current chairman Raymond Simmons, the idea was to produce inexpensive robots for the education market. They soon found out though that pharmaceutical laboratories had a special demand for their product, because it was reasonably priced and could be used to handle potentially hazardous biological materials.

CRS launched its first commercial product at a Toronto CAD/CAM and robotics show in 1985, after nearly four years of development. They soon went international, using distributors. Key sales were made in the United States and then Europe, especially Germany and the United Kingdom. Their relationship with their German distributor started when he came to Canada one week after they issued a German press release. Their second German distributor was later turned into a CRS subsidiary.

As CRS sold in more markets, they developed a formal process for choosing distributors. CRS demanded they be "established," a good fit, and willing to invest at least $30,000 to learn how to service the robots. The latter is especially critical in CRS's case, because as Simmons puts it "You just can't take one of our robots out of the box, plug it in, and use it." The product needs to be fine-tuned to its task and environment.

CRS looked into Japan after they were approached by a distributor from that country at a 1989 New Orleans trade show. They made their first sale in 1991 after a successful Osaka product launch. Unfortunately they eventually discovered that their first Japanese distributor was not willing to devote sufficient resources to learning about their product. By late 1992, they had built a relationship with another firm which both manufactures and sells related products. This tie worked better, especially as CRS made special efforts to build a close personal relationship with the firm's owner. For example, CRS hosted his son for about a year in Canada and also sent an engineer to Japan for a while.

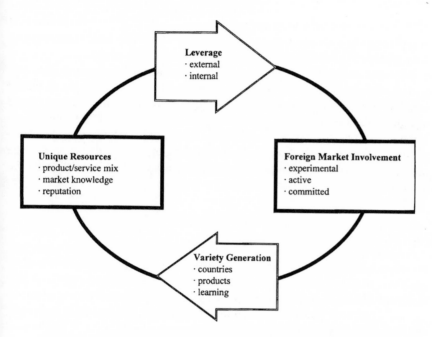

Figure 1. An Entrepreneurial Model of SME Internationalization

CRS's Japanese sales under the new distributor were good for several years. They sold robots to manufacturers, laboratories, and even a cake maker, for icing. However, Japan's recession hit hard, severely harming equipment sales, especially those of foreign makers. CRS though used their position in Japan to sell elsewhere. A key outcome of their Japanese experience was learning to design a robust flexible product. For example, they now make robots that use 100v electrical sources as in Japan, as well as the 110v standard in North America. Further, their Japanese customer's insistence on quality led them to secure ISO certification. The other key benefit of selling in Japan was to increase CRS's reputation as a high quality producer, like in the Sunset Neon case above. The fact they have sold in Japan, home to the world's leading robot makers, gives them legitimacy in third markets.

V. THE MODEL

We analyzed the six cases above using Eisenhardt's (1989) framework to produce the model shown in Figure 1. This model builds on the earlier work of Johanson and Vahlne (1977, 1990) in particular, as well as that on the importance of firm resources (for example, Barney 1991; Oliver 1997). The six cases suggest the need to extend this work to more explicitly include the entrepreneurial functions of leveraging and generating variety. These two entrepreneurial functions add a more dynamic element, in the sense that the movement from one state of market commitment to another is triggered by the two entrepreneurial activities. Our analysis also identified two modifying environmental variables, the domestic industry sector's capacity relative to the domestic market size, and the level of market accessibility.

Below we first describe the four core aspects of our model. We then show how it unfolds using evidence from the six firms studied here. For clarity, we describe the effects of the modifying variables in the "Discussion" section following the analysis.

A. Unique Resources

A company's unique resources are those which provide competitive advantage, its ability to offer a desired package of differentiation, quality, and price in its products and/or services (Hymer 1976; Barney 1991; Oliver 1997). These resources comprise a firm's resource and institutional capital (Oliver 1997), or "owner-specific advantages" (Dunning 1991), which are a combination of the physical, human, and organizational factors available to the firm. A firm's competitive advantage will be sustainable if its resource package is not easily acquired or imitated, and the firm's institutional context promotes the effective development and deployment of the resources it has access to (Oliver 1997).

In our study the initial set of resources often reflected superior product design, product or processing. However a key finding is that this initial set of resources was quickly expanded to include reputation developed through dealing with difficult markets. This meant the firm's exports contributed both to foreign and domestic sales.

Three key resources relevant to all models of internationalization are the firm's product/service mix, market knowledge, foreign business management ability (Johanson and Vahlne 1990; Aaby and Slater 1989), and reputation. An innovative mix occurs when an entrepreneur combines resources in a novel (Schumpeter 1968) or gap-filling (Kirzner 1985; Cheah 1990) way to produce the unique products associated with high levels of export commitment (Aaby and Slater 1989; Cavusgil and Nevin 1981). Market knowledge, which includes familiarity with marketing channels and distributors (Dunning 1991, p. 27), generates business opportunities and lowers uncertainty, enabling firms to increase their commitment to foreign markets (Johanson and Vahlne 1990). This type of knowledge is a source of sustained advantage because it is gained through experience (Johanson and Vahlne 1990), so is not readily acquired by other firms.

Firms seeking new markets must convince potential customers that they are credible and can deliver the goods and services they promise (Ganesan 1994). Though buyers can learn through trial and error, they would prefer to avoid the latter when costs are significant. Therefore exporters can facilitate overseas sales by establishing a reputation for competence, a type of "institutional capital" (Oliver 1997), by demonstrating their competence in competitive markets.

B. Leveraging

Having unique resources is a necessary, but not sufficient condition of entrepreneurial activity. Firms also need to leverage these resources so they can enter new markets (Tiessen 1997). Leverage enables firms to "pursue opportunities without regard to the resources they already control" (Stevenson and Jarillo 1990, p. 23). Hamel and Pralahad (1993, p. 78) describe this process as "creating stretch, a misfit between resources and ambition." Such an approach to management contrasts with an administrative stance which focuses primarily on deploying the resources at hand.

Entrepreneurs can get more out of their own resources by fostering teamwork and motivating themselves and workers with challenges (Hamel and Pralahad 1993; Stewart 1989). As well, they can gain the use of external resources, especially those of other organizations through networks and alliances (Jarillo 1989; Hamel and Pralahad 1993; Zacharakis 1998). These mechanisms are critical to SMEs which often use agents, distributors, or cooperative strategies because they typically cannot afford to own distribution networks. Governments, through export promotion programs, act to facilitate exports, especially those of small and medium businesses, by extending SME resources.

The entrepreneurial focus on leverage contrasts with the approaches to opportunity pursuit undertaken by two types of comparable non-entrepreneurial firms. The first type, larger administrative-focused companies (Stevenson and Gumpert 1985), allocate existing resources to their international activities. The other, non-entrepreneurial SMEs, dismiss overseas opportunities because they are not moved to assemble the necessary resources.

C. Market Involvement

The concept of market involvement, the second state, comes primarily from the research which identifies several levels of firm commitment to exporting, as discussed earlier (e.g., see Leonidou and Katsikeas 1996). We use Cavusgil's (1984) three categories in our model because they are conceptually clear and succinct. "Experimental involvement" is when companies act as passive exporters, filling unsolicited orders on an ad hoc basis. The next stage is "active involvement" when senior management formally recognizes the importance of exports, and firms begin to tailor their product and marketing efforts to foreign consumers. The last stage, "committed involvement" describe firms who prospect in several countries, and have reduced the distinction between domestic and foreign markets. The most committed firms, especially those that deal in products and services which have a high knowledge component, may invest in foreign facilities. If firms are very concerned about the dissipation of their firm-specific knowledge assets, they may in fact choose to enter foreign markets through foreign direct investment rather than exporting (Rugman 1980). Companies may, due to factors such as resource shortages or shifts in market importance, move to lower levels of commitment in certain markets (Calof and Beamish 1995).

Companies tend to progress through these stages as their foreign activities both demonstrate the benefits of exporting and help develop their market knowledge and export capability (Johanson and Vahlne 1990). However, if entrepreneurs have sufficient knowledge at the time of startup, they may skip the "experimental" stage and become "active" from the start (McDougall, Shane, and Oviatt 1994; McDougall and Oviatt 1996). This was a key finding of Reuber and Fischer's (1997) study of Canadian software companies which found that the international experience of top management teams was positively related to the speed at which their companies entered foreign markets.

D. Generating Variety

Generating variety is firm activity which develops its capacity to enter new markets. Companies do this by both making and finding opportunities which arise through either Schumpeterian "new combination" innovations or Kirzian gaps in markets, as discussed above (Cheah 1990). Specifically, generating variety has three aspects: entering (1) geographic and (2) product markets, and (3) learning. The latter refers to developing market and exporting knowledge by gaining experience (Johanson and Vahlne 1977, 1990). Most of the processes associated with generating variety involve generic marketing activities, such as differentiation and research, because like all firms, exporters need to identify and meet demand for their output. What differentiates the entrepreneurial from others is that the former are constantly engaged in creating innovative product-market combinations.

It is critical to stress that variety generation does not occur merely through exporting; managers need to maintain an entrepreneurial approach to ensure the knowledge is captured and used. Important market knowledge is related primarily to the processes of finding good distributors, understanding consumer needs and executing product or service delivery from a distance. Firms also can identify opportunities as they make changes in their product/service mix to address the needs of consumers in different types of markets.

VI.   THE MODEL IN ACTION

The entrepreneurial processes drive SME internationalization. Companies already resource-constrained may be reluctant to subject themselves to the costs

Table 2. Internationalization of Six Canadian SMEs

Company	Unique Resources	Leverage Mechanisms	Stages of Commitment Reached	Variety Generation † countries, ‡ products § learning
Sunset	• sign design and production • Japan reputation	• consortium	• experimental	† US
Canadiana	• raw material supply • manufacturing and design ability • package assembly • Germany reputation	• industry association • government	• committed	† Europe, Japan ‡ adaptation § foreign agent management
Fjord	• raw material supply • processing quality and cost	• agents	• experimental • active	† Australia, US, Japan, Europe § export skills
Protexion	• patent and trademark • product development & manufacturing	• licencees • distributors	• experimental • active • committed	† Europe, Japan ‡ adaptation § customizing for distance customers; delivery
Bartek	• manufacturing process • reliability	• distributors	• active • committed	† 30 countries § distributor selection, product delivery
CRS Robotics	• product • cost • service and reliability • Japan reputation	• distributors	• active •committed	† Europe, Japan § distributor selection, long distance service

and uncertainty inherent in markets which are geographically and culturally distant (Johanson and Vahlne 1990). An entrepreneurial stance though leads decision-makers to focus on spotting opportunities and assembling the means to exploit them, rather than on attendant risks and potential losses. Such a stance is consistent with the positive approach to risk demonstrated by successful export firm managers in the research cited above (e.g., Aaby and Slater 1989). All six companies exhibited a strong entrepreneurial stance: they leveraged their domestic capability internationally, though to much different degrees.

SME internationalization unfolds in the following fashion. Firms first develop unique resources which are leveraged into foreign markets. This leads to greater stages of foreign commitment and more generation of variety which in turn creates more unique firm resources, starting the cycle again. Next we illustrate the model's features and dynamics by analyzing the internationalization processes of the six firms studied. This analysis is summarized in Table 2.

A. Unique Resources

The cases demonstrate that exporters have a broad range of unique resource mixes which enable them to compete internationally. Most of the firms developed their reputations through their overseas activities, so their exports contributed both to foreign and domestic sales.

Two of the companies described here started with a tangible unique idea, Protexion's athletic supporter design and CRS's low cost small robots. Bartek's unique resource on the other hand, was its mastery of a production process and small lot delivery for a niche. The three smaller firms offered more complex mixes. Fjord and Canadiana add value to traditional Canadian exports, seafood and wood, in which Canada has a competitive cost advantage. Canadiana and Sunset are both nimble small firms able to execute complex custom orders efficiently.

It is notable that all but Fjord found the positive reputations developed through their overseas activities supported their marketing efforts in other countries. By being able to bear up to stiff competition in Japan's sign and robot markets, Sunset Neon and CRS became known as top level producers. This is especially important for these companies because their applications require significant customization. Canadiana, similarly, uses its ability to negotiate Germany's rigorous standard to sell in other house markets. Bartek valued its reputation so much that it delayed selling in the United States until they had a record selling in Europe. Protexion, the oldest and largest firm, had established its reputation through its trademarks and patents. Fjord, in contrast, amongst the group, is closest to operating in a commodity business, so does not depend on this resource as much as the other firms.

B. Leveraging

All of the firms used cooperative strategies to leverage their resources. The type of approach to stretching their resources varied by firm however, and some firms have shifted their approach with time and experience. The case studies overall suggest that government plays a limited role in leveraging SME resources.

Protexion began in the pre-free trade period by using licensees, and then distributors in foreign markets. This was possible because they had a patented product and trademark. Fjord and Bartek both work with distributors in foreign markets because they do not have the resources to concentrate on each market.

Distributors were vital to CRS's export thrust. This was important because robots are complex products and require effective follow-up service. This led to

em developing a rigorous selection process which required partners to commit
ınsiderable resources to the relationship. These close ties evolved into direct
vestments by CRS to form subsidiaries in Europe. These subsidiaries facilitated
e secure transfer of knowledge from Canada to European markets.

Sunset and Canadiana, both small firms, also used collective approaches to
wer risks and costs. Sunset took part in a consortium in Japan, which lowered its
sk, yet gave them access to another market. This was not unusual for them
:cause large jobs in North America develop in the same manner. Canadiana,
ough, adopted a deliberate strategy tailored for exporting, forming the manufac-
red housing association. The owner, Mayer, knew that fellow association mem-
:rs would benefit from pooling their resources and reputations in world markets.
his effort was assisted by the Canadian government which is eager to foster both
ports and small business.

The Canadiana case suggests governments can play a key role in helping SMEs
:tend their resources. Canadiana and its counterparts were supported by efforts
foster their association, as just mentioned. The government, in addition, acted
reduce trade barriers, such as the lumber approval standards in Japan. They
ve also produced market reports which are used by exporters. Even Japan's
vernment, through its semi-governmental agency JETRO, contributed to train-
g Canadiana for that market. These government efforts were effective because
anada has a supplier advantage and there is sufficient clientele to warrant
forts.

The other firms, in contrast, did not expect government to play a significant
le. For example, Sunset did not use the government funding it was offered later
explore other markets, because the firm was pre-occupied with its U.S. activi-
:s. Fjord, Bartek and CRS have used Canadian government and consulate
urces to identify possible distributors. All said that while overall they were not
ssatisfied, the assistance received varied greatly with the initiative of the indi-
dual providing it.

C. Market Involvement

The firms in our study have reached different levels of export involvement and
ken different routes to do so. Protexion was the only one which evolved from
perimental to active to committed stages, in the fashion predicted by incremen-
l models. This is because it internationalized during a more restrictive trading
vironment. For the others, it was unlikely they would begin as experimental
porters because they were too small to attract unsolicited orders. Only two
rms, Canadiana and Protexion, made substantial adjustments in their products to
it foreign needs.

Sunset Neon, the smallest firm, took an experimental approach, "piggyback-
g" (Terpstra and Yu 1990) on a consortium doing work in Japan. They have
mained at that stage, and are focusing on the neighboring U.S. market which

offers them sufficient sales. Fjord, though they export substantially, have un
now stayed as active exporters, are becoming more committed and prospecting
other markets. They may need to adapt more to different markets because they a
near-commodity exporters facing significant cost competition.

Bartek, CRS, and Canadiana all skipped the experimental stage of export cor
mitment. All three knew from the outset that the Canadian market could not su
port their business goals. This was especially the case for Bartek and CRS whi
produce niche products and now have significant world market shares in their sp
cific segments. Bartek's product, additives, is straight forward in its use, so the
do not feel compelled to support their distribution with foreign direct investmen
CRS's robots, in contrast, can require significant post-sale service so that firm h
invested in securing a reliable presence in their key overseas markets.

Canadiana went directly to the committed stage of exporting. This strategy w
required in their sector which competes with producers in several countries. The
strategy of linking with other Canadian producers to market their homes intern
tionally helped differentiate them in world markets, and associate their produ
with Canada's reputation as a wood producer.

D. Generating Variety

All six firms sustained their competitive positions by finding opportunities
new product and geographic markets, and developing their unique resources.
key capability learned was the ability to select and manage long distance ties w
distributors. Further, as mentioned above, the experience of some firms selling
tough markets has strengthened their reputation. Together this has allowed mo
of the firms to successfully sell in other markets, and increase their position
current ones. Most of the firms, except Canadiana and Protexion of course, se
fairly standard products which serve fairly standard needs. The firms to son
degree all generated variety through their activities, and transformed their lear
ing into more unique resources, starting the cycle again.

Protexion over 40 years has become an international marketer, and developed
broad line of sporting goods to serve several markets. They have learned how
service many types of buyers from a distance. For example, they develop
hockey equipment prototypes with their Japanese buyer, and learned to deliv
small shipments to the small shops in that market. Protexion, while committed
exporting, focuses on selling in the United States, which has proven to be a lucr
tive market.

Bartek's owners deliberately set out to learn from their overseas experienc
They first proved themselves capable of producing and serving European marke
before taking on the role as supplier to major US food processors. They ha
become proficient exporters, selling in more than 30 countries. A key to their su
cess, beyond product quality, has been their ability to select and offer effecti
service to their overseas distributors.

CRS similarly built their market serving ability through their exports. The disibutor selection process they developed was critical to their offshore success, ecause their product needs special installation and maintenance services. Failure) uphold that end of the transaction would have spelled failure. They also apply :ssons learned across all markets. A key one is the importance of frank communication which is needed to identify problems before they become critical. CRS's ophisticated product sells in the world's richest markets, North America, Europe nd Japan, all regions with substantial pharmaceutical companies.

Fjord has only recently taken significant steps to generate variety. Until then leir long term Australian, Japanese and European ties were seen as sufficient. he loss of a major U.S. customer though has shifted their focus to looking at ther Asian markets. The key market knowledge they have acquired also is how) work with distributors. As they become more active in new Asian markets they re becoming more experienced in the distributor selection process.

Canadiana's overseas experience has turned them into very proficient exportrs. They have learned how to produce customized work at a distance for very different market types, Germany and Japan. A key skill they developed was ecoming a good listener, and being responsive to customer demands as conveyed y their distributors. This allows them to adapt their product for different emands. As mentioned earlier, they gained a good reputation in Europe by being ble to address Germany's building codes, again from a distance. They now focus n three markets, Germany, Japan and Spain, and for now will continue to ecause they are currently limited by the small size of their firm.

Sunset has not entered any new country or product markets since their first verseas sale. The reason is, as mentioned above, they have ample opportunities nmediately available in the more convenient U.S. market. They are, though, pen to further consortium deals overseas. This is a sensible strategy for the firm s it stands now. However, if they wish to expand substantially they could be posioned to deliver to distant markets and capitalize on what they learned selling in apan.

VII. DISCUSSION

)ur model offers a generalizable, dynamic view of how SMEs expand their activies into international markets. Overall, our two main claims are that the level of)reign market involvement is positively associated with the (1) initial state of nique product and market servicing resources, and (2) the degree of entrepreeurship practiced by a firm. These relationships are modified by the size of the omestic market relative to the firm's capacity and the level of market accessibily. The latter term refers to the degree of market protectionism and logistic diffiulty of serving customers in a country. These links can be seen by briefly revising the case data.

The Protexion case highlights the effects of the modifying variables because of its long history and the sector in which it operates. Protexion did have a unique resource, its patented athletic supporter, which enabled them to take on international apparel/sporting equipment markets. However, protectionist policies in the pre-World War II period caused them to license this patent in these poorly accessible markets, rather than export. The growing openness of western economies in the 1950s and 1960s allowed them to sell a made-in-Canada product, increasing their commitment to foreign markets. Protexion, driven by an entrepreneurial owner in the 1970s, continued to grow by generating variety. They developed new products, based on their sewing and design ability, and entered other overseas markets, such as Japan, as they built their export skills. But, only 10% of their sales are outside North America. This is because the market for their main products, hockey and other sports equipment, is relatively large in Canada and the United States.

The firms with the lowest levels of overseas commitment were Sunset Neon ("experimental") and Fjord Pacific ("active"). Sunset Neon is for now at the "experimental" level because its capability, making signs, is not internationally unique and they have practiced moderate levels of entrepreneurial behavior. Their "American" cache, and cost competitiveness, in concert with the leverage of the consortium allowed them to work in Japan. However, they are now content to seek modest growth in the nearer U.S. market. This is because the logistics associated with designing, shipping, and building signs are simpler in a neighboring market. As well, the U.S. offers vast opportunities relative to their size.

Fjord's capability to make processed seafood is relatively more unique in world markets, because less countries produce salmon and herring in commercial quantities. This means the relative demand for Fjord's product is greater outside North America than it is for Sunset's signs. So, despite not undertaking high levels of leverage and variety generation, they have reached an "active" level of exporting.

The three other cases analyzed, Bartek, CRS Robotics and Canadiana, were instant internationals. Bartek and CRS both had unique resources, Bartek's manufacturing capability and CRS's robot size and cost, made them world leaders in their segments. Both needed overseas markets because the North American demand they face is, though significant, relatively limited for their niche product. Bartek and CRS both leveraged their resources by using distributors, and continued to generate variety as they established their reputations and deliberately learned from their overseas sales and service experiences. CRS, because it has foreign subsidiaries, may seem more internationally committed than Bartek. However, this difference is largely because robots require more before and after sales service, which is difficult to properly provide at a great distance. The main logistic issue faced by Bartek, in contrast, is efficient delivery.

Canadiana, on the other hand, is a different, more unlikely instant international. In some respects it resembles Fjord, because one of its unique resources is its supply of domestic raw materials, Canadian lumber. But unlike the fish processor

Canadiana operates in markets rendered quite inaccessible by building codes and logistical problems of designing and building at a distance. Further, the North American market for wood homes is very large for Canada's manufactured home sector. Canadiana, however, overcame these factors by undertaking high levels of entrepreneurial behaviors. The owner employed leverage via the trade association he helped found, and converted a market barrier, the need to comply with German's building regulations, into a resource used for further sales. This, and his learning on serving overseas markets augmented his original resources which he leveraged these into more markets.

VIII. IMPLICATIONS FOR MANAGERS

Our model of internationalization identifies the key issues faced by SMEs thinking of expanding their business overseas. It does this by offering guidelines in response to two key questions: (1) How much should we commit to foreign markets? and (2) How can we increase our chances of success? The answers to both are related strongly to the level of entrepreneurship practiced.

All firms, not only exporters, require unique resources if they are to survive in the markets they serve. Those wishing to exploit these resources in foreign markets though must also have the willingness to grow by effectively leveraging these resources, typically but not always by using intermediaries. If a firm has a very unique product/service for which there is limited domestic demand and faces relatively accessible markets, they may very quickly go international. It should be noted, however, that an owner who takes extraordinary steps in terms of leveraging these resources and generating variety, may overcome export-inhibiting conditions. If a firm does not possess an entrepreneurial stance, and/or there are profitable and more accessible domestic markets to tackle, they may make sufficient profits without going overseas.

To succeed as exporters, SMEs must conscientiously, and continuously generate variety by converting their experience into further resources and seeking other market opportunities. The core skills identified in these cases were the abilities to identify and work with agents and distributors and to address problems of providing service at a distance. Most successful firms will not rest easy. Those seeking further expansion will seek to leverage these newly created resources into higher levels of foreign market involvement and actively accumulate more resources, such as a reputation, needed to expand or maintain their position in competitive world markets.

IX. CONCLUSION

The paper reports on six Canadian case studies which were analyzed to produce an entrepreneurial model of SME internationalization. This model highlights the linkages between unique resources, leveraging, market commitment and variety generation. Although all phases are important, the novel contribution of this paper is the incorporation of the two entrepreneurial functions, leveraging and variety generation. These two functions are the catalysts or triggers which enable higher states of market commitment to be reached. As such the paper contributes to building theory at the intersection of international business and entrepreneurship, as proposed by Brush (1995).

Further, our approach accounts for the instant international firm, because it does not presume an evolutionary approach. Firms may jump up and down stages of commitment, depending on their unique resources and approaches to leverage and variety generation.

Although the paper provides a preliminary account of the role of leveraging and variety generation as critical elements of SME internationalization process, more research is needed on these functions. For example, Table 2 shows that leveraging is associated with different types of strategic alliances. However, in some cases it transpires in a more spontaneous way, like Protexion's move to Japan. As well, variations in the sources of leverage in SME internationalization warrant further study. Similarly, more research could reveal how SMEs learn, or not learn, through their international experience.

Future investigations would also more widely sharpen and test the generalizability of the constructs unearthed in the current study. A broader survey of firms, ideally in more than one country, could confirm that the model offers a reasonable representation of the SME internationalization process. The results could then be brought back to another series of case studies.

Today's competitive global economy has room for good SMEs. To survive however, these firms must exploit their entrepreneurial qualities, because they do not have the market power of large multinationals. Our model helps us identify how the key entrepreneurial functions, leverage and variety generation, contribute to firms creating competitive advantage through their unique resources and building greater commitment to foreign markets. These functions, practiced by firm entrepreneur/founders must be fostered if firms are to contribute more to the export performance of nations.

REFERENCES

Aaby, N., and S. F. Slater. 1989. "Management Influences on Export Performance: A Review of the Empirical Literature." *International Marketing Review* 6(4): 7-26.

Amit, R., L. Glosten, and E. Muller. 1993. "Challenges to Theory Development in Entrepreneurship Research." *Journal of Management Studies* 30(5): 815-834.

Barney, J. 1991. "Firm Resources and Sustained Competitive Advantage." *Journal of Management* 17(1): 99-120.

Beamish, P.W., R. Craig, and K. McLellan. 1993. "The Performance Characteristics of Canadian Versus U.K. Exporters in Small and Medium Sized Firms." *Management International Review* 33(2): 121-137.

Bilkey, W.J. 1978. "An Attempted Integration of the Literature on the Export Behavior of Firms." *Journal of International Business Studies* 9(1): 33-46.

Brush, C.G. 1995. *International Entrepreneurship: The Effect of Firm Age on Motives for Internationalization.* New York: Garland.

Calof, J. L. 1994. "The Relationship Between Firm Size and Export Behavior Revisited." *Journal of International Business Studies* 25: 367-387.

Calof, J., and P. W. Beamish. 1995. "Adapting to Foreign Markets: Explaining Internationalization." *International Business Review* 4(2): 115-131.

Carland, J. W., F. Hoy, W. R. Boulton, and J. A. C. Carland. 1984. "Differentiating Entrepreneurs from Small Business Owners: A Conceptualization." *Academy of Management Review* 9(2): 354-459.

Cavusgil, S. T. 1984. "Differences Among Exporting Firms Based on Their Degree of Internationalization." *Journal of Business Research* 12: 195-208.

Cavusgil, S. T., and V. H. Kirpalani. 1993. "Introducing Products into Export Markets: Success Factors." *Journal of Business Research* 27: 1-15.

Cavusgil, S. T., and J. R. Nevin. 1981. "Internal Determinants of Export Marketing Behavior: An Empirical Investigation." *Journal of Marketing Research* 28: 114-119.

Cheah, H. 1990. "Schumpetarian and Austrian Entrepreneurship: Unity Within Duality." *Journal of Business Venturing* 5: 341-347.

Dunning, J. H. 1991. *Explaining International Production.* London: HarperCollins.

Eisenhardt, K. M. 1989. "Building Theories from Case Study Research." *Academy of Management Review* 14: 532-550.

Ganesan, S. 1994. "Determinants of Long Term Orientation in Buyer-Seller Relationships." *Journal of Marketing* 58: 1-19.

Hamel, G., and C. K. Pralahad. 1993. "Strategy as Stretch and Leverage." *Harvard Business Review* 71(2): 75-84.

Holzmüller, H. H., and H. Kasper. 1991. "On a Theory of Export Performance: Personal and Organizational Determinants of Export Trade Activities Observed in Small and Medium-sized Firms." *Management International Review* 31 (Special Issue): 45-70.

Hymer, S. H. 1976. *The International Operations of National Firms: A Study of Direct Investment.* Cambridge, MA: MIT Press.

Industry Canada. 1996. *Small Business in Canada: A Statistical Overview.* Ottawa: Industry Canada.

Jarillo, J. C. 1989. "Entrepreneurship and Growth: The Strategic Use of External Resources." *Journal of Business Venturing* 4: 133-147.

Johanson, J., and J. Vahlne. 1977. "The Internationalization Process of the Firm—A Model of Knowledge Development and Increasing Foreign Market Commitment." *Journal of International Business Studies* 8(1): 23-32.

Johanson, J., and J. Vahlne. 1990. "The Mechanism of Internationalization." *International Marketing Review* 7(4): 11-24.

Kilby, P. 1971. "Hunting the Heffalump." Pp. 1-40 in *Entrepreneurship and Economic Development,* edited by P. Kilby. New York: Free Press.

Kirzner, I. M. 1985. *Discovery and the Capitalist Process.* Chicago: University of Chicago Press.

Leonidou, C. L. and C. S. Katsikeas. 1996. "The Export Development Process: An Integrative Review of Empirical Models." *Journal of International Business Studies* 27(3): 517-551.

McDougall, P. P., S. Shane and B. M. Oviatt. 1994. "Explaining the Formation of International New Ventures: The Limits of Theories from International Business Research." *Journal of Business Venturing* 9: 469-487.

McDougall, P. P., and B. M. Oviatt. 1996. "New Venture Internationalization, Strategic Change, and Performance: A Follow-up Study." *Journal of Business Venturing* 11: 23-40.

Miller, D. 1983. "The Correlates of Entrepreneurship in Three Types of Firms." *Management Science* 29: 770-791.

Oliver, C. 1997. "Sustainable Competitive Advantage: Combining Institutional and Resource-based Views." *Strategic Management Journal* 18(9): 697-713.

Reuber, A. R., and E. Fischer. 1997. "The Influence of the Management Team's International Experience on the Internationalization Behaviors of SMES." *Journal of International Business Studies* 28(4): 807-825.

Rugman, A. M. 1980. "A New Theory of the Multinational Enterprise: Internationalization versus Internalization." *Columbia Journal of World Business* 15(1): 23-29.

Schumpeter, J. A. 1968. *The Theory of Economic Development*. Cambridge, MA: Harvard University Press.

Stevenson, H. H., and D. E. Gumpert. 1985. "The Heart of Entrepreneurship." *Harvard Business Review* 63(2): 85-94.

Stevenson, H. H., and J. C. Jarillo. 1990. "A Paradigm of Entrepreneurship." *Strategic Management Journal* 11: 17-27.

Stewart, A. 1989. *Team Entrepreneurship*. Newbury Park, CA: Sage.

Terpstra, V., and D. J. Yu. 1990. "Piggybacking: A Quick Road to Internationalisation." *International Marketing Review* 7(4): 52-63.

Tiessen, J. H. 1997. "Individualism, Collectivism, and Entrepreneurship: A Framework for International Comparative Research." *Journal of Business Venturing* 12(5): 367-384.

UNCTAD (United Nations Conference on Trade and Development). 1993. *Small and Medium Transnational Corporations*. New York: United Nations.

Wiedersheim-Paul, F., H. C. Olson, and L. S. Welch. 1978. "Pre-Export Activity: The First Step in Internalization." *Journal of International Business Studies* 9(1): 47-48.

Zacharakis, A. L. 1998. "Entrepreneurial Entry into Foreign Markets: A Transaction Cost Perspective." *Entrepreneurship Theory and Practice* 21(3): 23-39.

PART IV

THE GLOBAL FIRM OF THE FUTURE

PROFILING THE TWENTY-FIRST-CENTURY KNOWLEDGE ENTERPRISE

Len Korot and George Tovstiga

I. INTRODUCTION

As we move into the Network Age, organizations are placing high priority on understanding and managing their knowledge-based intangible assets such as technological know-how and innovation. Firms are realizing that there is no sustainable advantage other than what they know, and how quickly they can learn something new. People-embodied knowledge has become the only meaningful resource in the new networked society, irrevocably replacing Industrial Age factors of production such as labor, capital and land (Drucker 1993).

The new Network Age is characterized by the proliferation of "knowledge enterprises." In the Silicon Valley alone, 1,500 new ventures were launched in 1997. This new generation of entrepreneurially driven SME's are unrestrained by historical models of organization and strategy. Rapid advances in technology are creating a boundaryless world. Increasingly, sophisticated computer software, accompanied by leaps in chip development and bandwidth, is exerting an unprec-

Research in Global Strategic Management, Volume 7, pages 157-172.
Copyright © 1999 by JAI Press Inc.
All rights of reproduction in any form reserved.
ISBN: 0-7623-0458-8

edented impact on the pace of business all over the globe. The Internet has become the major vehicle for information transfer, communication, commerce, and cross-boundary problem solving, thus creating extraordinary opportunities for the creation of new ventures.

These new ventures are erasing the traditional, textbook model of incremental internationalization in which companies solidify their domestic market before cautiously moving into carefully selected foreign markets (Oviatt & McDougal 1998). Knowledge-based services and products are being created and launched throughout the globe by new and existing high-technology SMEs. Cross-national strategic alliances and mergers among SMEs are becoming commonplace, no longer the exclusive domain of major multinationals.

Thus, major economic discontinuities such as the one currently driven by the surge in new technologies are allowing new, key drivers of sustainable competitiveness to emerge. Knowledge is quickly becoming *the* key determinant of competitive advantage in enterprises *of all sizes*. Justifiably, we can now already discern the emergence of a new *Knowledge Economy*.

We argue that as we move into the new Knowledge Economy, most traditional management constructs and approaches to management need to be challenged and much of our thinking on what constitutes competitiveness in the new economy will need to be reframed. A case in point involves the notion of protection of intellectual assets: Recognizing that most of the firm's truly competitive knowledge resides in its tacit realm—which therefore makes it inherently difficult to access, replicate and transfer—the notion of "protecting the firm's intellectual assets" takes on an entirely new meaning. The traditional fear that a firm's competitive position is jeopardized through the exchange of competitive knowledge within strategic alliances and networks becomes largely baseless when we recognize that the knowledge-based enterprise's real competitive position is—at least from a knowledge perspective—largely well protected. The firm's real determinants of competitiveness are, in fact, highly complex, multifaceted and therefore as difficult to capture and transfer as it is to transfer knowledge from the tacit to the explicit realm. In fact, quite the opposite may be at stake. According to one of the prime corollaries of the new, networked Knowledge Economy, the "law of increasing returns," value explodes with sharing. Firms, which are reluctant to share and exchange knowledge, are punished in the new, networked economy. Evidently, more and more small and medium-sized firms are grasping the strategic implications of networking, as is shown by the growing number of dynamic business networks and alliances in various industry sectors. Size of firm becomes increasingly irrelevant in this context. Indeed, even many large firms are increasingly functioning as networked satellites rather than as centralized behemoths.

The purpose of this chapter is to provide a framework for deepening our understanding of the twenty-first-century knowledge enterprise. We begin by examining the way in which it manages its knowledge base, its internal culture infrastructure, and its management practices. At a deeper level, we will then proceed to look at the role(s) played by the knowledge worker in the knowledge-based firm. The concepts and insights presented in this paper are drawn from our on-going research with a select group of pace-setting enterprises.

A. The Network Age Enterprise

From time to time, new management challenges emerge that have no precedent. Managing the emerging networked age enterprise, we feel, rightly deserves this distinction. This new era is emerging in the wake of unprecedented technologically and socioeconomically driven change. It is ushering in its own new rules and distinct opportunities (Kelly 1997), while at the same time clearly showing up deficiencies of existing organizational forms and practices. Throughout, managing knowledge assets has become the major organizational imperative. The payoff to managing knowledge astutely, Teece (1998) points out, has significantly been amplified due in part to (a) the phenomena of increasing returns; (b) new information and communication technologies; and (c) the changing role and positioning of intellectual property. Competition and competitive advantage are being dramatically redefined as a result of these developments.

Indeed, Amidon (1997) points out that the knowledge-intensive organization is more appropriately viewed from the perspective of a "strategic business network" (SBN) rather than the traditional "strategic business unit" (SBU). What are the organizational imperatives driving the emergence of the new networked organization? Bahrami and Evans (1987) suggest that in the emerging network age, technologies, markets, and competitors are in a state of perpetual flux. Consequently, the networked organization has to constantly focus on emerging technological innovations and short-lived market opportunities. We begin to see the emergence of so-called fluid-network organizations—organizations featuring permeable boundaries, minimal critical rules and flexible architectures (Maira and Thomas, 1998). It needs to be fast on its feet and act quickly as new developments and opportunities unfold. Furthermore, the networked organization needs to be flexible and accommodate impermanent tasks; all the while retaining the spirit of entrepreneurship in order to sustain the flow of innovative ideas.

Some of the characteristics, which describe the new Network Age, include:

External Environment: Fluid, global, unpredictable, complex, churning.
Work Processes: Automation and computerization of routine tasks, application of new technologies to the management of more complex, information-loaded processes.
Organizational Structure: Networked and fluid, built around self-managing "competency teams."
Decision Making: Made by self-managing units. Hierarchical command and control disappears.

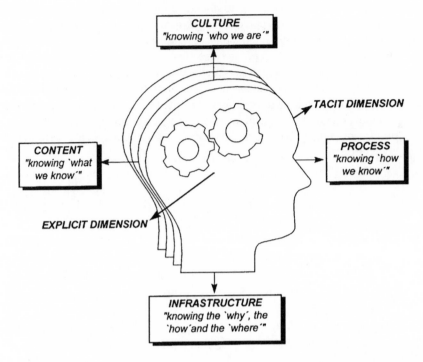

Figure 1. Organizational Knowledge Domains and Dimensions

Knowledge Workers: Equal status, self-managing teams are a blend of skills and talents; all members contribute to firm's knowledge creation and conversion processes.

Knowledge: Intelligence and experience-based; intuition, emotion and wisdom-based.

Learning Process: Double-Loop, trying and failing is viewed as a necessary transaction cost, assumptions are continually challenged.

B. Knowledge in the Network Age Enterprise

Knowledge, Pederson (1998) points out, can be described as the integration of ideas, experience, intuition, skill, and lessons learned; that has the potential to create value for all stakeholders of the respective firm. These may include the firm's employees, its customers, and ultimately the business and its networked environment. Value is created through knowledge by providing a more informed basis for decision making and improving actions. Nonaka and Takeuchi (1995) take the notion of knowledge in the firm further and define two realms of knowledge: tacit and explicit. Explicit knowledge is easily identifiable, easy to articulate, capture, and share. It is most readily apparent, but forms only the tip of the firm's knowledge iceberg. Pederson (1998), on the other hand, has described tacit knowledge, as "the difference between good and excellent performance." It resides in the heads of people and therefore consists predominantly of intuition, insight, perception, and beliefs and is to a great extent experiential. It is deeply entrenched in the culture of the firm and is therefore elusive, difficult to capture, and even more difficult to transfer. Of the two, tacit knowledge carries the greater value. It is a key determinant of competitiveness and forms the basis of exceptional performance and breakthroughs.

Managing knowledge in the networked age is a truly multidimensional challenge. It requires the simultaneous management of four inextricably linked domains (Figure 1): content, process, infrastructure and culture, all of which also have a tacit as well as an explicit dimension (Birchall and Tovstiga 1998; Chait 1998).

Knowledge Content or "Knowing What We 'Know'"

This domain comprises the firm's stock of strategically relevant knowledge—knowledge that enables the firm to perform competitively in its marketplace. Knowledge content can exist at various levels within a firm (Ives and Torrey 1998). Broadly categorized, we find knowledge existing in a firm in the form of:

- *experiential knowledge*—highly tacit and non-generalized, of high momentary and contextual value;
- *formal knowledge*—refined, generalized and highly explicit in nature; or
- *emerging knowledge*—both tacit and explicit, emerging at the interface of highly innovative and cross-disciplinary interactions in the firm, such as in the new product development projects.

Knowledge content, in its various forms, is embedded in the firm's business processes, infrastructure and organizational culture. Increasingly, firms are recognizing that the bulk of their competitive knowledge content lies in the *tacit* realm.

Knowledge Process or "Knowing 'How We Know'"

A firm's knowledge process domain encompasses that cluster of processes by which knowledge is managed within that firm—how knowledge is created, converted, transferred, applied, and ultimately discarded. In their work on knowledge creation in firms, Nonaka and Takeuchi (1995) have identified four key knowledge conversion processes—socialization (tacit to tacit), internalization (explicit to tacit), externalization (tacit to explicit) and combination (explicit to explicit).

Of these, the process of knowledge externalization (conversion and transfer of knowledge from the tacit into the explicit realm) is probably of key strategic importance; a key determinant of a firm's competitiveness is the extent to which it succeeds building capabilities in this process.

Knowledge processes can also involve roles played by the knowledge workers in the firm. The emphasis here is on *roles;* these differ distinctly from *job* descriptions. In our estimation, half of a firm's knowledge processes lie in the tacit dimension. The role of the knowledge worker focuses on executing knowledge management tasks within the virtual knowledge management processes. For example, knowledge workers perform key tasks in the various knowledge conversion processes of the firm.

Knowledge Infrastructure or "Knowing the 'Why,' the 'How,' and the 'Where'"

This knowledge domain encompasses all functional elements in the firm that support and facilitate the management of knowledge in a firm. Information and communication technology is one such element. For many managers, this is where the automation aspects of knowledge management reside and where knowledge management stops. Knowledge infrastructure encompasses much more, however. It also includes "carriers of knowledge" such as cross-functional project teams that facilitate the flow of knowledge between repositories and processes. Knowledge infrastructure, therefore, connects, binds, and involves individuals throughout the organization—those seeking specific knowledge and those capable of providing it. In this way, it supports the creation, transfer and leveraging of the firm's stock of knowledge (content) throughout the firm.

More importantly, however, *the* critical element of a firm's knowledge infrastructure consists of its network morphology. Increasingly, intra- and inter-organizational networks are easing aside the traditional Industrial Age hierarchical structures and rapidly becoming the predominant basis of the firm's infrastructure, giving rise to what Maira (1998) has termed the *"fluid-network organization"* of the networked era. Fluid processes and flexible teams are ensuring the rapid transfer of knowledge across complex and shifting internal and external organizational boundaries. While the exact outlines of this new organizational infrastructure are still evolving, we do already envisage some of its key features: It combines the "hard" aspects of the firm's organizational structure such as decision-making, boundaries, performance measures, and incentives, with the "soft," predominantly tacit aspects involving values, visioning, new ways of thinking, and new means of influencing mindsets. Powerful competitive multiplier effects are then achieved when the fluid-network organization links and integrates its internal network with any of a possible variety of external networks. These may include regional economic hubs, clusters, or business networks (Roy 1998).

Much of the knowledge infrastructure exists in the firm's *explicit* domain—as much as perhaps 75 percent—in the form of technology supporting the storage, transfer, and retrieval of information across the networks. The glue, however, that holds the networks together lies deep within the tacit realm of the firm's culture and processes—its conversational and knowledge sharing practices, modes of communicating and relationships embedded in the way the organization does things.

Knowledge Culture or "Knowing 'Who We Are'"

The last of the firm's four knowledge domains, culture, is perhaps the most elusive one. Yet research has shown culture to be the principal determinant of the success of knowledge management. A firm's knowledge culture consists of that set of organizational realities that act either as barriers or as enablers for the effective management of the firm's knowledge. It is also often the most neglected knowledge domain. An organization's knowledge culture may, for example, include any of the following dimensions (Korot and Tovstiga 1998):

- learning focus
- orientation with respect to experimentation
- leadership
- rewards and incentives
- information sharing tendencies
- organizational structure
- team collaboration (cohesiveness and problem-solving)
- degree of self-management

The culture domain exists at various levels in the organization. With reference to Schein's (1992) three levels of culture, these may range from the highly explicit visible organizational structures and processes (artifacts) to those highly tacit, unconscious, taken-for-granted beliefs and perceptions, thoughts and feelings (basic underlying assumptions). We estimate that perhaps as much as 70 percent of a firm's knowledge culture lies in the tacit dimension.

The Knowledge Dichotomy

Knowledge, on one hand, is an intensely personal entity. Much of it, by its very nature, lies deep in the tacit realm of *individuals*. On the other hand, we recognize that it is really only the (un-)bundling of, and providing access to, a firm's deeply embedded *collective* knowledge that ultimately yields competitive advantage. This requires a conscious transfer of knowledge from the tacit realm to the explicit realm. In this work, we try to delve into this knowledge dichotomy by focusing on the intersection of the firm's *knowledge culture* and *knowledge process* domains. Both of these domains exist, to a significant extent, in the tacit realm and have inextricable individual/collective dependencies. As we move into the Network Age, an entirely new dimension is added, however. We argue that real competitive advantage is gained only when a firm succeeds in capturing and transferring knowledge within a network extending beyond the boundaries of the firm, within a knowledge-driven network of firms.

C. The Knowledge Worker in the Network Age Firm

As organizations are becoming more knowledge-focused, new demands are being made on their primary source of competitive advantage—their knowledge workers. New functional descriptions are evolving which significantly transcend traditional knowledge roles such as that, for example, of the technological gate-keeper. In fact, the scope of the new knowledge worker role, we feel, will likely not even be confined to a single person's portfolio of skills and expertise. The new role encompasses a hybrid combination of hard and soft skills. It is more easily perceived as a non-discrete, kaleidoscopic entity that extends and retracts in the ebb and flow of the organization's information-rich environment. It calls for a much broader and flexible range of skills and attributes that is more aptly described in terms of metaphorical roles. Typically, these are carried out within the framework of informal functions within firms, for example, as part of the innovation process. A critical question in this context is: What is the *balanced* set of knowledge-based skills and capabilities that is desirable for a firm given its competitive environment?

II. RELATED RESEARCH

A. Organizational Knowledge Creation

One of the most comprehensive conceptual frameworks for knowledge creation and conversion is the theory of organizational knowledge creation of Nonaka and Takeuchi (1995). This theory constitutes a major building block of the profiling instrument developed in this paper. In their theory, the authors describe how knowledge-intensive organizations, when innovating in response to a changing environment, create new knowledge as a result of knowledge conversion between either of two forms or modes of knowledge—the tacit and the explicit forms. Conversion can take place in four ways: socialization (tacit to tacit), externalization (tacit to explicit), internalization (explicit to tacit), and combination (explicit to explicit). Knowledge creation occurs as a result of a spiral interaction between the two knowledge modes and at various organizational levels. The authors point out, though, that the key to knowledge creation really lies in the externalization process that involves the mobilization and conversion of tacit knowledge. When shared across the organization, the newly created knowledge, in turn, contributes to increased learning in the organization. Nonaka and Takeuchi point out that it is the role of the organization to provide the proper context for knowledge processes to run their course effectively.

B. Organizational Culture Profiling

Korot (1997) pursued the hypothesis that there is a high technology corporate culture that transcends national identity. The original research was based on a survey of 17 start-ups in Ireland, the United Kingdom, and France. The survey instrument is based on Schein's (1992) definition of organizational culture and assesses respondents' perceptions of the effectiveness of their organization in dealing with the problems of external adaptation and internal integration.

The study concluded that by contrast to previous research done by investigators such as Hofstede (1991) and Laurent (1983), remarkable "convergence" rather than "divergence" was found among the corporate cultures of these diverse enterprises. The addition of five U.S. high technology start-ups to the study sample confirmed the findings of the earlier study leading to a profile that characterizes "technocultures" (Korot 1989, 1997).

C. Knowledge Worker Profiling

In examining the emerging role of the knowledge worker in the knowledge-based organization, the essential question posed by Tovstiga (1998) in his recent study is: "How do we capitalize on the capabilities of our knowledge workers; that is, how do we capture, store, and feed forward the knowledge of our people in ways that contribute to the sustained well-being of our firm?"

Recognizing that much of the knowledge in firm with real competitive impact lies in the tacit knowledge domain (the proverbial nine-tenths portion of the iceberg submerged beneath the surface of the water), the challenge was: "How does one elicit knowledge which by its very nature lies in the tacit realm (that is, the knowledge workers' understanding of their contribution to their firm's various knowledge creation and conversion processes)?"

A diagnostic approach was developed on the basis of a conceptual framework that describes the knowledge-intensive organization's knowledge creation/conversion processes and metaphorical role descriptions used to elicit the relative contributions of the knowledge worker to each of the knowledge processes. What emerges is a pattern of behavioral and functional attributes showing the knowledge worker's role consisting of a potentially hybrid, composite, and flexible portfolio of competencies and attributes, all of which contribute to the organization's knowledge creation and knowledge conversion processes.

Empirical evidence based on an in-depth study of a Dutch-based international corporate engineering and research center suggests that the role portfolio is not necessarily concentrated within a single knowledge worker; rather, that it is distributed across boundary-crossing "communities of knowledge practices" on various levels within and external to the knowledge-intensive firm. Furthermore, there is evidence suggesting that, in the contemporary knowledge-based organization, there is a shift from an emphasis on traditional "explicit" knowledge conversion processes to an increasingly greater emphasis on "tacit" knowledge creation and conversion processes.

III. PROFILING OF THE KNOWLEDGE-BASED ORGANIZATION: RESULTS AND DISCUSSION

A diagnostic instrument for profiling the knowledge-based firm was developed on the basis of (i) a knowledge profiling approach proposed by Tovstiga (1998), and (ii) findings derived from research into the cultures of 22 start-up high technology firms in the United Kingdom, France, and the United States (Korot 1997).

The instrument is based on a questionnaire that was used to survey the organizations studied. The instrument taps into two major areas. In the first part, respondents are asked to assess their organization's *knowledge culture and processes.* These are reflected by the firm's:

Management of its *Knowledge Resource Base:* examining (i) where knowledge resides in the organization, (ii) how it is sourced and (iii) how it is disseminated within the firm.

Culture: what the learning focus of the firm is, its orientation toward experimentation, the firm's nature of leadership, rewards and incentives, information sharing and organizational structure.

Enabling Practices: including its strategic intent, autonomy, creative chaos and disequilibrium, overlap and redundancy, and information variety.

The second part of the instrument seeks to elicit a better understanding of *the emerging role of the knowledge worker* in the firm. Respondents are asked to reflect on and evaluate the range of roles played by the knowledge worker in their firms and the extent to which those roles contribute to the firm's knowledge creation and conversion processes.

The questionnaires were evaluated; on this basis a comparative analysis was carried of the four firms studied—Inhale Therapeutic Systems, a U.S. Silicon Valley start-up; SKF Engineering & Research B.V., the Netherlands-based corporate engineering and research center of the Swedish multinational; the Geneva-based European Laboratory for Particle Physics (CERN); and an R&D group at Palo Alto-based Hewlett-Packard. The results are presented in Table 1.

The sample sizes of the responses of the four firms studied were: 28 (Inhale); 11 (SKF); 4 (CERN); and 27 (Hewlett-Packard). The positions of the people surveyed ranged from CEO to specialist and/or first-level management. The resulting profiling represents an "organizational fingerprint" of the respective firms, reflecting the prevailing knowledge-related management systems, culture and practices. For Part I, we argue that a shift toward the right (or higher number values) represents a shift from Industrial Age organizational systems, culture and practices to Network Age organizational systems, culture and practices. For Part II, a shift from *combination* to *socialization* related processes (Nonaka and Takeuchi 1995), we argue, suggests a growing awareness of the potential competitive impact residing in the firm's tacit knowledge domain. This we would expect to be the case in the Network Age firm.

A comparison of the four firms evaluated in Table 1 suggests that both the Hewlett-Packard R&D group and Inhale, the U.S. Silicon Valley start-up, are closest to our profile of the Network Age firm. Both firms exhibit a strong "technoculture"; yet in both, this is well balanced with entrepreneurial and commercial attributes (see also Korot, 1989).

The CERN profiling results show an organization with a very strong technoculture, but with a considerable degree of variation in the cultural attributes assessed. As a non-commercial enterprise, technology at CERN is pursued largely for its own sake. Those cultural attributes supporting the advancement of new and highly sophisticated technology are generally well developed (for example, orientation toward experimentation and information sharing). Attributes supporting the commercial exploitation of technology, on the other hand, significantly lag behind. This hardly comes as a surprise since the commercialization of the numerous highly advanced new technologies developed has generally never been the mission of the CERN establishment (see for example the recent publication by Hamri and Nordberg 1998 describing the development of the World Wide Web at CERN). A unique technoculture has evolved in this environment; a technological breeding ground in the absence of any drive for commercialization. The question for the technology-based twenty-first-century firm is: "What mechanisms at CERN have supported the output of numerous remarkably successful products (from a purely technologically perspective), and how can these be interlaced and integrated into the technology-based commercial enterprise of the twenty-first century?"

The Netherlands-based engineering and research center also reflects a strong "technoculture"—suggested by the way in which its knowledge base is managed—but significantly lags behind in key cultural attributes, for example in the areas of learning, orientation toward experimentation, and leadership. In many ways, these relate to the entrepreneurial character of the firm. Thus, the engineering and research center unit examined reflects the more traditional knowledge environment of the large multinational of the current day. On the other hand, Brown and Duguid (1998) suggest that differences between start-up and large corporation might well become increasingly irrelevant when thinking about the competitive drivers of the twenty-first-century knowledge enterprise. We argue that a more dialectic approach focusing on how the two might be interlaced might yield a more meaningful approach.

Table 1. Comparative Evaluation: Profiling the Knowledge Enterprise

PART I. *Profiling the Firm's Knowledge Culture and Processes*

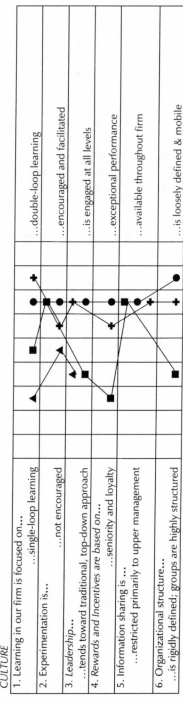

...mostly	1	2	3	4	5	6	7	8	9	...mostly
KNOWLEDGE BASE										
1. Knowledge in our firm resides primarily... ...with individuals										...collectively
2. Knowledge sourcing is primarily... ...internally focused										...outwardly focused
3. Knowledge dissemination occurs primarily... ...in structured, controlled ways										...through informal encounters
CULTURE										
1. Learning in our firm is focused on... ...single-loop learning										...double-loop learning
2. Experimentation is... ...not encouraged										...encouraged and facilitated
3. Leadership... ...tends toward traditional, top-down approach										...is engaged at all levels
4. Rewards and Incentives are based on... ...seniority and loyalty										...exceptional performance
5. Information sharing is... ...restricted primarily to upper management										...available throughout firm
6. Organizational structure... ...is rigidly defined; groups are highly structured										...is loosely defined & mobile

(continued)

Table 1. (Continued)

ENABLING PRACTICES ...not at all	1	2	3	4	5	6	7	8	9	...to a very great extent
1. Intention. Firm's strategic vision is clearly communicated and collectively shared...					▲	■	+ ● +			
2. Autonomy. Individuals have freedom to act autonomously; including self-organizing and cross-functional teams...					▲	■	+ ●			
3. Creative chaos and disequilibrium. Creative chaois encouraged in order to stimulate new ideas...			■	▲	▲	+ ●				
4. Overlap & Redundancy. Information available clearly goes beyond immediate operational needs...				▲	■	●	+			
5. Information Variety & Access. Conditions are created that maximize accessibility, variety & sharing of information...					▲	+ ■	●			

PART II. *Assessing the Individual's Contribution To the Firm's Knowledge Conversion Processes*

...irrelevant	1	2	3	4	5	...very important
SOCIALIZATION			▲ ■ ■	●		
INTERNALIZATION		▲	■ ▲ + ■	● ●		
EXTERNALIZATION			▲ ■	●		
COMBINATION						

KEY:
- ● Inhale Therapeutic Systems
- ▲ SKF Engineering & Research Centre
- ■ CERN (European Laboratory for Particle Physics)
- + Hewlett-Packard R&D

169

IV. CONCLUSIONS

Our understanding of the profile of the twenty-first-century, internationally competitive, entrepreneurial firm is truly nascent, as is our understanding of the implications of the firm's knowledge infrastructure and knowledge worker role on building sustainable competitiveness. The work presented in this paper represents a first thrust toward building a better understanding. The diagnostic profiling instrument discussed in this paper provides a vehicle for (1) thinking about key knowledge-related attributes and a profile of the Network Age firm and (2) gauging the progress of real-time enterprises toward achieving that profile, as was done in the case of two technology-driven firms.

We feel that the Network Age, knowledge enterprise will focus a disproportionate amount of effort on building their knowledge-related capabilities in terms of the way it manages its knowledge base, its culture and knowledge-related practices. Furthermore, we feel that there will be a much greater effort devoted to the mining of the firm's tacit knowledge reserves. This will likely become one of the primary management challenges of the twenty-first-century knowledge enterprise. All this will take place in the face of the inevitable increased scarcity and mobility of the knowledge enterprise's prime scarce resource: the knowledge worker.

We hope that this paper will serve to instigate further discussion of the relevant questions. One question requiring further scrutiny, for example, is: What are the relevant attributes and parameters which really capture and reflect the organization's knowledge culture and how do these impact the capture and transfer of knowledge, particularly *tacit* knowledge, within the firm? Knowledge infrastructure, we feel, is another area of immense strategic importance which is largely underestimated and misunderstood. In many firms, knowledge infrastructure is viewed largely only from the perspective of databases and hard-wired network technologies. Not surprisingly, these firms are then disappointed when the acquired technology fails to deliver on their expectations of creating a networked organization. By far, the important issues related to knowledge infrastructure lie in the tacit realm and are intimately linked to the firm's knowledge culture and practices. Even more importantly, the firm's knowledge infrastructure needs to provide the link with external "soft" knowledge network of the firm. The critical questions here are: What are the key attributes of a firm that describe its effectiveness in capturing and transferring knowledge, not only within its internal network, but also within its external network—its "community of knowledge practice." Much more work needs to be done in this area.

Finally, we argue that virtually all Industrial Age assumptions need to be challenged. Too many firms are still trying to cope with the emerging Networked Age using approaches firmly entrenched in the Industrial Age. A fundamental rethinking of what will drive human learning, cognitive assimilation, and the enterprise's innovation processes in the twenty-first century is needed. We also propose that in the Network Age, differences between start-up and large firms may increasingly become irrelevant as new knowledge-based drivers of competitiveness emerge. The cultural and management practices profiles of Hewlett-Packard and Inhale reported in this work appear to give an indication of this.

ACKNOWLEDGMENTS

The authors gratefully acknowledge those numerous people who participated in the empirical studies carried out in the three organizations. In particular, the authors gratefully acknowledge the support and input of Dr. Markus Nordberg of the CERN research establishment, Mr. Robert Chess, co-founder and CEO of Inhale Therapeutic Systems, Mr. Jos Bras, head of the SKF Bearing Theory & Testing Group and Mr. Rob Lawson of Hewlett-Packard.

REFERENCES

Amidon, D. M. 1997. *Innovation Strategy for the Knowledge Economy. The Ken Awakening*. Bostob: Butterworth-Heinemann.

Bahrami, H., and S. Evans. 1987. "Stratocracy in High-Technology Firms." *California Management Review* (Fall): 51.

Birchall, D. W., and G. Tovstiga. 1998. "Methodology for Assessing the Strategic Impact of a Firm's Knowledge Portfolio." Eighth International Forum on Technology Management, Grenoble, France, November 2-6.

Brown, J. S., and P. Duguid. 1998. "Organizing Knowledge." *California Management Review* 40 (3): 90.

Chait, L. 1998. "Creating a Successful Knowledge Management System." *Prism* (Second Quarter): 83.

Drucker, P. 1993. *Post-Capitalist Society*. Oxford: Butterworth-Heinemann.

Drucker, P. 1998. "Presentation." Third International Competency Conference, Royal Lancaster Hotel, London, September 7-10 (Linkage Inc.).

Hofstede, G. 1991. *Cultures and Organizations*. London: McGraw-Hill.

Ives, W., and B. Torrey. 1998. "Supporting Knowledge Sharing." *Knowledge Management* 1 (5) (April/May).

Kelly, K. 1997. "New Rules for the New Economy." *Wired* (September).

Korot, L. 1989. "Technoculture: Leading Edge to European Integration or an Organizational Anomaly?" Proceedings of the 1989 Annual Conference, European International Business Association.

Korot, L. 1997. "A Cross-Cultural Comparison of the Organizational Cultures of Hi-Tech Start-Up Ventures." Presentation, Executive MBA Group, Pepperdine University.

Laurent, A. 1983. "A Cultural Diversity of Western Conceptions of Management." *International Studies of Management and Organization* 3: 75.

Maira, A. N. 1998. "Connecting Across Boundaries: The Fluid-Network Organization." *Prism* (First Quarter): 23.

Maira, A. N., and R. J. Thomas. 1998. "Organizing on the Edge: Meeting the Demand for Innovation and Efficiency." *Prism* (Third Quarter): 5.

Nonaka, I., and H. Takeuchi. 1995. *The Knowledge Creating Company*. New York: Oxford University Press.

Oviatt, B. M., and P. McDougall. 1998. "Accelerated Internationalization: Why Are New and Small Ventures Internationalizing in Greater Numbers and with Increasing Speed?" Proceedings of the Conference on Globalization and Emerging Businesses, McGill University, Montreal, Canada.

Pederson, P. O. 1998. Contribution in *Knowledge Management Review* 1 (March/April): 3.

Roy, P. 1998. "Business Networks for SMEs: Powerful Synergy for Growth in the Emerging Global Market Place." International Conference on Globalization and Emerging Business: Strategies for the Twenty-First Century, McGill University, Montreal, Canada, September 26-28.

Schein, E. H. 1992. *Organizational Culture and Leadership* (2nd ed.). San Francisco: Jossey-Bass Publishers.

Teece, D. J. 1998. "Capturing Value from Knowledge Assets: The New Economy, Markets for Know-How, and Intangible Assets." *California Management Review* 40 (3): 55.

Tovstiga, G. 1998. "Profiling the Knowledge Worker in the Knowledge-Intensive Organization: Emerging Roles." Second World Congress on the Management of Intellectual Capital & Innovation, McMaster University, Hamilton, Canada (January 21-23); to appear in an up-coming issue of *International Journal of Technology Management*.

Tovstiga, G., and L. Korot. 1998. "Profiling the 21[St] Century Knowledge-Based Organization." Eighth International Technology Management Forum, Grenoble, France, 2-4 November.

TWENTY-FIRST-CENTURY LEADERSHIP
REALITY BEYOND THE MYTHS

Nancy J. Adler

I. INTRODUCTION

That the world is going global comes as a surprise to no one. Whereas world output grew by 600 percent in the past 50 years, world trade grew by over 1,500 percent (Hill 1998, p. 10). In just the last decade, the annual flow of foreign direct investment from all countries increased nearly sixfold (Hill 1998, p. 10). Will women join men as leaders in this increasingly global world of the twenty-first century? The answer is yes—across the full range of society's most influential roles, from political leadership to leadership in global entrepreneurial enterprises. The myth, however, is that there are either no global women leaders or very few. Yet we must challenge this and other myths about global leadership if we are to begin to understand the societal changes taking place, including the increasing importance of global strategy and entrepreneurial activity.

Research in Global Strategic Management, Volume 7, pages 173-190.
Copyright © 1999 by JAI Press Inc.
All rights of reproduction in any form reserved.
ISBN: 0-7623-0458-8

II.   WOMEN LEADING COUNTRIES[1]

Let us begin by looking at society's most visible leaders—political leaders. Are there women who are assuming the most senior level of leadership in their country? In recent history, how many have become president or prime minister ?

The Myth of Scarcity: There Are No Global Women Political Leaders

The myth of scarcity would suggest that there are few women leaders, perhaps three or four. Reality reveals 42.[2] Forty-two women have served their country as head of government or state in the last half century, considerably more than the myth of scarcity would suggest. However, given that there are more than 185 countries in the world, 42 is not a particularly large number.

The Myth That History Predicts: Is the Past a Good Predictor of the Future?

Should we expect the number of women political leaders to remain small, or, as some would even suggest, insignificant? Will nineteenth and twentieth-century history remain a good predictor for forthcoming twenty-first-century reality? Whereas the absolute number of women leaders raises such questions, the trend compellingly suggests an answer. No women presidents or prime ministers came to office in the 1950s, three came to office in the 1960s, five in the 1970s, eight in the 1980s, and 26 in the 1990s—and the decade is not yet over. Over 60 percent of women political leaders first came to office in the 1990s. Four out of five women who have held high political office this century served their country during the last decade. More women have come into office since 1990 than in the prior five decades combined.

Moreover, as shown in Table 1, among the 42 women leaders, almost 90 percent are the first women whom their particular country has ever selected to become president or prime minister. Among the few women who have followed another woman into office, all five came into office in just the last five years.[3] If patterns such as these continue—and there is every reason to believe they will—there is no question that more women will lead their country in the twenty-first century than have ever done so before. Based on such increases, we can easily predict that women's voices will become a more important, albeit unprecedented, addition to global strategy and world leadership in the twenty-first century than in any prior century.

The Minority Myth:
The Myth That Only a Few "Advanced" Countries Select Women as Leaders

Even with increasing numbers, don't most women leaders come from only a few, "advanced" countries? No, women political leaders neither come from a small cluster of similar countries nor disproportionately from countries that are considered politically, socially, or economically advanced. Rather than represent-ing a small, homogeneous minority, the countries that have selected women lead-ers represent the broadest range of cultures, geographic locations, political systems, and levels of economic and social development. Women leaders come from some of the world's richest and poorest countries; the largest and smallest countries; some of the most, as well as the least, economically advantaged coun-tries; and from countries with the highest and lowest levels of infant mortality, lit-eracy, and longevity. Women lead countries representing six of the world's major religious traditions. That the rapidly growing number of women leaders is based broadly throughout the world represents neither an aberration nor a coincidence. It clearly reflects a new, important, and pervasive global trend.

III.   WOMEN LEADING MAJOR CORPORATIONS[4]

Are there similar trends emerging among women business leaders as we see among the political leaders? While it is too early to know for sure, the emerging trends look familiar. Let's look at what we know versus what most people believe to be true about the world's business leaders.

The Scarcity Myth: Few, If Any, Women Lead Major Global Corporations

Do we see similar increases in the number of women CEOs and presidents of major companies as we are seeing in the number of women political leaders? The initial answer would appear to be *no*. Think for a moment about the number of women CEOs of major global corporations that you can name. Not many. Only in the late 1990s, for example, did Britain gain its first woman chief executive of a *Financial Times (FT-SE)* 100 firm, Marjorie Scardino at Pearson Plc. As the press has observed, "Twenty years after adopting equal-opportunity laws, Europe is still a man's world. [Whereas] women make up 41% of the European work-force...[they only] claim about 2% of senior management jobs" (Dwyer, Johnston, and Miller 1996, pp. 40-41). American women are not faring that well either. Only 2.4 percent of the chairs and CEOs of *Fortune* 500 firm are women (Wellington 1996, reported in Himelstein 1996).

Whereas the number of women leading major corporations remains exceed-ingly small, women are making progress. For the first time in history, one coun-try's largest company (albeit a subsidiary of an American company) is headed by a woman: Maureen Kempston Darkes, president and CEO of General Motors Canada's over $23.5 billion operations.

Kempston Darkes is not alone. Women now lead a disproportionate number of major Canadian corporations and the Canadian operations of major American multinationals. Canada, however, is not the only country in which corporations are now beginning to select women as their senior business leaders. In the 1990s, the

Table 1. Woman Political Leaders: A Chronology

Country	Name	Office	Date
Sri Lanka	*Sirimavo Bandaranaike	Prime Minister	1960-65;1970-77, 1994-*
India	(Indira Gandhi)	Prime Minister	1966-1977, 1980-1984
Israel	(Golda Meir)	Prime Minister	1969-1975
Argentina	(María Estela [Isabel] Martínez de Perón)	President	1974-1976
Central African Rep.	Elizabeth Domitien	Prime Minister	1975-1976
Portugal	Maria de Lourdes Pintasilgo	President	1979
Bolivia	Lidia Gveiler Tejadalnterim	President	1979-1980
Great Britain	Margaret Thatcher	Prime Minister	1979-1990
Dominica	Mary Eugenia Charles	Prime Minister	1980-1995
Iceland	Vigdís Finnbógadóttir	President	1980-1996
Norway	Gro Harlem Brundtland	Prime Minister	1981;1986-89;1990-1996
Yugoslavia	Milka Planinc	Prime Minister	1982-1986
Malta	Agatha Barbara	President	1982-1987
Netherland-Antilles	Maria Liberia-Peters	Prime Minister	1984; 1989-1994
The Philippines	Corazon Aquino	President	1986-1992
Pakistan	Benazir Bhutto	Prime Minister	1988-1990; 1993-1996
Lithuania	Kazimiera-Danute Prunskiene	Prime Minister	1990-1991
Haiti	Ertha Pascal-Trouillot	President	1990-1991
Myanmar (Burma)	Aung San Suu Kyi	Opposition Leader**	1990-**
East Germany	Sabine Bergmann-Pohl	President of the Parliament	1990
Ireland	Mary Robinson	President	1990-1997
Nicaragua	Violeta Barrios de Chamorro	President	1990-1996
Bangladesh	Khaleda Zia	Prime Minister	1991-1996
France	Edith Cresson	Prime Minister	1991-1992
Poland	Hanna Suchocka	Prime Minister	1992-1993
Canada	Kim Campbell	Prime Minister	1993
Burundi	Sylvia Kinigi	Prime Minister	1993-1994
Rwanda	(Agatha Uwilingiyimana)	Prime Minister	1993-1994

176

Table 1. (Continued)

Country	Name	Office	Date
Turkey	Tansu Çiller	Prime Minister	1993-1996
Bulgaria	Reneta Indzhovalnterim	Prime Minister	1994-1995
Sri Lanka	*Chandrika Bandaranaike Kumaratunga	Executive President & former Prime Minister	1994-*
Haiti	Claudette Werleigh	Prime Minister	1995-1996
Bangladesh	*Hasina Wajed	Prime Minister	1996-*
Liberia	*Ruth Perry	Chair, Ruling Council	1996-*
Ecuador	Rosalia Artega	President	1997
Bermuda	Pamela Gordon	Premier	1997-1998
Bosnian Serb Rep.	*Biljana Plavsic	President	1997-*
Ireland	*Mary McAleese	President	1997-*
New Zealand	*Jenny Shipley	Prime Minister	1997-*
Guyana	*Janet Jagan	Prime Minister, President	1997-*
Bermuda	*Jennifer Smith	Premier	1998-*
Switzerland	*Ruth Dreifuss	President	1999-*

Notes: () = No longer living
  * = Currently in office
  ** = Party won 1990 election but prevented by military from taking office; Nobel Prize laureate.

Source: Adapted and updated from Adler, Nancy J. (1996) "Global Women Political Leaders, An Invisible History, An Increasingly Important Future," *Leadership Quarterly,* 7 (1):136.

177

United States saw a record number of women assume the highest leadership position in their respective corporations, including, among many others: Jill Barad at Mattel; Carol Bartz at Autodesk; Diana Brooks at Sotheby's; Orit Gadiesh at Bain & Company; Katherine Hudson at W.H. Brady; Jeanne Jackson at the Banana Republic; Sally Frame Kasaks at Ann Taylor; Sherry Lansing at Paramount Pictures; Rebecca Mark at Enron Development Corporation; and Linda Joy Wachner at both The Warnaco Group and Authentic Fitness Corporation.

Whereas the numbers are smaller outside North America, women from around the world lead major corporations that are not controlled by their family. Examples include the Czech Republic's Zdena Homolkova, General Director and chairwoman of Sanitas, France's Colette Lewiner, chairman and CEO of SGN-Eurisys Group, India's Tarjani Vakil, former chairperson and Managing Director of the Export-Import Bank of India; Israel's Galia Maor, CEO of Bank Leumi le-Israel; Italy's Marisa Bellisario, former CEO of Italtel; Gloria Knight, former president and Managing Director of the Jamaica Mutual Life Assurance Society; Japan's Harumi Sakamoto, Senior Managing Director of The Seiyu, and Zimbabwe's Liz Chitiga, former CEO of Minerals Marketing Corporation of Zimbabwe. Women today lead major corporations in Africa, Asia, Europe, and the Americas. The myth that there are no women leading major corporations is simply not true.

The Female-Friendly Myth: The Myth That Averages Predict

Many people believe that only a few supposedly *female-friendly* countries—those providing women with equal property rights, equal access to education, healthcare, employment, and equal protection under the law—choose to promote women into senior leadership. The myth, however, similar to many other myths about global leadership, is simply not true. *Female-friendly* countries do not elect a disproportionate number of the world's women political leaders. In fact, countries—such as Bangladesh—that have neither legislated nor implemented equal opportunities and rights for women, have already elected two women prime ministers, whereas countries considered by many to be more female-friendly, such as Sweden and the United States, have yet to elect even one.

Similar to countries, most major corporations that select women as their most senior leaders are not those that have implemented the most female-friendly policies, such as providing day-care centers and flextime (Wellington 1996 as reported in Dobrzynski 1996). For example, among the 61 American *Fortune* 500 companies employing women as chairmen, CEOs, board members, or one of the top five earners, only three are the same companies that *Working Woman* identified as the most favorable for women employees (Dobrzynski 1996).

Although it should have been self-evident, we all seem to have missed the point. If we want to understand women's potential for global leadership, we cannot confuse leaders with the population as a whole, nor can we continue to confuse leaders with either managers or employees. Inadvertently most people assume that the dynamics that apply to women in the lower ranks of organizations as they move into and up through management, often getting stopped at the so-called *glass ceiling*, also apply to women who have made it to the top. That is, they seem to believe that being a woman is so salient that the difference between how a company treats its women working as entry-level employees and those promoted to senior executive positions is irrelevant. From a dynamic perspective, we have mistakenly assumed that the influence of being a woman neither interacts with role nor with level in the organization. As now seems self-evident, our assumption has been wrong: one cannot predict the probability of a company selecting a woman CEO based on how the company treats its women employees in general. Likewise, one cannot predict which country will elect a woman president or prime minister based on how that country treats the majority of its female citizens. Average behavior—whether in countries or companies—does not predict the behavior of the few people—women and men—who become leaders.

The Myth That History Predicts

Similar to the women political leaders, a disproportionate number of the women leading major corporations have only become leaders within the last decade; and almost all of them are "firsts." Only in a very few cases—such as Shelly Lazarus succeeding Charlotte Beers as CEO at Ogilvy & Mather Worldwide—do you see a woman following another women into office. Whereas the absolute number of women leading major corporations remains small, the trend indicates the beginning of a new pattern—a pattern in which more women are moving into the highest levels of corporate leadership. The myth that history predicts, that the past is a good indicator of the future, appears to be just as false for women corporate leaders as it is for women political leaders. Corporate strategy in the twenty-first century will be defined by both women and men; it will no longer remain the domain of men alone.

IV. WOMEN LEADING FAMILY BUSINESS

Contrary to popular belief, women's scarcity in leading major corporations does not mean that they are scarce as leaders of global companies. Most women have not attempted to climb the corporate ladder, and of those who attempted the climb, few succeeded. Unlike their male counterparts, who lead over 98 percent of the world's largest corporations, most women chief executives have either created their own businesses or have assumed the leadership of a family business.

Table 2. Women Leading Major Family Businesses

Country	Leader	Title	Company
Argentina	Amalia Lacroze de Fortabat	President	Grupo Fortabat
Canada	Martha Billes	Chairman	Canadian Tire
Brazil	Beatriz Larragoiti	Vice President	Sul America S.A.
Brazi	Zlata Sauer	President	Amsterdan Sauer
Costa Rica[i]	Donatella Zingone Dini	Chairman	Zeta Group
Finland	Liisa Joronen	President	SOL Cleaning
France	Dominique Hériard Dubreuil	President	E. Rémy Martin & Co.
France	Anne-Claire Taittinger-Bonnemaison	CEO	Baccarat & VP of ELM Leblanc
Germany	Eugenie Burgholte-Kellerman		Kamax-Werke
Hong Kong	Sally Aw Sian	Chairman & Managing Director	Sing Tao Holdings Ltd.
Hong Kong	Nina Wang	Chairlady	Chinachem Group
Ireland	Margaret Heffernan	Chairman	Dunnes Stores Holding Company
Japan	Mieko Morishita	President	Morishita Jintan Co.
Japan	Sawako Noma	President & CEO	Kodansha Ltd.
Norway	Anna Synnove Bye		Fosen Mekaniske Verksteder A/S
The Philippines	Elena Lim	President	Solid Corporation
Sweden	Antonia Ax:son Johnson	Chairman & CEO	Axel Johnson Gruppen
Switzerland	Elisabeth Salina Amorini	Chairman & Managing Director	Société Générale de Surveillance Holdings S.A.
Taiwan	Emilia Roxas	Chairperson, CEO	Asiaworld Internationale Group
United Kingdom	Janet Holmes à Court	Chairman	Heytesbury Holdings
United States:	Gertrude Boyle	Former CEO	Columbia Sportswear
	Katherine Graham	Former CEO & Chairman	The Washington Post Group
	Christie Hefner	CEO & Chairman	Playboy Enterprises
	Ellen Gordon	President & COO	Tootsie Roll Industries
	Martha Ingram	Chairman	Ingram Industries
	Barbara Levy Kipper	Chairman	Chas. Levy Company
	Loida Nicolas Lewis	CEO	TLC Beatrice Intl. Holdings
	Sally McClain	Chair	Mark III Industries
	Elizabeth Minyard & Gretchen Minyard Williams	Co-chairs	Minyard Food Stores
	Jane O'Dell	Co-owner	Westfall Investment Associates

Most businesses worldwide are family businesses. Even in the United States, family business comprises more than 90 percent of all business, with one-third of the country's largest, *Fortune* 500 companies being family led.[5] Historically, family businesses have been handed down from father to son, leaving women largely absent from their formal leadership. However, in the last few decades, the pattern has begun to shift. Influenced by dramatic increases in global competition, families are increasingly choosing to pass their businesses on to the most competent child—whether male or female—rather than automatically bequeathing it to a son. The death of a CEO-husband—which previously led most frequently to either the sale of the family's business or its inheritance by a son or brother—today leads more frequently to his wife taking it over.

As highlighted in Table 2, similar to women political leaders, women leading prominent family businesses come from around the world, not from just a few select countries. Many women-led family businesses are earning billions, not just millions, in annual revenues.

V. WOMEN ENTREPRENEURS: WOMEN LEADING THEIR OWN COMPANIES[6]

The most dramatic shifts in global leadership are taking place among global entrepreneurs, with contemporary reality overturning many of the myths of history.

The Scarcity Myth: There Aren't That Many Women Entrepreneurs

In striking contrast to the current situation of scarcity for women leading major corporations, a disproportionate number of women have founded and are now leading entrepreneurial enterprises. Women currently own one-third of all American businesses (Kelly 1996, p. 21). Across the United States, "enterprising women are forming businesses at twice the rate of men. At this pace, by the year 2000, women will own half the businesses in the United States. There is a revolution reshaping the business landscape" (Jung 1997).

Is the situation completely different outside of the United States? No, the increasing number of women entrepreneurs is a growing international trend, not just an American trend. "The number of women-owned enterprises is growing faster than the economy-at-large in many countries" ("Women Wanted" 1996, p. 1). In Poland, a transitional economy, "the number of women starting their own businesses almost doubled between 1989 and 1991...and the percentage of women among all entrepreneurs...[rose] to 33 percent," a 20 percent increase over the same three year period" (Mroczkowski 1995, p. 56). Polish women continue to start businesses at a higher rate than do Polish men (Mroczkowski 1995, p. 56).

Such rapid increases are not confined to transitional economies. In economically advantaged countries the pattern is similar. In Germany, for example, "one-third of all... start-ups are now woman-owned, up from 10" percent just two decades ago (Dwyer, Johnston, and Miller, p. 42). Similarly in Canada, the number of women-led firms, which now stands at one-third of all Canadian businesses ("Women Wanted" 1996), is growing at almost 20 percent per year—twice the national average ("Myths and Realities 1995 cited in "Growth of Women-led Businesses," p. 1). Worldwide, the number of women entrepreneurs is neither small nor shrinking. Based on current trends, the only valid prediction is that the proportion of women entrepreneurs will increase significantly in the twenty-first century.

*The Pink Ghetto Myth: Women Only Lead Businesses
in Female Industries, Such as Beauty and Fashion*

The numbers may be increasing, but the assumption—supported by press stereotypes—is that women only lead companies offering products and services primarily to women, such as fashion, health and beauty care, and childcare-related services. They certainly do not lead companies in such supposedly male domains as construction and heavy industry.

The myth is half true. Over the course of the twentieth century, a number of women have become prominent leading companies that cater primarily to women. The fashion industry, for example, includes a large number of highly successful women—both historically and currently—who became both extraordinarily creative designers and good business women. Coco Chanel is perhaps the *grande dame* of such fashion houses, but, the list goes far beyond Chanel. Prominent women have led major fashion houses headquartered in Asia, Europe, the Middle East, and the Americas, including, among many others, Sonia Rykiel and Agnès Troublé in France, Jill Sander in Germany, Joyce Ma in Hong Kong, Lea Gottlieb in Israel, Miuccia Prada and Donatella Versace Beck in Italy, Hanae Mori in Japan, and Josephine Chaus, Donna Karan, Carole Little, Paloma Picasso, and Susie Tompkins in the United States.

Further accentuating the *Pink Ghetto Myth* that women lead businesses offering their services primarily to other women are the set of prominent business women who have founded and successfully led cosmetics, beauty, and healthcare companies. Estée Lauder in the United States was one of the first such entrepreneurial women to create a worldwide beauty care company. Now a family business, The Estée Lauder Companies earn revenues exceeding $3.4 billion.[7] Similarly, Mary Kay Ash founded and led her U.S.-based beauty care company to worldwide success, with current revenues exceeding $1 billion.[8] More recently, Anita Roddick founded and led her U.K-based Body Shop to success, with operations in over forty countries and annual revenues exceeding $435 million.[9] At the same time, India's Princess Shahnaz Husain was creating Shahnaz Herbals and expanding

Table 3.   Women Leading Major Companies in Traditional *Male Industries*

Country	Woman Leader	Company	Industry	Sales-US$ (millions)
Argentina	Amalia Lacroze De Fortabat	Groupo Fortabat[f]	Cement	$700
France	Colette Lewiner	SGN-Eurisys Group[c]	Nuclear fuel processing	$800
Germany	Eugenie Burgholte-Kellerman	Kamax-Werke[f]	Bolts & other fasteners	$280[l]
Greece	Fonini F. Legaki	Hellafarm S.A.[e]	Pesticide manufacturing	$20.4[l]
India	Rita Singh	Mesco Group of Industries[e]	Industrial group including steel, pharmaceuticals, & leather	$612[l]
Italy	Lucia Manzoni	Manzoni Group[e]	Manufactures metal presses for auto & consumer goods manufacturers	$95[l]
Israe	Ruth Hirsch	Dubek Limited[c]	Cigarette manufacturing	$80
Norway	Anna Synnove Bye	Fosen Mekaniske Verksteder A/S[f]	Ship building	$75[l]
Philippines	Elena S. Lim	Solid Corp.[e]	Industrial group, manufactures & distributes cars & consumer electronics, and exports prawns	$114[l]
Taiwan	Emilia Roxas	Asiaworld Internationale Group[f]	Conglomerate, includes mining, construction, agribusiness, among others	$5bil[l]
USA	Patricia Gallup	PC Connection Inc.[e]	Computer products & information	$325[l]
USA	Christine Liang	ASI[e]	Computer equipment and systems	$325[l]
USA	Jane O'Dell	Westfall Investment Associates[f]	Truck & car dealership, including big-rig tractor trailers	$300[l]
Zimbabwe	Liz Chitiga	Minerals Marketing Corp. of Zimbabwe[c]	Sells/exports minerals	$400

Notes: Type of business:
   [c] = Public corporation, non-family held
   [e] = Entrepreneurial business
   [f] = Family business

Source: *Leading Women Entrepreneurs of the World and Women to Watch* (1997). Washington DC: National Foundation of Women Business Owners.

the company's operations internationally and its revenues to over $100 million (*Leading Women Entrepreneurs* 1997). Australia's Imelda Roche, with her husband as a partner, has grown Nutri-metics revenues to over $235 million.[10]

Do *Pink Ghetto* companies explain all, or most, of women entrepreneurs' stories? No. Whereas women certainly have created some highly visible and successful companies in industries serving primarily female markets, they have also gone far beyond the narrow confines of the *Pink Ghetto*. As highlighted in Table 3, women from around the world have led major companies in such non-stereotypically female industries as construction, nuclear fuel processing, pesticide production, auto parts manufacturing, ship building, big-rig truck leasing, and pharmaceuticals, among many others.

In the United States, "industry trends...indicate explosive growth in [women-led businesses in] non-traditional sectors" ("Women entrepreneurs" 1997, p. 1). Between 1987 and 1996, "the top growth industries for women-owned businesses...were: construction, wholesale trade, transportation, agribusiness, and manufacturing" (*Leading Women Entrepreneurs* 1997, p. 45). "In [just] the last decade, the number of women-led construction, transportation/communications, agriculture and manufacturing companies each grew by over 100%" ("Women entrepreneurs" 1997, p. 1). In being historically half true, the *Pink Ghetto* myth camouflages the success of today's women-led businesses across a full range of industries.

The Myth of Trivial Size: Women Only Lead Very Small Businesses

While increasing in number and expanding across industries, are most women-owned businesses remaining so small that they are, in fact, trivial? The majority of women-owned businesses are small: 85 percent have no employees (Fritsch 1998, p. E2). However, the myth that women lead only very small businesses is false. Many women entrepreneurs generate substantial revenues. The current top two women-owned entrepreneurial enterprises in the United States, for example, each generate annual revenues above $2 billion ("America's Top 500" 1998).[11]

Do women in other parts of the world also lead businesses of substantial size? Absolutely. To site but a few examples, Malaysia's Khatijah Ahmad, chairman and Managing Director of the KAF Group of Companies—a financial services conglomerate—earns annual revenues of $5 billion, as does Emilia Roxas' Asia-world Internationale Group—a Taiwan-based conglomerate involved in mining, construction, and agribusiness, among other industries (*Leading Women Entrepreneurs* 1997). Sweden's Antonia Ax:son Johnson's Axel Johnson Group also exceeds $5-billion in annual revenues (*Leading Women Entrepreneurs* 1997), while Ernestina Laura Herrera de Nobel's Grupo Clarin—the Argentina-based newspaper and news media empire—annually earns over $1 billion (*Leading Women Entrepreneurs* 1997).

The Myth of Trivial Impact: The Contribution of
Women-Owned Businesses to the Overall Economy Is Trivial

Similar to the misperception that individual women-owned businesses are so small that their impact remains trivial, many people believe that the collective impact on the overall economy of women-owned businesses is also trivial. Beyond leading a few very large businesses, what are women entrepreneurs collectively contributing to their respective national economies? The answer: substantial revenues and employment. In the United States, for example, in 1996 the "nearly 8 million women-owned firms...generated nearly $2.3 trillion in sales, and employed [more than] one out of every four company workers—a total of 18.5 million employees (Leading Women Entrepreneurs 1997, p. 45). Already by the mid-1990s, women-owned businesses employed 35 percent more people than the entire U.S.-based *Fortune* 500 companies employed worldwide" ("Women entrepreneurs" 1997, p. 1). In the past decade alone, the number of people employed by women-owned businesses in the United States grew by an explosive 183 percent (Dogar 1998, p. 36).

Similarly in Canada, women-led businesses provide more jobs than the *Canadian Business* Top 100 companies combined (M. Fraser in Kirbyson 1996).[12] More importantly, women-led businesses in Canada are creating new jobs in Canada at four times the national average ("Myths and Realities" 1995, reported in "Growth of Women-Led Businesses" 1996, p. 1). To say that the impact of women-owned businesses is trivial is to completely misunderstand the reality of the situation. Increasingly, to even begin to appreciate the dynamics of our national economies, we must understand the contributions of women-owned and women-led businesses.

The Domestic Myth: A Woman's Place Is in the Home

Many people believe that women-owned businesses stay home; that is, that most women entrepreneurs operate domestic businesses. However, reality no longer supports such a stay-at-home myth. A survey of women business owners in 15 countries found that 40 percent of women-owned businesses were not staying home (Wellington 1996, p. 1). Forty percent had gone beyond their own national borders and were conducting business internationally (Wellington 1996, p. 1). In Poland, for example, nine percent of women-owned businesses are now predominantly exporters, meaning that they have moved beyond the local Polish economy altogether (Mroczkowski 1995, p. 61).

Whereas women-owned businesses used to "stay home," they no longer do so. The recent and rapid expansion into international markets among women-owned firms is striking. According to the same 15-country survey, half of the women-owned firms that conduct business internationally only became internationally active within the prior year (Wellington 1996, p. 1). Moreover, almost half of those that still operate exclusively within their own domestic market expect to begin exporting and/or importing within the next three years (Wellington 1996, p. 1). Women entrepreneurs have discovered the global marketplace (or perhaps they never lost sight of it in the first place).

Not only are women-owned businesses going global in record numbers, their international expansion is succeeding. "Women-owned firms that operate internationally...grow more rapidly than do firms focused strictly on their domestic market" (Green 1998, p. 7). Fifty-seven percent of women-owned businesses that operate in the global marketplace developed a new product or service in the prior calendar year, whereas only 44 percent of firms not involved in international trade did so: a 30 percent innovation advantage for the international firms ("Going Global" 1995, p. 1). "Companies most likely to be involved in international trade are in" industries that are among the fastest growing for women-owned businesses ("Going Global" 1995, p. 1). The picture is clear: women-owned firms neither stay home nor fail when they venture abroad.

The Myth of Prejudice: Some Cultures Are So Prejudiced Against Women That They Could Never Succeed in Global Business

International business often includes expanding into areas of the world believed to be culturally hostile to business women. The most visible evidence of such cultural hostility is the apparent scarcity of local business women in many countries. However, generalizing from a country's treatment of its own women to predict how that country will treat foreign business women has proven to be neither accurate nor helpful. Most countries do not treat foreign business women in the same culturally limiting ways in which they often treat their own women.

Take, for example, the Arab countries. Similar to most cultures, Arab culture strongly differentiates between the male and female role. Many Arab cultures place restrictions on local women's behavior that inhibit their ability to conduct business. However, Arab cultures do not treat foreign business women in the same way that they treat local Arab women. They give more latitude to foreign women. Because the cultural norms are less restricting for foreign business women, they have been succeeding for years in the Middle East and will continue to do so.

The underlying dynamic is simple, although often misunderstood and therefore unexpected. Foreign business women are not treated like local women, they are treated like foreigners. As one Tokyo-based woman executive for a major financial institution explained, "Being a foreigner is so weird to the Japanese that the marginal impact of being a woman is nothing. If I were a Japanese woman, I couldn't be doing what I'm doing here. But they know perfectly well that I'm not" Japanese (Morganthaler 1978, pp. 1, 27). Foreign business women are given much more latitude in the range of behaviors that the local culture finds acceptable in them, and yet condemns in their own native women. The mistake, made all to frequently by both men and women, is to exaggerate the salience of being a woman. Arabs do not treat all women the same, nor do the Japanese. Each treats foreigners—whether male or female—with the respect necessary for them to succeed in business. As an added benefit, foreign women often gain much easier access to local business women than would any man representing a foreign enterprise. The cultural prejudice that often looks initially like a probable barrier to business success, in fact, often offers potential benefits.[13]

VI. TWENTY-FIRST-CENTURY LEADERSHIP: LEADING BEYOND THE MYTHS OF HISTORY

Focusing on the scarcity of women political leaders caused us to blind ourselves to the rapidly increasing numbers of women presidents and prime ministers. Similarly, focusing on the scarcity of women in senior corporate leadership, rather than highlighting the increasing number of women chief executives of global entrepreneurial and family firms, appears to be causing us to miss important societal trends and their implications for global strategy. Instead of considering the impact and potential advantages to society of the increasing number of women-led countries and companies, most scholars and executives appear to remain trapped in questioning why there are so few global women leaders. Moreover, given the pervasive societal focus on the apparent scarcity of women leaders and on society's prejudice against women in general, many scholars and executives misguidedly spend their time struggling with erroneous and misleading myths rather than beginning to understand women's new patterns of contribution. Global entrepreneurship, rather than traditional, hierarchical corporate leadership, is providing a particularly promising and important avenue for women's increasing prominence in the global business environment.

The twenty-first century will not replicate the twentieth century. The limited roles women that have historically played in society will not continue to constrain their future contributions either within their own companies and countries or within the greater society. The combined contribution of women's and men's best leadership bodes well, not only for entrepreneurs and global business strategy, but also for global society.

ACKNOWLEDGMENTS

This chapter was originally presented as a keynote address at the Globalization and Emerging Businesses Conference in Montreal, Canada on September 28, 1998. It was researched and written in collaboration with Sara Jean Green, *The Globe and Mail* (Toronto, Summer 1998). It is adapted, in part, from Nancy J. Adler's "Global Entrepreneurs: Women, Myths, and History," *Business and Contemporary World* (1999, in press, John Wiley & Sons, Inc). The author would like to thank Avon Products, Inc. for its generous research support and on-going commitment to women's global leadership. She would also like to thank the Social Sciences and Humanities Research Council of Canada for their support of her research on global human resource issues.

NOTES

1. For a more in-depth discussion of global women political leaders, see Adler's "Did You Hear? Global Leadership in Charity's World" (1998), "Global Leaders: A Dialogue With Future History" (1997), "Global Women Political Leaders: An Invisible History, An Increasingly Important Future" (1996), and "Societal Leadership: The Wisdom of Peace" (1998).

2. San Marino's head of state and government is the co-captain regent elected for a six-month term. Given the small population of San Marino (less than 25,000 people) and the short term of office, the five women who have held the role of co-captain regent have not been included with the 42 listed presidents and prime ministers. The five co-captain regents include: Maria Lea Pedini–Angelini (April 1 to October 1, 1981), Gloria Ranocchini (April 1 to October 1, 1984), Edda Ceccoli (October 1, 1991, to April 1, 1992), Patricia Busignani (April 1 to October 1, 1993), and Rosa Zafferani (April 1 to October 1, 1999).

3. Of the 42 women presidents and prime ministers, five are not "firsts," but rather their country's second woman president or prime minister. In 1994, Sri Lanka elected their current prime minister, Chandrika Bandaranaike Kumaratunga, whose mother served Sri Lanka as prime minister both in the 1960s and 1970s. In 1995, Haiti selected Claudette Werleigh as prime minister, whereas Ertha Pascal-Trouillot had served as Haiti's president in 1990-91. In 1996, Hasina Wajed followed Khaleda Zia into office as Bangladesh's second woman prime minister. In 1997, Mary McAleese became Ireland's president, following Ireland's first woman president, Mary Robinson. In 1998, Bermuda elected their second woman premier when Jennifer Smith followed Pamela Gordon into office.

4. For a more in-depth discussion of women business leaders, see Adler's "Global Leaders: A Dialogue with Future History" (1997), "Global Leadership: Women Leaders" (1997), "Global Leaders, Global Entrepreneurs: The Myths of History" (1998), and Adler, Brody, and Osland's "The Women's Global Leadership Forum: Enhancing One Company's Leadership Capability" (1999, in press). Note that although all types of business can be incorporated, only non-family controlled, professionally managed, publicly held companies are referred to as corporations.

5. As cited by Nan-b deGaspé Beaubien, director of the Family Enterprise Institute, Montreal, Quebec, Canada.

6. For a more in-depth discussion of women entrepreneurs on which this section is based, see Adler's "Global Entrepreneurs: Women, Myths, and History" Business and the Contemporary World (1999, in press).

7. 1997 revenues, as cited by Fortune.

8. See Mary Kay Website: 1997 revenues $1.1 billion.

9. 1997 revenues for The Body Shop were $416-$435, exact amount depends on the exchange rate between the British pound and the U.S. dollar. Anita Roddick, the founder, is currently co-chair (see The Body Shop Website).

10. After the acquisition of Nutri-metrics by Sara Lee Corporation, 1997 revenues for Nutri-metrics were announced as $200 million in a June 1998 Sara Lee press release.

11. The two are Marian Ilitch's Little Ceasar Enterprises and Mary Kay Cosmetics ("America's Top 500" 1998).

12. The Canadian Business Top 100 firms employed 1.5 million people in 1996 whereas women-owned businesses in Canada employed 1.7 million in the same year ("Myths and Realities" 1995).

13. For an in-depth discussion of the role of international and expatriate business women, see Adler's "Competitive Frontiers: Women Managing Across Borders" (1994).

REFERENCES

Adler, N. J. 1994. "Competitive Frontiers: Women Managing Across Borders." Pp. 22-40 in Competitive Frontiers: Women Managers in a Global Economy, edited by N. J. Adler and D. N. Izraeli. Cambridge, MA: Blackwell.

_____. 1996. "Global Women Political Leaders: An Invisible History, An Increasingly Important Future." *Leadership Quarterly* 7 (1): 133-161.

_____. 1997. "Global Leaders: A Dialogue with Future History." *International Management* 1 (2): 21-33.

_____. 1997. "Global Leadership: Women Leaders." *Management International Review* 37 (Special issue 1): 171-196.

_____. 1998. "Did You Hear? Global Leadership in Charity's World." *Journal of Management Inquiry* 7 (2): 135-143.

_____. 1998. "Global Leaders, Global Entrepreneurs: The Myths of History." Keynote address at the Globalization & Emerging Business Conference in Montreal, Canada. Montreal: McGill University, Faculty of Management.

_____. 1998. "Societal Leadership: The Wisdom of Peace." Pp. 205-221 in *Executive Wisdom and Organizational Change,* edited by S. Srivastva and D. Cooperrider. San Francisco: Jossey-Bass.

Adler, N. J., L. W. Brody, and J. S. Osland. 1999, in press. "The Women's Global Leadership Forum: Enhancing One Company's Global Leadership Capability." *Human Resource Management.*

"America's Top 500 Women-Owned Businesses." 1998. *Working Woman* (May): 54-72.

Dobrzynski, J. 1996, November 6. "Somber News for Women on Corporate Ladder." *New York Times,* p. D1.

Dogar, R. 1998. "The Top 500 Women-Owned Businesses." *Working Woman* (May): 35-40.

Dwyer, P., M. Johnston, and K. L. Miller. 1996, April 15. "Europe's Corporate Women." *Business Week,* pp. 40-42.

Fritsch, J. 1998, September 23. "Big is Small Business, Straining to Grow." *New York Times,* p. E2.

"Going Global: Women-Owned Firms Are Going Global." 1995. National Foundation of Women Business Owners, as cited in "Women-Owned Firms Are Going Global" (1995), NFWBO & Women's Connection Online, March 17, p. 1. (http://www.womenconnect.com/search/info/business/mar 1795b_bus.htm).

Green, S. J. 1998. "Women Entrepreneurs." Unpublished paper, Montreal, Canada.

"Growth of Women-Led Businesses in Canada Echoes Increases in the U.S." 1996. Washington DC: National Foundation of Women Business Owners. August 23, p. 2.

Hill, C. W. L. 1998. *International Business: Competing in the Global Marketplace* (2nd ed.). Whitney, MT: Irwin/McGraw Hill.

Himelstein, L. 1996, October 28. "Shatterproof Glass Ceiling." *Business Week,* p. 55.

Jung, M. 1997. "California: Enterprising Women Move Ahead." *Women's Resource & Yellow Pages.* http://www.workingwoman.com/articles/zjung.htm)

Kelly, C. 1996. "50 World-Class Executives." *Worldbusiness* 2 (2): 20-31.

Kirbyson, G. 1996. "Small Business Is a Significant and Growing Force." *The Financial Post.* Reprinted in *Women in Management* 7 (2) (December/January 1997): 6.

Leading Women Entrepreneurs of the World and Women to Watch. 1997. Washington DC: National Foundation of Women Business Owners.

Morganthaler, E. 1978, March 16. "Women of the World: More U.S. Firms Put Females in Key Posts in Foreign Countries." *Wall Street Journal,* pp. 1, 27.

Mroczkowski, T. 1995. "Shaping the Environment for Private Business in Poland: What Has Been Achieved? What Remains To Be Done?" *Law and Policy in International Business,* June 1. (http://nrstg1s.djnr.com/cgibin/DJIntera ...edPubLists=defaults&AdditionalSources=All).

"Myths & Realities: The Economic Power of Women-Led Firms in Canada." 1995. Bank of Montreal's Institute for Small Business & Dun & Bradstreet Information Services.

Wellington, S. W. 1996. "Women in Corporate Leadership: Progress and Prospects." New York: Catalyst.

"Women Business Owners Employ One in Four U.S. Workers." 1996. Washington DC: National Foundation for Women Business Owners. March 27, pp. 1-2.

"Women Entrepreneurs Are a Growing International Trend." 1997. Washington DC: National Foundation for Women Business Owners, March.
"Women Wanted." 1996, April 11. *The Province (Vancouver)*, p. A35.

AUTHOR INDEX

SUBJECT INDEX